"K FOR THE WAY"

Praise for "*K for the Way*"

"'*K for the Way*' is layered, joyful, and sonically sophisticated in style, tone, and technique. With lyrics, interviews, and the insight only a dope DJ/academic could provide, Craig reminds us of the responsibility of the DJ to inform the crowd as the sound of social justice movements. The rhetorical practices of the DJ are emancipatory with each cut. Craig's writing moves DJing back to the center of Hip Hop where it belongs."

—**Bettina L. Love, Columbia University, author of** *We Want to Do More Than Survive* **and** *Punished for Dreaming*

"I can't put this book down! A comprehensive exploration and examination of Hip Hop as a boundless resource, '*K for the Way*' is a tool that transcends time, race, gender, and socioeconomic status."

—**Bruce Campbell Jr., Arcadia University, founder of the Dust + Dignity Project**

"When we really come to terms with how the Hip Hop DJ reorganizes technology and popular culture, and how Hip Hop culture continues to remix modernity, the dangerous question is this: What is the humanities without an epistemology of the Hip Hop DJ? Todd Craig goes deep into the crates to keep us in the break, unleashing the neglected underappreciated rhetorical power of the Hip Hop DJ as a transformer, scholar, sponsor, and custodian of an essential 'way' that should be center stage in our scholarship."

—**Chenjerai Kumanyika, New York University, founding member of The Spooks**

"'*K for the Way*' is not just an interruption of writing and rhetoric as it has been taught in schools. It's flipping those scripts and crossfading what's been known with what's been felt through Hip Hop for at least the past fifty years. Academia should thank Hip Hop for Todd Craig and this contribution to scholarship."

—**A. D. Carson, University of Virginia**

"DJs are cultural creators. '*K for the Way*' is a strong addition to the larger move in rhet/comp toward cultural rhetorics and the broader tradition in Hip Hop studies that places Hip Hop creators as experts."

—**Emery Petchauer, Michigan State University**

"This is Hip Hop pedagogy at its best. Craig uses DJ techniques in the actual writing—he digs through crates, he writes an entire chapter on the 1s and 2s, he makes both hard and blended transitions, he lets the platter keep spinning even after he is finished—it's fun, smart, and virtuosic."

—**Justin Burton, Rider University**

"K FOR THE WAY"

DJ Rhetoric and Literacy for
Twenty-First-Century Writing Studies

TODD CRAIG

Foreword by Young Guru

UTAH STATE UNIVERSITY PRESS
Logan

© 2023 by University Press of Colorado

Published by Utah State University Press
An imprint of University Press of Colorado
1580 North Logan Street, Suite 660
PMB 39883
Denver, Colorado 80203-1942

 The University Press of Colorado is a proud member of the Association of University Presses.

The University Press of Colorado is a cooperative publishing enterprise supported, in part, by Adams State University, Colorado State University, Fort Lewis College, Metropolitan State University of Denver, University of Alaska Fairbanks, University of Colorado, University of Denver, University of Northern Colorado, University of Wyoming, Utah State University, and Western Colorado University.

∞ This paper meets the requirements of the ANSI/NISO Z39.48–1992 (Permanence of Paper).

ISBN: 978-1-64642-482-5 (hardcover)
ISBN: 978-1-64642-483-2 (paperback)
ISBN: 978-1-64642-484-9 (ebook)
https://doi.org/10.7330/9781646424849

Library of Congress Cataloging-in-Publication Data

Names: Craig, Todd, 1974– author.
Title: "K for the way" : DJ rhetoric and literacy for twenty-first-century writing studies / Todd Craig.
Description: Logan : Utah State University Press, [2023] | Includes bibliographical references and index.
Identifiers: LCCN 2023014123 (print) | LCCN 2023014124 (ebook) | ISBN 9781646424825 (hardcover) | ISBN 9781646424832 (paperback) | ISBN 9781646424849 (ebook)
Subjects: LCSH: English language—Rhetoric—Study and teaching (Higher) | Literacy—Study and teaching. | Hip-hop—Influence. | Music in education. | Culturally relevant pedagogy. | Disc jockeys.
Classification: LCC PE1404 .C66 2023 (print) | LCC PE1404 (ebook) | DDC 808/.0420711—dc23/eng/20230515

LC record available at https://lccn.loc.gov/2023014123
LC ebook record available at https://lccn.loc.gov/2023014124

Cover illustration © Cathey White

To Kaylee and Julia:
Daddy did it—so that means you can do it, too!

To Uncle Dea and Leo and Science and Mommy
Thanks to each of you for all you gave me to get here.

CONTENTS

vibe. When you got the party in *that*, that's all psychological. It's also something that's community-based. Then there's communal dances, and this goes all the way back to Africa: where we have conversations through dance and movement. There needs to be some sort of beat or rhythm that goes along with it. We're having conversation but not with words—it's conversation with tones, with movement and with attitude. The DJ sets that pace. You can't dance to silence. You need some sort of rhythm with some sort of beat, or some sort of music. The DJ is the foundation for that.

All of these different things were introduced to me through Hip Hop. From me trying to figure out how I put together a sound system, I become interested in physics and engineering because I want to master all of the things that I'm doing. All of this is predicated off of wanting to rock the spot as a Hip Hop DJ. Period! From my first party when I was twelve, and the first outdoor jam I did for Parks and Recreation at age fifteen for the Midnight Basketball tournaments. I was practicing on Matson Run with Jay, Joey, and DJ Shant Money on that Mickey Mouse turntable. I was building sound systems with Monte Hackett in Mrs. Hackett's basement, and listening to Jazzy Jeff and Ca$h Money. I was looking at DJ Too Tuff from Tuff Crew and a plethora of DJs that were in Philly at that time, because you had to be super nice at cutting, scratching, and blending in order to even be noticed. But *Project X*—a compilation record by Grand G (Wilmington, Delaware's Marley Marl)—was just as important. It's part of Wilmington, Delaware, history, part of my Hip Hop history, and the essence of the way I approach records, sound, and engineering. Record shop owners would be like, "Why is this fifteen-year-old kid here when I'm opening the store at seven in the morning, and doesn't leave until four in the afternoon?" They're not understanding I'm going through the whole "fifty-cent bin" to go record digging, trying to find particular records. I took DJing very serious. I DJed all the way through high school to college. That's how I got my name known at Howard University. From '92 to '96, I DJed every club that you could think of in DC along with people like DJ Iran, DJ Ceelo, and DJ Trini. I was part of that early '90s nightlife and DC club scene. Then I became a tour DJ for Nonchalant in 1996. Coming out of that, I went into engineering—but I started off as a DJ; that is my first love. That's the first thing I ever did connected to Hip Hop.

These ideas and these stories are important to tell and to document. One of the most critical moments of my music career was in 2010, when Jay-Z asked me to come on tour with him as his DJ. So 2010 was me stepping back out into the world as a DJ, because I had been in this enclosed room at Baseline making hits and having success with that for a long time. That was a huge education for me in terms of going back into the club where kids are now *not* playing third verses! You may play first verse, hook, and then you have to get out of the record. It was a whole different re-education on the flow of a party.

We've gone off a lot of lore and myth and storytelling from people's memory of Hip Hop's early days. We need to lock down what the actual history is, and there are very specific ways we can do that. We have the blessing that the people who created the culture are still alive and we can ask them very specific questions. There has been a focus on Bam, Herc, and Flash, because of media and the way Hip Hop has been reported. But there are a host of characters who may not have been reported about who were just as important. We also need to make distinctions about culture. Because a culture doesn't just start immediately one day; culture develops over time. So we have certain monumental points as to where things happen, but we need to lock in what those things are. I feel like it needs to be told by the people who were actually there, certain people who lived through it, and those who are speaking subjectively and not objectively. When I say subjectively, I mean from the standpoint that we are the subjects of it, I'm speaking from the inside of it, not looking at it as an object or from the outside. I am the subject that I'm talking about. We can get those people together. But there are certain things we do need to get absolutely correct: who did what and at what time. It's super important because it's the culture that we created, it's the thing that's going to live beyond us. And we want to make sure we get it correct for the children. If you love Hip Hop, you want to make sure that it's told in the right way. That part of it is important for me, because I am an educator. Someone who's looking at an eighteen-year-old, and having to remind my peers, when they say, "Oh, your students this" and "your students that" and I'm like, "Yeah, this person was born in 2000, born in 2003." So their perspective is not going to be our fifty-year-old perspective. So while giving them that history, we need to correct what those things are; specifically because I've watched other people who are not of the culture give the history but get it wrong.

Imagine I want to study Jazz as a foundation of what I do in terms of music, there's levels. If I was to write about it, or to research it, I'm looking at it from the outside looking in; I don't play Jazz, but I'm interested in it. It doesn't negate me from studying or learning Jazz, the same way someone else is not negated from studying or learning Hip Hop if they don't practice it. It's just the way you approach it. I wasn't at Minton's, so I would never walk amongst a circle of Jazz people and claim to be an authority above them. That's the problem: when people who are outside of the culture walk amongst people who are actually doing it and claim to have some sort of authority, because they're published. That doesn't matter in our world, it's how authentic your information is. If you're in it—you're going to have an intimate knowledge. And you're also going to be able to wipe away some of the mystery or the embellishment, when other people start coming in and talking. It's how you approach it, and the respect level that you have for it.

That's why *K for the Way* is exciting for me. Someone of the culture, writing about the culture number one. Number two being specific to the literary sense of it. What is your definition of writing? What is your definition of literacy and how are you trying to use it? To be able to answer those questions and put it in Composition and Rhetoric is something that's exciting for me to see. Third, there is an intimacy with the people in the book. I know them personally. So it's very exciting for me to see those people be translated. I'm very proud of them. Look at Natasha—this woman is incredible. I'm at "Mobile Mondays" every Monday night when she's holding it down with 45s. I might DJ "Mobile Mondays" sparingly. She's there *every* Monday, playing a different set, different records, every time. Whether it's on-time blending, cutting, or scratching, she can hold her own wherever. Rich Medina, that's my guy! Or BreakBeat Lou: a close and personal friend who helped start the break beat compilations with his partner, BreakBeat Lenny. Those sorts of things are exciting for me. I know those stories and how they can translate. The point of interjecting these stories into academia is to show some of the restrictions that traditional writing may have held over Hip Hop. You may need to change the formula or the criteria for what you consider a proper paper. In Hip Hop, your sources may not be published, or people that you can necessarily refer to on a page in a book. But an interview with them should hold just as much weight, because my research needs to come from someone who may not be published, but they have the actual information on the subject matter.

So even though the Hip Hop spirit says, "I don't need your approval," what this book does is looks at writing, at Hip Hop culture, and says, "Let's get this story right." And it looks at the DJ and says, "We deserve to be here."

ACKNOWLEDGMENTS

So it seems really odd to me that in academic texts, this section comes first and not at the very end . . . but since that's what it is, I'ma go in . . . cue that theme music, yo!

> *. . . BEM Bem bi-BEM, BEM Bem bi-BEM . . .*
> *. . . Woah, woah, woah, woah, WOAH . . .*

First and foremost, I need to thank the Higher Power I rock with for getting me to this spot and making this truly possible . . . indeed all praises are due. To the #ThreeGirlSquad I spend each and every day with. Stefanie: who would've thought that meeting in 1616 Locust and then Cue Records would lead to all this?!? Thank you for being the best partner and friend imaginable! To my favorite oldest daughter, Kaylee, and my favorite youngest daughter, Julia: I love you one million! To Ruth Muchita (RIP): Mommy, I wish you were here to see this, but I know you do. Thank you for making sure I got here.

> *. . . MOMMY . . .*

To George Muchita: thanks for helping me get to this place. Todd and Jay Muchita for all the years of seeing me through. To Tameka Muchita (the bestest sister-cousin ever) and Kejuan Muchita (H—I'm officially here now!)—I appreciate y'all beyond measure. Betty Jean Mattson and Nicole Mattson. To my crew of nieces and nephews: Kejuan Muchita Jr., Cee'Asia and Atiya Daste and Maxwell Muchita: it's been an honor to watch y'all grow up. Anissia and Aaliyah Paulino: Uncle Todd is always here for y'all. Mercedes and Kelvin Thomas; Jeremy Portje and family. To Jeanie and Bill Smerkers: thanks for always supporting us and your grandkids! And to the Craig, Cannon, Davis, High, Black, and Ellis families in North Carolina, Oklahoma, Arizona, and all over: what up y'all!

https://doi.org/10.7330/9781646424849.c000b

. . . bring friend, friend, friend, friend . . .

There are some shoulders that I stand on in this moment that must be mentioned: First and foremost, to Carmen Kynard—the illest water-walking mentor one could have! Thanks for always keepin' it 1000, and for helping me see this when I almost couldn't. To Dr. John Lowney (RIP) and Lee Ann Brown: thank you for giving me an early forum to think through connecting Hip Hop, Jazz, African-American music, poetry, poetics, creative writing, and the Black literary tradition.

. . . forearm tattoo, that's squad, squad, squad, squad . . .

Of course, to Ravenswood and Queensbridge Houses, and ALL of my peoples— y'all know who y'all are, word! Special shout to Gotti, Chinky, Noyd, Twin, G.O.D., Nitty, Alchemist, Fly, Jose, and the whole Infamous conglomerate. Good lookin' out for the love throughout all the years of my education, for real. To Patricia (since 8AC4), Bilal, Ali-Asha, and Malachi Polson (Bilal—thanks for walking with a brother on this one, word!) To every single DJ I interviewed: all of you are listed hard-body in the bibliography! This project is NOT the same without each and every one of you and your influences. A special thanks goes out to Mas Yamagata: you was the FIRST one who really believed this could happen . . . good lookin out homie! DJ Spinna, Clark Kent, BreakBeat Lou (I'm done now, Lou . . . you know what that means—we got work to do!), Boogie Blind, A.Vee, Ca$h Money, Freddie Foxxx, and Christie Z-Pabon. To Mr. Len, Rich Medina, Phillip Lee, and Sonny James: y'all dudes have been family since Day Numero Uno . . . infinite thanks and blessings to y'all, for real.

. . . I got bigger plans than stayin' rich /
I been tapped in since I was six . . .

To that Black Rhino Crew: especially Dr. Rich Alexander, Travell Summerville, Kevin Barton, Rob Ricketts, Jason Monroe, Greg Bedward, Ron Young, Damon Pace, Cornell Caines, Dr. Nkem Okpokwasili, and all the families: y'all saw me through some dark times and made sure I got through in one piece—blessings! To my man Marcus Todd Lewis—thanks for being the dopest ear and harshest critic early on. I appreciate all those invaluable DJ moments in RI, word. To Sarah and Rich Kim and family (Scrappy—look what all those Stretch and Bob tapes did for me!!!); To my Williams crew: Henry, Tashon, and Madison McKeithan Miller (Scott—thanks for the decades of friendship); Mike Humphreys and family; Chris Jones and family; Heather Mitchell and family;

Bill Wood, Frank Rosado, and family: Bill and Frank—thanks for continuing to keep me pushin' on the 1s and 2s, word!

To Dr. Eileen de los Reyes, Hal Smith, Vikas Srivastava and family, Lauren Ferguson and family. Donna McCleary, Theresa and Jon Gaskin, and family, Dinorah Rodriguez and family, Carol Moore and Phil! Jan Ramjerdi and Ron MacLean for that early book-writing faith. Furqan Khaldun and family, Takbir Blake and family (appreciate the brotherhood Furqan and Tak)—Young and Informed Media all day! Marcos Ramirez, Stephen Quinones and family, Alexander Soltero: thanks for family vibes and fresh footwear!

> *. . . get out the way, get out the way, get out the way, YEAH . . .*
> *. . . you either wit' me or . . . WAIT . . .*

Chenjerai Kumanyika and family, A. D. Carson, Tara Betts, Regina Duthely-Barbee and family, Laquana Cooke and family, Khirsten Scott and Lou M. Maraj (DBLAC, what up!!!), Sherita Roundtree, and Victor Del Hierro. Yolanda Sealy-Ruiz, Emery Petchauer, Bettina Love, John Jennings, and Lauren Leigh Kelly. To the CCCC/NCTE Black Caucus. Special shout to Ben Ortiz and Caroline Reagan at the Cornell Hip Hop Collection. To Monique Ferrell and Julian Williams (my CUNY siblings from some other parenting).

> *. . . I put the beats on 'em like Dre outside . . .*

To Marta Effinger-Crichlow: the first person to have me teach a Hip Hop class in the academy—infinite thanks! Renata Ferdinand: appreciate you letting me rock out!!! To LeBrandon Smith and James Horton: thanks for a new chapter of brotherhood, word! Amy Wan and Neil Meyer: thanks for being great colleagues and collaborators. Shereen Inayatulla and Sara Alvarez. To the English Department at the Graduate Center and all the students I've been able to rock with so far!

> *. . . I can tell real by who you runnin' wit . . .*

To Tonya Hegamin, Maria DeLongoria, Aisha Williams, LeVar Burke (this is what longer arms looks like!) Kevin Adams, Rogelio Knights and family, Jeff Sigler and family (I'm forever thankful for that phone call), Jackie Rosseau, Kareen Odate, Wes and Ebonie Jackson and family, David Hatchett, Shakima Scott, Judy Morgan, Hector Dominguez, Eric Pellarin, and Chi Koon. Support for this project was provided by a PSC-CUNY Award, jointly funded by the Professional Staff Congress and the City University of New York. To the good folks at the Charles Evans Inniss Memorial Library: thank you for helping me secure each and every book I needed for this project. And thanks to Judith Schwartz for extending the deadlines on each and every book I needed for this project! Finally, to all the students I've been blessed to interact with at Medgar Evers College, City Tech, QCC, KBCC, QC, CSI, NJCU, HCCC, Montclair State, GEAR-UP at UPENN, and all the way back to that first teaching internship at Community Prep in Providence, Rhode Island, circa January 1995: thanks for making me a better educator by pushin' me to be at my best each and every day, for real, for real.

> . . . *Hit my plug just to re-up and he was like "Boop–here"* . . .

Much appreciation to the whole Utah State University Press Crew, with a special thanks to Michael Spooner for taking a chance on me to get this project across the finish line and making sure that vision was seen through to completion. To Rachael Levay: thanks for being the most patient and supportive editor in the game! Special thanks to Cathey White for the cover art and to Kevin Monko for permission on the Rich Medina x TEDxPhilly picture.

> . . . *I'm all in the wind wit' it* . . .

RIP Cue Records, Fluid Nightclub, Clara C. Park, Don Oliver, Leo Stehle, Kim Glowark, James "Uncle Dea" Miller Jr., Delores Wright, Todd "Killer Black" Muchita Jr., Albert "Prodigy" Johnson, Deanna Cameron, Aunt Cathy Cannon, Tonnie Muchita, Lynn "Aunt Lydia" Ferguson, and RiShana Blake.

Shouts to all of the true Hip Hop scholars who are really trying to rep Hip Hop to the fullest from an informed perspective, who aren't trying to front with Hip Hop 'til they git to where they goin'. Super shout to every dope Hip Hop beat that helped to birth the words I write on the daily . . . and *that's* on God! And finally, to the haters, nah-sayers, path-blockers, and obstructors of justice: this one's for all y'all, too! Salute!

> . . . *championship goin' dumb, nufin to sumthin, I WON* . . .

And to anyone else who may feel left out or forgotten: I ain't forget you . . . see: THANK YOU!

> . . . *win, win, win, WIN, YeAHHHHHhhh* . . .
> . . . *BEM Bem bi-BEM, BEM Bem bi-BEM* . . .

"K FOR THE WAY"

1

PLANTED SEEDS GROW TREES

The Impetus for the Urgency of "K for the Way": DJ Rhetoric and Literacy for Twenty-First-Century Writing Studies

P.S.K. we're makin' that green / people always say "what the hell does that mean?" /
P is for the people who can't understand / how one homeboy became a man /
S for the way we scream and shout / one by one, I'm knockin' em out /
K for the way my DJ kuttin' /
other MCs, man ya ain't say nufin! /
rockin' on to the break of dawn . . .

Schoolly D, "P.S.K. (What Does It Mean?)" *Schoolly D*, Jive Records, 1986.

. . . one of the records I'd always have on deck for my old-school set was
"PSK" by Schoolly D. It was an undeniable record when it came out,
and still is an undeniable party-rocker, a tune that
truly stood the test of time sonically. I always thought
Schoolly D killed that song. His flow was dope and innovative,
no one was really rhyming like that just quite yet,
the beat was hard-hitting, and the vibrations from
the overly reverbed TR-909 drum through the speaker woofers
will still rattle your chest cavity. Almost twenty years later,
I'd start my tenure-track gig wanting to buy decorative letters
to put "PSK" in my office . . .

https://doi.org/10.7330/9781646424849.c001

I start this book by thinking back to how I gained my sense of literacy—specifically in regard to writing, reading, and critically thinking. I have to pay homage to Hip Hop. My first life memories revolve around my two uncles: one I was named after, and his partner in crime DJ Jam aka Dea Mill. I was spending the night at my cousins' house. Just imagine three young boys—no more than three or four years old. It's late Friday or Saturday night, and this blaring noise won't let me sleep. So I walk out the bedroom into a dark sound-filled living room. I didn't know what was happening, but I knew there were a lot of cool-sounding noises and sparkly lights shining through the darkness; some colors bounced up and down, while some were stationary, jutting out of nowhere, from left to right or vice-versa. I can still see it, being a little boy and getting a little closer while trying not to distract these two men— 'cuz we all know as a kid, if you made your presence felt this late in the evening, it'd be off to bed for dat ass! So I crept up on them, their backs were turned, with these funny-looking things on their heads and ears that stopped them from noticing I'm *not* where I'm supposed to be. Peering through the darkness, I could distinguish the items we were told NOT to touch: the "records." These two men kept picking up those records, and then they'd put them right back . . . and every time that happened, soon after the sound changed, and the colored lights moved differently. I was young, and this was nothing short of absolutely incredible.

And I can *still* see it.

So I went back into the bedroom, woke my two cousins up, and made them come into the living room to see this whole operation going down. And don't get me wrong, I remember the sonics just as clearly as the visuals: the multicolored lights that floated and cascaded like a Christmas tree in front of a background of fireworks, or even the Empire State Building on a clear night. But then we started running around and playing; at first, the two men were so caught up in their zone, they didn't even sense our presence. After all, they never caught wind of me standing there by myself for so long. Something in me knew—there was a power in their actions, because nothing seemed to matter but the changing sounds and the dancing lights. But as all little kids do, someone knocked something down, something got broke, and alas, the moment was ALL over. Those two men were my two uncles: one is still alive; one has passed on—both were DJs. The other two boys were my two cousins: one is still alive; one has passed on—the remaining two of us were influenced by this moment for the rest of our lives. One became a successful music producer. Some of his hit songs were created with some of those "records" we were told not to touch. I went on, with some of those "records," and became a DJ, taught by James Miller Jr., my Uncle Dea—who passed away a week before I started my doctoral coursework—the same uncle who stood there in that zone with my other Uncle Todd. This is one of my top-three earliest life memories, and one of the most formative, as it is the cornerstone to my understanding of DJ culture and literacy.

In his book *Reading for Their Life: (Re)Building the Textual Lineages of African American Adolescent Males*, Alfred Tatum argues that one way to reinvigorate African-American adolescent males in the subjects of reading and writing is to help them understand their "textual lineage." This textual lineage is comprised of students' favorite authors; as students see the value in the authors they choose, this should translate into an eagerness to read and explore more literature of varying authors writing similar work or coming from a similar background to the authors originally presented in their textual lineage. This concept perfectly captures spoken and unspoken mentorship in Hip Hop DJ culture; thus, as Tatum describes it, my introductory story sparks the initial stages of my DJ textual lineage.

This developmental stage in my early childhood would forge my initial understanding of Hip Hop culture and how DJs were integral in its early formation. As a product of Queensbridge and Ravenswood Houses, my literacy evolved once I realized that on Friday and Saturday nights, between 9 p.m. and 1a.m. (sometimes 2 a.m., depending on the station), there were these DJs who followed the philosophy that Red Alert detailed in our interview, when he said, "Kool Herc I always felt was considered a Pied Piper of the culture, because his vibe and his music embraced a little bit of everybody to be under one roof. That's what I feel the importance of a DJ is: he helps lead the audience through whatever the whole [musical] form is at that time" (KOOL DJ Red Alert). These DJs introduced me to what Hip Hop music and culture would be: from the early idea of the "Hip Hop sounds" (KOOL DJ Red Alert) to what would later become Hip Hop music. It was a schizophrenic learning; I would sit, glued to the old-school one-piece stereo system with the record player on top, a cassette deck, an 8-track player, and the AM/FM stereo. I'd be in my bedroom next to the stereo, with a blank cassette tape I bought from the bodega earlier that week for 0.75¢ in the "record" position, spanning the analog dial between "home team"—Mr. Magic with DJ Marley Marl (who was from Queensbridge)—and "away team"—with DJ Chuck Chillout on Fridays and

KOOL DJ Red Alert on Saturdays. Here's how it worked: The recording would start with home-team . . . after all, I'm from Queens. If the first song was hittin', I'd immediately start recording. And I'd rock with Mr. Magic and Marley until one of two things: a wack song or commercial break. On the other hand, if the first song was wack, overplayed, or on one of the many cassette tapes I'd already made, I'd quickly spin the chunky silver analog dial from 107.5 WBLS counterclockwise to 98.7 KISS-FM. Honing in to catch the right spot was a craft in itself. These were *not* the digital-tuning days, when you punch in a number that takes you right to the station . . . these were the days of armgrease, where hand and eye coordination met each other, as I quickly cranked the dial counterclockwise, while watching the orange-yellow hued line move to the left. Getting from 107.5 to 100 was easy, especially since I didn't know the Awesome Two were on 105.9 WHBI. The difficulty was honing those spins to catch 98.7. There were a cluster of radio stations in that area of the FM dial: too far left, you'd be in dance music zone . . . too far right, you'd be in Rock or Oldies. So precision became crucial. This was how Friday and Saturday nights would go, back and forth between these two, with one ninety-minute tape always in the cassette deck, and another ninety-minute tape on-deck. You didn't want to miss this four-to-five-hour window, because once it was gone, the lesson was over, and the "Hip Hop sounds" would not be back for another six or seven days. That was back when our DJs were the pied pipers to the subculture emerging from the Bronx, and arguably Queens, depending on who's talking. This was the foundation of my formative teachings in Hip Hop literacy and DJ culture. These childhood moments also became literacy sites for many young members of Hip Hop and DJ culture, because this was where Hip Hop really began to get consistent exposure amongst people who subsequently became the culture's community members and practitioners.

Decades later, I evolved from studying the craft with Uncle Dea in QB on the sixth floor of 41-05 12th Street, to high school and college radio, club residencies in New England, and parties up and down the Eastern Seaboard, including a DJ set where I opened for DJ Premier of Gang Starr in one of Philadelphia's most well-known nightclubs. My journey had come full circle: from the first piece of vinyl I bought with my allowance (Whodini's *Back in Black*), to scratching the bells on the intro of Bobby Brown's "Don't be Cruel" with my cousin on that same old-school one-piece component system, I had walked the DJ journey. My first pair of turntables were from a pawnshop; it took both belt-drive Technics I bought for my uncle to help me build one that was fully functional. And the second turntable: a Fischer direct drive with three AAA batteries taped to the tone arm as a counterweight. And in the middle was the all-black Realistic 32-1200B Radio Shack DJ mixer. Any DJ worth their weight in Hip Hop gold understands this struggle and has walked that mile in a pair of shell-toed moccasins!

"When Needle Meets Wax": The Effects of Broken Grooves, Broken Promises, and Breaking BIPOC Spirits in Academia

Skip stage from my humble DJ beginnings to over twenty years later, when I'm preparing for a conference presentation. A senior scholar in Composition/ Rhetoric (or Comp/Rhet) unexpectedly asked me to join a conference panel. The invite was based on a referral from an elder statesman in the field, and it led me to an intriguing search involving Hip Hop scholarship.

For this panel on innovative writing strategies and first-language teaching, I wrote an abstract using Hip Hop scholarship as an example of a marginalized field in Comp/Rhet. I wanted to investigate how our discipline could begin to counteract discriminatory language, literacy, and pedagogy practices. How might we include various voices and sources of cultural capital that now serve as more "standard" in American society than "Standard English?" Finally, where in this paradigm might Hip Hop scholarship fit and serve as a learning tool?

This brings me to two specific texts. On the song "No Role Modelz" by J Cole, he says, "Fool me one time, shame on you / fool me twice, can't put the blame on you / fool me three times, fuck the peace sign / load the chopper / let it rain on you." The second text is the classic Comp/Rhet document "Students' Right to Their Own Language" (CCCC; hereafter SRTTOL), which presents a loophole: to promote students' language rights, instructors and scholars who teach those students require the same right(s) to said language(s) in both teaching and research. Here, I contend SRTTOL acts as a hegemonic mantra: while the field may purport its validity, the scholarship of teacher/ researchers enacting and engaging in Hip Hop Nation Language (Alim, *Roc the Mic Right*) practices both with and for students becomes marginalized by Composition/Rhetoric in conference appearance(s) and publication(s). For example, the 2016 program for one of the premier Comp/Rhet conferences revealed that in 300 pages' worth of panels over four days, there was only *one* Hip Hop panel: Saturday at 9:30 a.m. (the last day of the conference, typically labeled the most undesirable time slot, as people usually leave on Friday night or early Saturday morning).

I want to quickly make the connection here with SRTTOL and Hip Hop scholarship, as Hip Hop was, is, and continues to be based in African American Vernacular English (AAVE). We know from Geneva Smitherman to Valerie Kinloch to myriad others, that there are sociocultural and political values ascribed to, as well as rhetorical strategies exhibited within, AAVE. These same strategies and values help set the stage for the emergence of Hip Hop culture and its shift from "underground" to mainstream popular culture. For more clarity, consider this: both Mina Shaughnessy and Geneva Smitherman published *Errors and Expectations* and *Talkin and Testifyin*—respectively—in 1977. Both books engage poignant discussions about writing, language structure and formation. Meanwhile, Kool Herc was on Cedar and Sedgewick birthin' Hip Hop in August 1973 . . .

In other words, during a critical moment where dialogue about writing, language use/construction, and their connection to racial and cultural enclaves is happening in Comp/Rhet, Hip Hop has already been birthed, uttered its first words, and even completed the arduous task of potty training. The point here is these pieces of cultural activity and a particular push toward a critical consciousness of how the teaching of writing and language education take place are transpiring around the same time in the mid-1970s. Yet almost fifty years later, while Hip Hop remains more prevalent than ever, it seems less prominent, or even relevant, for Composition/Rhetoric as a field. But why?

To further demonstrate the lack of representation in Hip Hop scholarship in Comp/Rhet, I did some scholarly crate-diggin'. By no means is this mini research dive scientific or extraordinarily futuristic. But the cursory search is helpful in exposing a larger point. I took one of the premier journals in Writing Studies and looked at its content over a ten-year period. This small-scale perusal entailed using college databases and two physical library spaces to locate copies of the selected journal. In this premier journal in the field, the editor wrote that in over four years, there have been over 697 submissions; of that number, I counted 187 publications (including articles, reviews, symposia, conference addresses, and awards speeches). Thus, the journal had a 26.8 percent acceptance rate. In this 26.8 percent acceptance rate, I could roughly account for the following: nine scholars of color; six of the nine were Black scholars and "usual suspects," and of those six, four were "executive addresses." So of the 187 publications, roughly 4.8 percent are scholars of color; 3.2 of the total 187 were Black and identify as "active Hip Hop" scholars.

"Fool me one time, shame on you!"

In five and a half years, there were two book reviews of Black authors who actively cited Hip Hop as a location of scholarship in their work. Three addresses actively cited Hip Hop as a location of scholarship, and one person cited an author whose work is Hip Hop specific (note this person was not of color). One person cited the DJ as the impetus for how a student understood the writing process. However, the same scholar ignored the Hip Hop DJ's influence on said student, yet *sentences later* the author summarizes the student's understanding of writing. At this time, there were at least three contemporary publications that identified the Hip Hop DJ as a source of intellectual query—specifically in writing (Paul Miller [DJ Spooky], *rhythm science*; Jabari Mahiri, "Digital DJ-ing"; Jeff Rice, "The 1963 Hip Hop Machine").

In one issue of this Comp/Rhet journal, both a writer *and* the editor evoke Hip Hop by referencing a website. They mention the website in name only to spark possible interest around this article. But like "clickbait headlines," they just evoke the name. So here, we see Hip Hop as a flashy hook or catchy chorus that becomes critical to this publishing structure. These editors understood evoking Hip Hop was a way to keep their journal "relevant."

In combing through the 5.5 years of journal issues, the last time a Hip Hop–centered piece was published *in this journal* was in 2007.

"Fool me twice, can't put the blame on you . . ."

It seemed that active Hip Hop scholars of color working within Comp/Rhet were not appearing in the journal as were their white colleagues. Even though this spoke volumes, I dug back into the Comp/Rhet digital crates, finishing the remaining four and a half years. Extrapolating from the 26 percent acceptance rate calculated above, I made a rough calculation that in this ten-year timespan, there have been 1,476 submissions and 396 acceptances. As well, in this ten-year period, there were four citations, one article, and one book review in 2007 that have a Hip Hop focus.

Why does this statistical set become integral to this already difficult conversation? Honestly, there was—and still is—no way to ignore the obvious impact of race here. After all, this same journal documents the resignation of a BIPOC conference chair but does not explain why or deal with the reinstatement or controversy surrounding said resignation.

"Fool me three times, fuck the peace sign / load the chopper let it rain on you . . ."

In fairness to the journal in question, I cannot account for how many BIPOC scholars submitted Hip Hop–based articles for publication, or if those articles met the journal's publication criteria. What I can share, however, is much of the field's folklore among colleagues, elders, and peers was the gatekeeping practices of this journal were overtly aimed at keeping Hip Hop scholarship (specifically coming from BIPOC scholars) out of the publication mix. Meanwhile, you can peruse the same ten-year time span to see how Hip Hop scholarship was thriving in other fields and intellectual locations.

"This right here is word on the streets . . ." aka Literature Review

During the same time period (2007–2017), I identified over forty books and articles privileging Hip Hop Based Education (HHBE) from BIPOC scholars, engaging with Hip Hop on Hip Hop's terms, or pinpointing the DJ as a figure worth investigating. I'll quickly highlight this vast range of Hip Hop scholarship to lend clarity to this argument.

H. Samy Alim's "The Whig Party Don't Exist in My Hood" (Alim and Baugh, *Talkin Black Talk* [2007]) highlights an interview with American Cream Team rapper Bankie, while focusing on his work with middle school students in creating a Hip Hop–based student magazine. Both Brian Coleman's *Check the Technique* (2007) and Bill Brewster and Frank Broughton's *The Record Players: DJ Revolutionaries* (2010) use narrative and direct artist/DJ commentary to illustrate Hip Hop practitioners' voices around Hip Hop cultural practices.

William Jelani Cobb's *To the Break of Dawn* (2007) examines how the MC/emcee's artistic choices affect aspects of Black language arts and revolutionized storytelling in Hip Hop music. H. Samy Alim, Awad Ibrahim, and Alastair Pennycook's *Global Linguistic Flows* (2008) addresses Hip Hop's global expansion, with Hip Hop Linguistics evolving from "English-imitating" versions of Hip Hop, into more region-specific, localized language that occupies pockets of resistance and struggle. While Adam Bradley reviews emcees' poetic structures in *Book of Rhymes* (2009), Gwendolyn Pough explores the rhetorical savvy of women MCs who are able to "catch wreck" in navigating the complex connections between Hip Hop culture, feminist philosophies, and Black womanhood in *Check It While I Wreck It* (2015). Sophy Smith interrogates Hip Hop DJ turntablist teams' composing practices in *Hip-Hop Turntablism, Creativity and Collaboration* (2013), situating the work of the DJ and probing DJ notational practices—a technique used to chart DJs actions from a musicality perspective.

The Real Hiphop (2009) finds Marcyliena Morgan documenting Project Blowed (a West Coast–based Hip Hop freestyle/improvisational group) and exploring intrinsic connections between youth, Hip Hop culture, and language practices. Greg Dimitriadis analyzes Hip Hop's influence on identity formation and construction with midwestern youth in *Performing Identity/Performing Culture* (2009). In 2012, Bettina Love and Emery Petchauer share two critical HHBE books: *Hip Hop's Li'l Sistas Speak* and *Hip-Hop Culture in College Students' Lives*, respectively. Both texts grapple with how students both embody and negotiate their relationships with Hip Hop, as they experience the culture within academic confines and outside of academia in their everyday lives.

Marc Lamont Hill and Emery Petchauer's collection *Schooling Hip-Hop* (2013) includes HHBE scholars Chris Emdin, David Stovall, Joycelyn A. Wilson, Decoteau J. Irby, H. Bernard Hall, and others who contribute perspectives on the current and future climate of HHBE practices. Envisioning digital sampling as a special case of musical borrowing in the newly formed art world he labels "hip-hop's imagined community," Justin A. Williams in *Rhymin' and Stealin'* (2014) contemplates the nuance created when DJs and producers engage in sample practices responsible for inventing completely new sounds and sonic compositions.

With an acute focus on the DJ, Felicia Miyakawa's "Turntablature: Notation, Legitimization, and the Art of the Hip-Hop DJ" (2007) examines Turntablist Transcription Methodology (TTM) created by John Carluccio, and DJs catfish and Raydawn, and what this notation means both rhetorically (thinking about the language practices used in notating and describing turntablist's musical actions) and culturally (expanding the legitimacy of the DJ into music canon's "high art"). In *Capturing Sound* (2010), Mark Katz investigates both digital sampling (again, part of the DJ/producer pedagogy and discourse) and Hip Hop turntablism. Examining this specific subset of DJ culture allows Katz to pinpoint the modes, operations, and practices of many turntablists. Jared A. Ball embraces elements of Hip Hop DJ discourse in *I Mix What I Like! A Mixtape Manifesto* (2011). Ball reflects on "the mixtape" as a source of "Emancipatory Journalism": a form of media and communication disbursement that revolves around decolonizing practices. The title itself, "A Mixtape Manifesto," is a clear indication of rhetoric rooted in DJ practices.

Dating back to the early 2000s, there are a series of books, anthologies (Forman and Neil), and articles that reflect on the impact of Hip Hop music and culture, whether from a sociocultural or historical perspective (Chang, *Can't Stop Won't Stop* [2005]; Kitwana [2002]; Spady, "Mapping and Re-Membering" [2013]), a sociolinguistic perspective (Alim, *Roc the Mic Right* [2006]; Richardson, *Hiphop Literacies* [2006]), Hip Hop based–educational practices in K–12 (Hill [2009]; Low [2010]; Mahiri [2006]; Morrell and Duncan-Andrade [2002]; Petchauer, "Framing and Reviewing" [2009]; Rodríguez [2009]; Sánchez [2010]), or specific college-classroom-based perspectives (Campbell [2005]; Rice, *Rhetoric of Cool* [2008]; Sirc [2006]; Wakefield [2006]). DJ Spooky's *rhythm science* (Miller [2002]), Carol Becker and Romi Crawford's "An Interview with Paul Miller aka DJ Spooky—That Subliminal Kid" (Becker, Crawford, and Miller [2002]), and Tim Lawrence's *love saves the day* (2003) all engage with the DJ; the most formative text that begins to do this work is Joseph Schloss's *Making Beats* (2004), even though this book primarily focuses on the Hip Hop producer.

There are three notable DJ-centered texts published just outside the ten-year window of the journal that sparked this exploration. Victor Del Hierro's "DJs, Playlists and Community: Imagining Communication Design through Hip Hop" (2019) specifically addresses Hip Hop DJs as technical communicators within their local communities, who build complex relationships that translate into accessible and localized community content. Jenny Stoever's "Crate Digging Begins at Home: Black and Latinx Women Collecting and Selecting Records in the 1960s and 1970s Bronx" (2018) inserts the oft-removed narrative of mothers, aunts, and sisters who helped birth Hip Hop culture by essentially serving as the cultural curators who taught foundational Hip Hop DJs how to listen to, play, and synthesize records. Finally, DJ Lynnée Denise's "The Afterlife of Aretha Franklin's 'Rock Steady': A Case Study in DJ Scholarship" (2019) explores the practices and four different tenants she identifies in labeling a form of DJ scholarship: "'Chasing samples', 'Digging through the crates', 'Studying album cover art', and 'Reading liner notes'" (Denise 64). These practices inform a specific type of DJ praxis she builds through the lens of Aretha Franklin's "Rock Steady" alongside EPMD's "I'm Housing." These three texts show the rich and complex site of inquiry for Hip Hop DJ research.

In contrast to the premier journal that started this conversation, over half the authors listed in this review of Hip Hop–based texts identify as BIPOC scholars. Furthermore, there are many more texts rooted in HHBE as well as other disciplines that critically engage Hip Hop culture as a viable source of knowledge and meaning-making for young people in classroom settings. But the truly uncharted territory is how the Hip Hop DJ can serve as an example of twenty-first-century new media reader and writer in the college setting, specifically in Comp/Rhet spaces. Thus, it becomes imperative to remember the earlier scholarship comparison between the premier journal versus the pool of sources listed above to situate the importance of the work *K for the Way* will tackle when thinking about DJ Rhetoric, Literacy, and Pedagogy in the twenty-first century.

Finally, I bring these two instances together to spotlight the schism I've experienced between understanding aspects of my own literacy acquisition via the DJ and Hip Hop culture on the one hand and entering a field that seems to diminish the relevance of this same culture, on the other. This moment is not an exercise in the essentialist mantra that "only Black and Brown" folks can speak on Hip Hop. Quite the opposite. I maintain that damn-near *nobody* gets to talk about the music and life stylings that currently dictate global popular culture in Comp/Rhet and Writing Studies. Furthermore, when Hip Hop is evoked, it is clearly misused (like the earlier journal article author who fumbled the moment when the student cites the Hip Hop DJ as a source for understanding the writing process). It is this misusage that *K for the Way* aims to address.

"Houston: We Have Lift-Off . . . Everywhere Else but Here . . ."

How might this conversation extend past English Composition and Rhetoric, and infiltrate other disciplines across the Humanities? And why is it so problematic? Let's explore this difficult conversation together to make sense of this quandary.

If you currently have a stake in teaching K–12 and believe in the Houston Baker mantra, you will understand that by 2017, Hip Hop is completely ingrained in the psyche of our young people, from ages two to twenty-two (Baker). As clearly identified by various HHBE scholars, if you have spent time helping students become invested in their cultural awareness and identity formation educationally, and Hip Hop is a piece of the culturally sensitive and responsive pedagogy you have engaged in through your K–12 work, know that when these same students enter college, they are *all* required to take two specific classes: First-Year Writing I and II, also known as English Comp. But as evidenced in the Comp/Rhet journal discussed in the preceding section, there seems to be an investment from Comp/Rhet as a field to diminish Hip Hop culture—and thus, a specific contingent of racial, cultural, ethnic, and sociopolitically marked bodies—within the landscape of the field. This move by Comp/Rhet, one of the few required courses in the undergraduate experience, suggests to students that bringing one's culture to the college writing classroom will quickly become problematic, thereby compromising the choices students need to make in order to be considered "proficient" or "competent" (Flores and Rosa; Kynard, "I Want to Be African").

Because First-Year Writing is an introductory class in every collegiate General Education program nationwide, it is essential that the academy at large works to strengthen students' undergraduate experiences by reinforcing their racial, ethnic, and cultural ties. Let's also think about how the BIPOC community affects the landscape of New Media Studies, with a barrage of contemporary "texts": images, sonics, and technology—from Black Twitter and @HipHopEd to *Power* and *Atlanta*, from *Luke Cage* and *Fresh Off The Boat* to ESPN and HGTV (rockin' the "Ante Up" instrumental on *Flip or Flop* commercials), and even *The Life of Pablo* and *DAMN*—erased from a twenty-first-century landscape to instead perpetuate twentieth-century models of reading, writing, and two-dimensional text-on-the-page. Meanwhile, Hip Hop has healed our souls during a pandemic, and sold us everything from food, clothing, and shelter within the last fifteen minutes if you're not living under a rock. However, instead of utilizing students' inherent cultural capital, marrying it with intellectual sensibilities to create a unique form of critical consciousness, Comp/Rhet seems to be moving in the opposite direction. And if First-Year Writing courses set this tone at the start of college, one can see how it could easily cast a shadow on the rest of a student's journey through the undergraduate experience.

So when people ask why I feel Comp/Rhet has shunned Hip Hop, or even diminished Hip Hop scholarship as part of the intellectual conversation, *this* is why. It's not a "Mad Rapper moment" for me. It is truly an instance where I'd like to have a formative, and probably difficult, conversation with my elders and peers in the field. The same culture that is currently global popular culture is the very same culture that gets delegitimized by the field my doctoral degree requires me to claim. So how does one navigate this quagmire? Or to repose the question many BIPOC have posed throughout academia: Who gets to tell our story, and what perspective gets privileged in the telling? For me, the dismissal of Hip Hop culture in the field for the students I teach sits on my soul, in the same way Aja Martinez describes the importance of and her

Figure 1.1. Rich Medina at "TEDxPhilly: The City." November 2011. *http://www.flickr.com/photos/tedxphilly/6352000667/in/photostream/. Photo by Kevin Monko.*

connection to counterstory. Thus, *K for the Way* aims to tell a Hip Hop–centered story that includes the culture, "and will always include my family, nonacademics, because the work is for them, is sometimes about them, and is nearly *always* inspired by them" (Martinez 19; emphasis mine).

"So Why Tell That Story, Sun?" aka the Rationale of It All

K for the Way addresses the story of the DJ. To introduce that idea, we start with international club DJ Rich Medina. In Medina's TEDxPhilly talk, he names Philadelphia as the mother city that nurtured his "musical muscle." In the days before his DJ career exploded, Medina talks about how he kept his day-job, but notes,

> All along I was still nurturing my musical aspirations . . . 3–5 workdays a week, you could find me in Armand's Records, Sound of Germantown, Funk-O-Mart, suit on, tie undone, spending ALLLL of that gigantic paycheck on records and equipment and things that were gonna help me take care of my craft. I say my "craft" being DJing because it was my shrink when my basketball career ended. I moved to Philadelphia, I went home, I got my turntables, I got my records, I put them in my apartment and every day: right hand, left hand, right hand, left hand, right hand, left hand (Medina, "TEDxPhilly").

DJs within DJ culture have countless stories like this, sharing anecdotes about the modes, methodologies, and practices used toward perfecting their individual crafts and acquiring an acute DJ literacy. While the DJs may be different, many of these stories converge in similar ways on similar meeting grounds surrounded by similar landmarks and sponsors, benchmarks, and cornerstones within DJ culture. This book aims to collect and retell some of these stories, constructing an argument for DJ Rhetoric, Pedagogy, and Literacy.

Finally, Medina was writing a recurring weekly column with *Complex* magazine (www.complex.com) called "On the Road with Rich Medina." In this column, Rich usually recapped his week's events with pictures accompanied by his own blurbs, including club appearances and performances, special edition sneakers gifted to him, and family moments. His column extended an up-close and personal view into the life and times of an internationally known DJ (for perspective, on the *Master of the Mix* TV show, DJ Scratch said, "Rich Medina is my FAVORITE club DJ"). In his weekly update from January 21 to January 27, 2012, Rich posted a blog called "Head Start" which included a picture of his son's room. The image captured a colorful kid's table with matching chairs, in front of a small set of shelves containing children's books, with turntables and studio monitors on the top level. The caption of the picture reads as follows:

The State of Things: On the Road with Rich Medina (Jan. 21–27)

Head Start

WHERE: My Son's Room
WHEN: Every Day
Lil' man's new set up. Had the CDJs in his room, but he was whining about wanting to have "reow turntaybows" . . . so he can start practicing "wiffout" me. I second that emotion like Smokey Robinson . . . wax on, wax off . . . (Medina)

Anyone familiar with Rich Medina knows he was exposing his son to DJ practices since Kamaal Nasir could fit functionally in the front-facing Baby Bjorn. From outdoor festivals in the summer to practice sessions in Rich's home studio, Kamaal has been surrounded by records, CDJs, Technic 1200s, DJ and studio mixers, and all the other necessary pieces included in the DJ's intricate educational puzzle. For Kamaal's three-year-old birthday party at Fluid Nightclub in Philadelphia (they rented the club out during the day), Kamaal—aka DJ Snacks—made his first public debut on the turntables. Since then, a small internet video collection posted by Medina and friends shows Kamaal flexing his then four-year-old DJ muscle—even scratching on 45s. After Medina developed DJing as a passion for Kamaal, at four years old, his son was asking to move up from CDJs to real turntables. Showing Kamaal DJ modes and discourse fostered within him the desire to follow in his daddy's footsteps. This moment shows the DJ's ability to enact what Adam Banks notes as griot: an orator of sorts, passing down traditions, stories, and practices of the culture not only through storytelling but also by allowing those stories to unfold live in praxis, thus demonstrating the DJ as a writer and digital storyteller.

"The DJ Literacy Sound-Off"

Rich Medina's TEDxPhilly lecture that highlighted early moments in his DJ career and his son Kamaal's budding DJ talents demonstrate a highly functional set of practices and language that can be categorized as DJ Rhetoric, or the pedagogy of the DJ. Thus, the idea of DJ as a twenty-first-century new media reader, writer, and literary critic is long overdue, as the craft of DJing is indeed its own unique form of rhetoric and literacy. The Hip Hop DJ's modes and methods comprise a distinctive set of discursive practices, stemming from the Black tradition of a shared sonic and life experience in the early 1970s, and have since evolved in forty-plus years to become a very well-popularized position and title in popular culture. And the logic is quite simple: while there were many before the Hip Hop DJ to engage in the craft of "spinning" records, it was the Hip Hop sounds coupled with the creation of the "scratch" (shouts to Grand Wizzard Theodore and Grandmaster Flash) and manipulating the breaks that revolutionized the craft of DJing into what we know it to be now. As said by Grandmaster Caz in Ice T's documentary *Something from Nothing: The Art of Rap*: "Hip Hop didn't invent anything. Hip Hop RE-invented EVERYTHING!" (Grandmaster Caz). The scratch and the break are part-new-invention while also part-reinvention building blocks when thinking about Hip Hop culture's origins. Since the formation of Hip Hop culture, the DJ has always served as the premier "tastemaker" for not only music but also product branding and technology. Frankly, if the Hip Hop DJ plays it, "it's lit." Having the right DJ at your event hits different and can catapult brand visibility and consumption. Finally, turntables, headphones, mixers, and computer software have been engineered and manufactured with the Hip Hop DJ in mind, tweaked out of beta phases *after* DJ usage and feedback. Indeed, the Hip Hop DJ is integral and irreplaceable in this process of "reinvention."

"From 'Nas Album Done' to 'I Got It on Me'": DJ Literacy and Research from the Folklored Perspective

It becomes important to situate this study in the scope of Hip Hop scholarship; a huge majority of research on Hip Hop's elements addresses either the emcee, the b-boy/b-girl, or graffiti (aka graf) writers. While there have been contributions on the DJ, there is still a limited range of work on this seldom-addressed topic. And the work that has been produced tends to focus on the metaphor of the DJ as writer or the DJ as collager and examines metaphoric analyses of what the DJ does and how the DJ does it. For example, in his book *Digital Griots: African American Rhetoric in a Multimedia Age* (2011), Banks identifies the metaphor and thus opens the door to the idea of the DJ as griot, as the DJ initially gave the storytelling MC that first opportunity to shine on the M.I.C. This thinking builds upon earlier work from Jeff Chang; in exploring the importance of foundational DJs to Hip Hop culture's formation, Chang identifies the myriad roles DJs occupied in the early to mid-1970s: "Godfather, yes, but also original gangster, post-civil rights peacemaker, Black riot rocker, breakbeat archaeologist, interplanetary mystic, conspiracy theorist, Afrofuturist, Hip Hop activist, twenty-first-century griot" (Chang, *Can't Stop Won't Stop* 92).

One does not have to look too far in today's society to find examples of griot-rockin-DJs. First, let's look at DJ Khaled. A quick listen to HOT 97 the weekend his album *Major Key* dropped, and you could hear Khaled killing the airwaves with that left-hand-right-hand DJ business. He ran the record gambit from dropping the latest and greatest, back to "Wu-Tang Forever." While the HOT 97 crew was rocking the first-ever Summer Jam Japan in June 2016, Khaled was providing an extended DJ set featuring records on his new album, but he was especially excited about "Nas Album Done." After playing it on at least five different occasions, DJ Khaled took to the microphone with his signature style: "Tri-State:

somebody call Nas and tell him I'm makin' this movie right now!!!" From there, it took about three years before Khaled was hosting Nickelodeon's 2019 Kids' Choice Awards. This range of settings—which display part excitement, part enthusiasm, part "fingers on the pulse of the culture," and part "know he's ahead of the curve"—makes Khaled the DJ/Producer enigma we all know and love.

For the next example, the Mid-Atlantic's tristate area (New York, New Jersey, and Connecticut) hears him almost every night on HOT 97. His name: Funkmaster Flex. Any example of Flex premiering a new record will do. Whether Flex showcased Jay-Z and Kanye West's "Otis," Rick Ross's "3 Kings," or Pop Smoke's "Got it on Me," his attitude and bomb-dropping approach can be likened to a historical survey of Black griotic tradition. Don't get me wrong—many people, myself included, have said the following about Flex over the past twenty years: "PLEASE shut up and let the damn record play!?!" But the fact that we've all been saying the same thing for the past twenty years is a testament to who Flex is, what he has done, and continues to do for Hip Hop culture via his position as DJ/radio personality. Put simply, his iconic relevance in Hip Hop DJ and radio culture cannot be dismissed or overlooked. An unmistakable radio personality, Funk Master Flex was one of the first DJs who stood at the apex of Hip Hop going mainstream. This is documented in his long-standing history on New York City's HOT 97. Mounting his milk crate with megaphone in hand, Flex serves as part Malcolm Little and Martin King Jr., part Alex Haley and Ralph Ellison, part Louis Armstrong and Langston Hughes, and even part Muhammad Ali and Miles Davis: African-American griots who encompass the tradition of our great orators and cultural historians, storytellers and record keepers, folktale chroniclers, shit-talkers, and back-turners who back that shit up properly. Only a small few could hold a candle to Funk Flex when he presents the theatrics of the modern-day Black Hip Hop moment. He also served as record producer, working alongside Big Kap (RIP) to release a series of DJ-inspired Hip Hop compilation albums that stood as the blueprint for a kind of legal "mixtape as album": approved by record labels, and pushing the taste-making DJ back to the forefront of Hip Hop culture. Each of those four mixtapes (released on Loud Records) as well as his album *The Tunnel*, further propelled Funk Master Flex into a three-decade-plus career in radio, TV, and entertainment. Add into the mix his LitDigitalDJs movement, where he has combined forces with DJ pioneers like KOOL DJ Red Alert and Chuck Chillout, alongside his contemporaries and younger DJs like Bobby Trends and DJ Spazo. This endeavor to bridge the gap between generations of Hip Hop DJs is invaluable, making Flex the griot who communicates on the 1s and 2s, while also living out a particular narrative of how Hip Hop DJ culture should look.

Finally, a quick perusal of Arbitron and Nielson radio ratings of decades past will help identify Funk Master Flex's radio relevance in his primetime evening slot of 7 p.m.–10 p.m. At one time, when the Arbitron radio ratings released for the quarter, you could hear Flex in rare form, taking a musical "victory lap": always talking with his hands, but evoking the griot in telling the story of the record, of the ratings or of certain situations in grandiose fashion. After one of these broadcasts, listeners cannot mistake his positioning in Hip Hop culture.

K for the Way stands as a text about the Hip Hop DJ that inhabits Comp/Rhet, while also straddling Hip Hop Studies, to contribute perceptive scholarship to both fields. Hip Hop music—and specifically the Hip Hop producer—utilizes the sample to capture various sonic moments that get chopped, flipped, and reconstituted to form unique sonic compositions. As well, the Hip Hop DJ manipulated the breaks from various genres live to present what was known as "the Hip Hop sounds." So too, does *K for the Way* utilize a New Literacy Studies approach that cultivates interdisciplinary insights in order to explore and (re)envision DJ Rhetoric as a means of twenty-first-century new media reading and writing. This book will read as an amalgamation of DJ conversations, theories, and scholarship from Hip Hop culture, Composition/Rhetoric, Hip Hop Studies, New Literacy Studies, Ethnomusicology, and Education. *K for the Way* will achieve praxis in its embodiment—showing, telling, and doing DJ culture.

Because the Two Do Connect: The Hip Hop Lens in Academic Practice

Many people can tell you about the transformative nature of Hip Hop music and culture. Hip Hop has truly saved my life—it comes back and forth in various iterations of savings. Most recently, Hip Hop rejuvenated my academic soul with the Hip Hop Institute. This type of lifesaving happens when you see your dreams come true and unfold right before your eyes.

The first year Wes and Ebonie Jackson came to our college with programming for the first two days of the Brooklyn Hip-Hop Festival, my friend and colleague Kareen Odate coordinated the programs through the Women's Center. Soon after, Kareen coordinated a meeting between Ebonie, Wes, her, and me. Of course, I gave my ultimate pitch about preserving Hip Hop in New York City from an academic lens. My argument was clear: we've spent a lot of time traveling hours to get to intellectual spaces that honor and chronicle Hip Hop. Why do we not have that same physical space at home, where Hip Hop was born, grew up, and came of age before going off to conquer the world? Couple that pitch with my wife working with Wes back in the day when she was at

Footwork in Philadelphia, and there you have it. I would help them coordinate the next three years of programming through the English Department. After watching the second year of the Hip-Hop Institute and Dummy Clap Film Festival happen at my home institution, I realized I had witnessed a dream come true. That dream culminated on Saturday during a Brooklyn Hip-Hop Festival performance.

We attended the festival, initially running around to different booths and vendors while Rapsody was rockin' in the background. She left the stage to overcast. The cloudy darkness turned to monsoon status, raining through Talib's whole set. I stood in line for food during Fabolous's set but was still in-tune when Lil Fame joined Fab on stage and dropped that infamous "Ante Up" verse. I made everyone with me as comfortable as possible before the moment of my own truth, one of the main reasons I was in attendance.

It happened right there in the VIP area, under the cement and metal suspension we like to call the Brooklyn Bridge. And it was during the headlining act with a dude named Nasir Jones. His set started with his band playing the Black National Anthem, "Lift Every Voice and Sing." But then his band and DJ started to play the Sting record "The Shape of My Heart." Anyone who knows the record recognizes that signature string introduction. After about four bars of the solitary guitar rift, there's a brief pause, right before Sting goes in with the lyrics. The strummed melody on that Sting tune sonically pulls on an emotion that matches the name of the song. I remember closing my eyes for a second and hearing Nas talk about "this was Sting's version . . . let's rock to my version." So when Nas's band and DJ rolls right into "The Message" from *It Was Written*, the interconnectedness and intertextuality of the sound came full circle for me. Some people around me didn't know exactly what was happening. But as a DJ, I knew this roadmap because I had studied both records, so I could see/hear the exact course Nas had charted for his listeners. There was a younger dude, no older than thirty, sportin' multicolored Flyknits, who knew every word of every verse. A few people made the sonic connection, but once Nas started his verse, it all came into form for the community of avid Hip Hoppers. This moment was special for me: imagine the kid from Queens listening live to the kid from Queens with the lethal first verse on the first full track of his highly anticipated second album. I was in undergrad rockin' that album on cassette in the '83 Mazda 626 when it came out. And now, I was hearing that verse live, only a few years after I had used that same verse in my own work.

On July 2, 1996, Nas released his second album, *It Was Written*. The first lines Nas spits on the first full-length song "The Message" are specifically directed at members of the Hip Hop community claiming to be gangsters in their written music, while their lives stray quite far from the lifestyle they portray. When Nas says: "Fake thugs / No Love / You get the slug / CB4: Gusto," he is referring to artists who are exploiting the monetary gain seen during the time when rappers—who come from a mainly urban underclass wrought with sex, drugs, and violence—discuss that life in the content of their songs (Nas, "The Message"). This idea springs from the film *CB4—The Movie*, where one of the three protagonists, Gusto (Chris Rock) is the lead member of gimmick-snatching gangster rap group CB4—even though Gusto's personal background and musical preferences do not match the music his group makes as gangster rappers. They insert themselves into the "gangster" trope of Hip Hop music solely for monetary gain and popularity. This immediately resonates in academia, as we have seen in the past few decades how Hip Hop has been embraced but also at times intellectually used to exemplify or epitomize the latter construct. The irony is many academics were never in a position to dictate what Hip Hop is in any circle beyond limited academic ones. In fact, the temporary utility of Hip Hop to such academics leads them to reject the tenants and cultural background of the people who created Hip Hop in the first place. By doing so, they are in effect rejecting the students they claim to love working with so much via "Hip Hop in the classroom." People who engage in this type of activity can be seen as the CB4-Gusto types Nas references.

Carmen Kynard addresses this very notion in "'Looking for the Perfect Beat': The Power of Black Student Protest Rhetorics for Academic Literacy and Higher Education." In thinking about her student Rakim and the sophisticated sense of political and cultural capital he brought with him to college through his organizing with the Universal Zulu Nation, Kynard identifies not only how racism has permeated various facets of higher education, but also offers a solution:

> While the dominant discourse of literacy educators today often centres on how to create bridge models for students of colour to take their "street codes"/(neighbour)hood/community literacies and translate them into academic literacy and/or the norms of a "culture of power," the history of black student protest rhetorics and activism flow in the opposite direction. It is the university and school structure, including its literacies and rhetorics, that are in need of change, not the students and thereby, the communities and cultural histories that they represent. (Kynard, "I Want to Be African" 393)

Here, Kynard captures two ideas. First is the academy must change and shift based on the importance of Hip Hop culture—as it has indeed become popular culture. Second, Kynard connects Hip Hop to its lineage and legacy, which are intrinsically connected to a Black diasporic tradition of literacy. Similarly to Travis Harris's definition of Hip Hop as "an African diasporic phenomenon" (Harris 21), I contend the DJ (and thus, Hip Hop DJ culture) is the epicenter of Hip Hop culture's creation, which includes aesthetic and cultural values and sentiments, that springs forth from the African-American social and lived experiences in the Bronx, Queens, and other New York City boroughs—specifically impoverished urban communities. Although graffiti emerges before the DJ, the Hip Hop DJ brings all the cultural elements together, mixing more than just records on turntables. Therefore, the DJ is the glue of Hip Hop culture as we know it. Understanding Hip Hop culture as an African diasporic phenomenon accounts for foundational Hip Hop DJs whose roots and origins stretch into the Caribbean, Puerto Rico, and other areas. Asian Americans and white folx were there too, no doubt. But the universality of Hip Hip's global inclusivity happens in the urban inner-city epicenters of New York—BIPOC melting pots—which, frankly, were inherently Black by design. I don't find labeling this origin to be exclusively limiting or creating a narrow binary. Hip Hop started as a multicultural happening that emerges from the Black experience. Hip Hop deejaying is an act that emerges as the sonic foundation of Hip Hop culture, with DJ elements convening a Black sonic experience. And because the DJ has always sat at the forefront of Hip Hop, it makes sense that the DJ sits as a griot, in the forefront of this cultural phenomenon called Hip Hop.

The intentionality of highlighting Hip Hop in the academy can become problematic when scholars fall short in the very place Kynard pinpoints when defining rhetoric. While some may find the stakes to be high in research and the paradigm of "publish or perish" in academia, some teacher/researchers do not want nor try to understand the paradigms involved for African-American youth in Hip Hop culture. This is an important distinction to recognize and is illuminated by Kynard. In her article "'Looking for the Perfect Beat': The Power of Black Student Protest Rhetorics for Academic Literacy and Higher Education," when redefining rhetoric in regard to African-American student protest history in the 1960s, she states:

> I am using rhetoric to encompass much more than the art of persuasion and stylised speaking. I mean the qualities of language, both oral and written, through which cultural meanings and histories are communicated and thus, where attitudes towards language and life are central. Rhetoric is, thus, a means of discourse, where what gets said in stories, dance, song, paintings and

everyday banter communicates belief systems, social values, a sense of the past, notions of shared identity and communal aspirations. (Kynard 396)

So when Comp/Rhet scholars utilize traditional notions of rhetoric when engaging Hip Hop culture, they may not coincide with the belief systems, social values, historical and contemporary shared identities, or communal aspirations. Without the cultural or social connections to the communities about which they speak and "teach," we see years later that their research does not speak to the ideas of rhetoric Kynard presents. This idea is also fleshed out further by Banks, as he quickly establishes the pitfalls of such careless choices in scholarship, as it "risks becoming yet another in a long line of those who have 'taken our blues and gone,' as Langston Hughes would call it, if we somehow build our theorizing on individual practices without full recognition of the people, networks, and traditions that have made these practices their gift to the broader culture" (Banks 13). It is further explicated by Travis Harris, when he states, "While writing about Hip Hop may be an academic exercise, the experiences of colonization, coloniality, hegemonic Whiteness, dispossession and other oppressive events that have destroyed African diasporic lives raises the stakes and brings a heaviness to this subject. As a result, non-Black scholars and especially White scholars need to recognize their position when studying, researching and writing about Hip Hop" (Harris 64).

Here I define DJ Rhetoric as the modes, methodologies, and discursive elements of the DJ. DJ Rhetoric encompasses the quality of oral, written, and sonic language that displays and expresses sociocultural, historical, and musical meanings, attitudes, and sentiments. From what gets said in the songs to what gets looped in the break in the mix, from the part of the song that gets cut up and scratched on the 1s and 2s to what gets chopped and flipped in the sample. DJ Rhetoric communicates the values of Hip Hop culture, (re)shaping it as we have known, now know, and will continue to know it (Craig, "Tell Virgil Write BRICK"). With this definition in mind, DJ Literacy stands as the sonic and auditory practices of reading, writing, critically thinking, speaking, and communicating through and with the rhetoric of Hip Hop DJ culture.

Thus, *K for the Way* aims, on the one hand, to examine and present a Hip Hop DJ Rhetoric and Literacy that includes ideas about poetics, communicative practices, and language formation and clearly demonstrates, on the other hand, the social, cultural, and political values ever present in DJs' roles and actions. This brings us back full-circle to Banks's understanding of the DJ as a particular type of griot: communicating the pulse and the evolution of a culture that once sat as "underground" but now has dramatically evolved to "mainstream."

But is this movement from forefront to background then back to the fore-front some sort of mysterious happenstance? I argue not, because anyone who knows Hip Hop cultural history knows full well it was the DJ first and foremost making the culture move. In my interview with God's Favorite DJ and acclaimed producer DJ Clark Kent, he describes the DJ's historical function as "the style of DJing, the cutting up the breaks, the making the break the most important part of a record: that was the DJs fault and that is the 100 percent beginning of what we understand Hip Hop to be—it's what the DJ created. You ain't hear about no rappers before you heard about DJs. We are the cornerstone, DJs *are* the cornerstone of Hip Hop . . . the DJ—first, always!" (DJ Clark Kent). While many people might gravitate toward the movie *Scratch* when thinking about the DJ (since it focuses solely on the DJ and the turntablist), I think one of the most compelling movies for our contemporary generation is *Something from Nothing: The Art of Rap*. Director/narrator Ice-T's extraordinary documentary on the art of the MC shows many of "your favorite rappers' favorite rappers" (Styles P from "Ryde or Die"), highlighting their entrance into Hip Hop via DJ positionality. For example, stories tell how Redman, who early in his career at his shows would come out on stage and, before even touching the mic, first push the DJ on the set out the way and start rocking on the turntables (Redman currently DJs on his Sirius/XM show, *Muddy Waters Radio*). In my interview with triple-threat (Emcee/DJ/Producer) Lord Finesse—who is probably best known for being an MC and later a producer—he told me the story of his Hip Hop his-tory behind the turntables:

> Back in the day, the DJ was the thing to be . . . I always wanted to be the DJ first, I ain't want to be a rapper. And people go, "how'd that happen?" I always wanted to be the DJ, the DJ was the dude! I just got real nice at [rapping], to the point where people were like "you need to pursue THAT!" So I got into rapping heavy, that took priority first. And in my spare time, I was still practicing and practic-ing until it got to the point where I *know* I'm nice, lemme start entering these DJ battle competitions . . . I'm doing the tricks, I'm doing the blindfolded thing, I'm doing ALL of that! (Lord Finesse)

Lord Jamar of Brand Nubian also discusses in *Something from Nothing: The Art of Rap* how he started as a DJ. Finally, Q-Tip of A Tribe Called Quest states, "In the beginning it was sound systems. Because the DJ was probably more prevalent than the MC actually, when the shit started off" (Q-Tip). Around the same time, Smirnoff was at the forefront of showcasing and highlighting the DJ within their company branding. Along with Smirnoff's *Master of The Mix* DJ reality show, the company also launched a campaign that premiered legendary DJ Kid Capri as the cornerstone of the party in a series of commercials. So to find the DJ sitting at the forefront of mainstream culture only shows the cyclical nature of history.

Given the modes of new technology—as DJs move between vinyl and computer-based software to manipulate turntables, CDJs, DJ controllers, and other devices—we, too, see our students in English Studies moving toward the need for more technology-based discourse. While the discipline thus begins to move in directions toward a type of Digital Humanities, part of the work we must do as English scholars is think about giving students captivating examples of writers. DJ Rhetoric and Pedagogy could have intriguing implications on how students in English Studies examine and (re)approach the modes and methods of writing and composing. In my interview with internationally renowned DJ Spinna, he stated very clearly, "We ARE writers, we are ABSOLUTELY writers!" (DJ Spinna). Spinna voices this sentiment because DJs program music, construct playlists, (re)write songs, compose digital sets with the new advancements in technology, and then make the natural progression into music production. Spinna pulls together these elements in DJing in the same way, conversely enough, that English Studies makes distinctions between and fractures itself into English Literature, Composition/Rhetoric (or Writing Studies), and Creative Writing. However, would any of these elements exist without its second or third counterpart? Not at all. So as we move forward from the two-dimensional sense of text given to us by twentieth-century English Studies into a more multidimensional idea of twenty-first-century writing exhibited by the new push toward the Digital Humanities, we must examine different types of writers and composers, orators, and storytellers. If we can explore the idea of the Hip Hop MC as a writer within English Studies, why not equally explore the DJ as new media reader and writer, in the creation of DJ Rhetoric and Pedagogy? Spinna has captured it best in saying, "I tell a story with a beginning, middle and end . . . we ARE writers" (Spinna). It follows that if our argument is English Studies is a discipline that functions around the construction of and subsequent analysis of "the word," we must investigate the meaning-making writer known as the DJ. But as I showed earlier in this chapter, we must do this work in a manner that responds to the ways Hip Hop scholarship within English Studies has shunned community members of the culture in that scholarly conversation. I argue this approach will require a change in perspective and the need to privilege a different set of voices in this integral cultural conversation.

So to collectively push toward an ecology that bridges scholarship in English Studies with voices of the cultural practitioners and communal meaning-makers in Hip Hop culture, *K for the Way* highlights DJ voices through conversations grounded in hiphopography, a philosophy introduced by James G. Spady. In promoting the advantages of an emic view when conducting research in the Hip Hop community through the lens of hiphopography, H. Samy Alim states:

> hiphopography can be described as an approach to the study of Hip Hop culture that combines the methods of ethnography, biography, and social and oral history. Importantly, hiphopography is not traditional ethnography. Hierarchical divisions between the "researcher" and the "researched" are purposely kept to a minimum, even as they are interrogated. This requires the hiphopographer to engage the community on its own terms. Knowledge of the aesthetics, values, and history as well as the use of the language, culture, and means and modes of interaction of the Hip Hop Nation Speech Community are essential to the study of Hip Hop culture. (Alim, "The Natti Ain't No Punk City" 969)

With this philosophy in mind, the premier voice in *K for the Way* is the DJ. And to ensure those voices resonate and shine throughout the research, you'll see every DJ's name quoted in parenthesis, just as MLA instructs us to do for academic voices. In *K for the Way* the voice of Hip Hop will be prevalent and the voice most paramount will be the DJ.

The Method to the Madness: The Research Roadmap of "K for the Way"

K for the Way deploys James G. Spady's hiphopography as the methodological process of data collection. With a philosophy that embraced the avant-garde meaning-making of Hip Hop artists, Spady defined hiphopography by stating:

> Our objective was to present a shared discourse with equanimity, not the usual hierarchal distancing techniques usually found in published and non published (visual-TV) interviewers with rappers. That is why we decided to do a HipHopography of the Bronx rather than an Ethnography of the Bronx. The crucial difference is the fact that in our case, we shared the cultural, philosophical values embedded in Black life stylings. HipHopography provides unique means of assessing and accessing the word/world realities found therein . . . as

> Hip Hop investigators we saw it as crucial to render the subject's cultural realities as accurately as possible (Spady and Eure vii)

Hiphopography allowed me to engage a variety of Hip Hop DJs while also maintaining my own shared values and sentiments around my love of Hip Hop culture and DJ practices. My intricate understanding of both Hip Hop and DJ culture transformed many discussions with participants to quickly turn from "formal interview" to friendly conversation. I also conducted more interviews by asking DJs to refer me to people they felt I should include in the project; this was an unscripted question I quickly began to ask at the very end of every interview. Because one of the main goals of *K for the Way* was to have an interview with "your favorite DJs' favorite DJ," it was critical and mandatory that I organically circulated through the DJ community with the organic intellectuals of the landscape—mainly through word of mouth, peers, and sponsors who experienced the process and understood the direction of this project.

Since there is not an expansive body of research on the DJ that springs directly from the DJ, hiphopography was favored simply because understanding DJ Pedagogy must come from the DJ and not from the abstract perspective of a certain type of "wax poetic" theorizing of the DJ from afar. In this regard, *K for the Way* strives to achieve praxis: the theory emerging from this research study is primarily based in the practice of DJs who participated in this study. The data accumulated from interviews reveal the life practices of various DJs; these practices dictate the theory and intellectual body of knowledge *K for the Way* aims to interrogate when discussing the Hip Hop DJ.

Whether overtly quoted or subconsciously embedded in the thinking and theorizing, various DJ voices drive this book. Furthermore, the Hip Hop aesthetics both Alim and Petchauer identify—the ways of knowing and being "Hip Hop"—serve as the theoretical skeleton. While my experiences as a DJ serve as bone marrow, hiphopography is the theoretical lens that adds the research meat on this book's bones. Yet, it is also innately dwelling as the backdrop—to discuss DJs, I could not afford the haphazard musings of a "whatever" moment. I have a responsibility as a DJ and Hip Hop participant/practitioner *to* the culture to present it properly. DJ Rhetoric is an explicit form of Hip Hop aesthetics; it is a way of knowing and being Hip Hop without even really laying claim to that label. For example, DJ Clark Kent would not call himself a "Hip Hop DJ." However, his DJ style—the way he knows and breathes the rhetorical savvy of his sonic communication through his hands with records and two turntables—is very much Hip Hop knowing and being. Hiphopography lends itself to a conversational practice that brings forth meaningful qualitative data. Yet at the heart of this methodology is the humanizing of participants; the knowledge and cultural capital DJs shared in our interviews truly became the privileged knowledge source.

A technique used in *K for the Way* was member-checking: using cross-referential information from participants to gauge the importance and relevance of data given from their peers. While I began with an initial set of DJs I wanted to interview based on my knowledge of DJ culture, those interviews happened organically only after being referred to those individuals by other peers in the community. For example, while KOOL DJ Red Alert was on my personal "Wish List" of participants, he was interviewed very late in the process. It took an earlier interview with Christie Z-Pabon alongside numerous other interviews before Red Alert contacted me and said he heard about my project and would like to be involved.

"The Hiphopological-Semi-Structured-Methodological Movement"

A semi-structured interview method rooted in hiphopography was used for *K for the Way* for several reasons. An interview technique that encompasses elements of both the traditional standardized interview guide with open-ended interview strategies allows for greater rapport with participants and consistency within every interview so that each participant is asked the same set of questions. There is an interview matrix, but it is not necessarily the only roadmap within the interview. This flexibility encourages participants to offer important content that might be absent in the interviewer's questions; it also affords the interviewer flexibility in further exploring a respondent's unanticipated ideas (Patton 347). This transactional relationship between interviewer and respondent fosters more organic dialogue, eliminating some of the power dynamics that may arise in most interview formats (Cohen and Crabtree). This sentiment also falls directly in line with the tenants of hiphopography.

The semi-structured interview approach through the lens of hiphopography in *K for the Way* empowered the participants, their thoughts, and ideas throughout the process and in the research itself to let participants' voices shine. I found myself interviewing DJs on their own terms, many times on-location at Hip Hop events. For example, Mr. Len and I went to "Toca Tuesdays" in LES (aka the Lower East Side) so I could interview DJ Tony Touch. While I was there, DJ Clark Kent made sure I connected with the guest DJ: a young Chi-Town DJ named Timbuck2 (RIP and "throw two fingers in the air for Timbuck"). DJ A.Vee connected me with Prince Paul at the "Donuts Are Forever" J Dilla Tribute at Brooklyn Bowl. These interviews were entrenched in the DJ's world of nightclubs and venues known for hosting Hip Hop events. These location-based interviews further exemplify Alim's premise that "hiphopographers have the chance to document the lives, narratives, and practices of Hip Hop's culture creators while they are actually living and engaging in Hip Hop cultural practices—it's a living history, a history in motion. This enhances the power and accuracy of our interpretation of Hip Hop cultural production exponentially" (Alim, "The Natti Ain't No Punk City" 972). As both Spady and Alim have said, you gotta be in the place to be with the people who make the place to be *the place to be*.

Part of how I built rapport with DJs who participated in this research project was linking the perspective of the research to our collective connections via Hip Hop culture, which superseded many of the formalities presented in "standard academic research." Since my perspective and approach were different, more aligned with Hip Hop and "Black life stylings" as presented by Spady, the lens for what information was privileged shifted. For example, during my interview with BreakBeat Lou in my home office, his interest in the project grew exponentially upon seeing my DJ equipment sitting right underneath my framed master's degree. My genuinely tangible love of DJ culture in my questions and our conversations coupled with a framed MA degree sparked a special interest in the research. He veered off-course in our interview to address seeing all sides of my researcher/practitioner/participant spectrum merge:

> On the real right now—I'm gonna say it, I know he's not expecting this—and I'ma be a little extra right now, but [picks up the framed master's Degree from the desk shelf]. The reason I don't mind doing this, and I'm being forward, but somebody that has this right here, this is worth more than anything that I'm saying. Someone who has this, and has an appreciation for the culture that we call Hip Hop, and even more so as to rep the DJ, git ya game right, for real! And that's one of the main reasons why I'm here right now! (BreakBeat Lou, personal interview)

BreakBeat Lou highlighted my positionality in the interview, and then became an ally for me within the DJ community. If you let Lou tell it, "Todd is the truth—he's REALLY part of our culture" (BreakBeat Lou talking to Ben Ortiz of Cornell's Hip Hop Archive at "Diggers Delight" in Harlem, summer 2012). This natural rapport was established by the connectivity hiphopography lends as methodology using the semi-structured interview method. Since the goal of this qualitative study is to give life to DJ culture through the experts and participants in the culture, it made the most sense to sit down with various players throughout the community and capture their voices in terms of how they envision the reality they participate in and represent.

Narrative analysis will be crucial throughout *K for the Way*. While the academy might occasionally indulge in narrative driving sections of academic manuscripts, we typically don't permit narrative to be integral in the process of sponsorship and fact-checking for who gets to tell a story and how the story is actually told. Because of my positioning as a DJ and my membership within both the DJ community and Hip Hop culture, there are aspects to the DJ community most people would not be able to access or analyze, as well as aspects to DJ modes and practices to which I am already innately familiar and connected. This positionality allows me an uncanny insider perspective to successfully complete this research and to foster a sense of trust within the community the average researcher might not gain. There is a saying in the Hip Hop community that "real recognize real." Even though I am a researcher and English scholar, my DJ peers understand and trust my commitment to the DJ community, to Hip Hop culture, and to ensuring this research presents DJ Rhetoric, Literacy, Pedagogy, and culture objectively, by presenting an honest portrait of the cultural, communicative, and discursive practices of the Hip Hop DJ to an academic community.

Questions That Drive the Movement:
"K for the Way" Research Questions

If we take into consideration the aspects of previous scholarship about the DJ from scholars like Jeff Rice, Paul Miller, and Adam Banks, one of the major questions of this research is how can the DJ's rhetoric, practices, and modes compel us to (re)envision writing as we know it? Other questions include:

- What is the history and lineage of the Hip Hop DJ? What is the main role of the Hip Hop DJ in popular culture in the twenty-first century?
- How can the Hip Hop DJ be included in the category of new media reader and writer?
- What is the evolution of the DJ as writer? How do contemporary Hip Hop Studies help in framing Hip Hop DJ Rhetoric and poetics?
- What implications might a Hip Hop DJ Rhetoric, Literacy, and Pedagogy have on English Studies for (re)imagining and (re)envisioning contemporary Writing Studies?

These questions all strive toward elucidating an overarching research question: How can we better understand the previously presented metaphor of "DJ as writer" and "DJ as Griot" or the connections between the DJ as orator and the linkages between African-American rhetoric, sonics and technology?

When the Headline Reads, "Todd Craig Leaks 'K for the Way' Tracklist": The Project Creation and Content

K for the Way's structure is steeped in honoring DJ practices. Chapter 1 states the primary goals of the book and introduces an argument for DJ Rhetoric and Literacy. Chapter 2 explores aspects of the author's acquisition of DJ Rhetoric and Literacy alongside narrative taken from DJ culture to expand on the idea of "sponsors" within the DJ community. The narrative is coupled with sponsorship/mentorship theories provided by Eric Pleasant and Gail Okawa, alongside commentary from Antonio Gramsci and Morris Young.

Chapter 3 examines more tangible implications for DJ Rhetoric and Pedagogy in writing by exploring how sampling techniques and practices in Hip Hop DJing and production can challenge the ideas of citation and plagiarism. Chapter 4 hones in on theoretical quandaries around DJ Rhetoric and Literacy, using narrative to probe the practice of "DJ as educator" when applying revision strategies in student writing.

Chapter 5 introduces and interrogates the meaning-making of six groundbreaking women DJs: Spinderella, Kuttin Kandi, Pam the Funkstress (RIP), Reborn, Shorty Wop, and Natasha Diggs. How these super-bad record-rocking sisters make their way through the testosterone-heavy Hip Hop industry is a story to be told and heralded both within and outside of DJ culture. Chapter 6 utilizes a "contact zone" framework in order to both define and explore the positionality of the DJ. This chapter also highlights interviews with DJs Mr. Len, Rich Medina, Sonny James, Phillip Lee, and Boogie Blind to examine ideas we see in Comp/Rhet from scholars such as Scott Lyons, Karla Holloway, Kermit Campbell, and others. Finally, chapter 7 examines the different directions scholarship on DJ Rhetoric can go and grow in envisioning "Comp3.0."

Each chapter starts with a quote, followed by a written excerpt, which consists of either prose or music lyrics, from somewhere else in the book. Each chapter ends with either a quote from an artist, an action that is demonstrated in the chapter or should be acted upon by the reader, or prose and music lyrics from somewhere else in the book. The formatting evokes how

DJs dig for records: you go into a record store, grab a set of records, and make your way to the turntable, or "listening station" to get a sonic snippet of your selections (when there's no listening station, you might be savvy enough to break out your Vestax or Columbia portable). In a store, there is no time to listen to 15 or 115 records from start to finish. So as a DJ, you take the stylus and needle-drop through the record, trying to get a feel based on thirty-to-forty-five-second segments of sonic sensings. The quotes from the chapter intros and outros aim to embody diggin' for the DJ: what BreakBeat Lou aptly titled "The Diggin' Exhibition" and what Lynnée Denise highlights as one of DJ Scholarship's four cultural practices—"Digging through the crates" (Denise 64).

"K for the Way": DJ Rhetoric and Literacy for Twenty-First-Century Writing Studies samples from a larger research project entitled "SPINificent Revolutions: 360 Degrees of Stylus as Pen" and uses over twenty (20) interviews from DJs who are scholars, "curators" (Chairman Mao), historians, and experts in their field. The work they have amassed in their world equates to, or possibly overtakes, much of the work done by scholars examining the culture. And because there hasn't been much work done by scholars in this particular field, the experts are the DJs who were interviewed. My job as researcher is to serve as a conduit that frames the information in these DJs' voices (Creswell 18–19), illuminating potential possibilities for English Studies. While part of DJ Rhetoric sits with quotes and extensive conversations with DJs that can't all be included here, DJ Rhetoric is embodied in both the writing and analysis. These DJs have become friends and mentors, and they create a familial culture through the bloodline of 1200s and Radio Shack Realistic mixers. Again, I'm reminded of Aja Martinez, who says if this work doesn't include family, then what good is it, and what's the use? Spady also addresses the importance of conversations about Hip Hop with Hip Hop participants: "In this connection it is necessary to realize that the interviewers/editors were as interested in the rap artists' narrative discourse as its historical content. An interview is a speech event. You should have been physically on location as these visionaries/knowers rapped" (Spady and Eure vii). The same approach that Spady deployed with the emcee was my approach with the DJ.

Thus, one of the objectives of *K for the Way* is to engage Hip Hop DJ Rhetoric and Literacy from the Hip Hop DJ's perspective, privileging their voices as opposed to someone who may have never touched a turntable, or even know what a 1200 is. Second, *K for the Way* approaches this topic from a different perspective; instead of privileging aspects of scholarship in the field while using participant interaction, interviews, and narrative as supplemental, this book will explore the outcome of research that privileges the narrative experiences of both the participants and the author/researcher/scholar and will tell stories as a way to "get at the details of one's life and all of the factors that shaped that particular Hip Hop artist . . . individual life histories become especially powerful when collected into a large body of representative participants who are active in the culture" (Alim, "The Natti Ain't No Punk City" 971).

Finally, the structure of *K for the Way* aims to replicate the machinations of a DJ set. Digging and listening; twisting and turning; cutting and scratching; blending, dropping, and spinning between modes, genres, and musical selections, this book aims to navigate aspects of memoir and storytelling with research-minded creative nonfiction and interview data. *K for the Way* will not only talk about the DJ; it will also embody the DJ. In any live DJ set, there are deft moments of cutting and scratching. There are crescendos through blends and beat-matching that boggle the mind and ear. There are abrupt drops that get the listeners from one record to another . . . and there are also those moments of "trainwrecks"—where everyone looks at the DJ, knowing full well that was *not* supposed to sound the way it did! *K for the Way* hopes to achieve at its best a conversation about DJs as an enactment of DJ Rhetoric and Pedagogy. Whether in written dialogue about other DJs, MCs, or producers, the twenty-first-century practices of reader, writer, and literary critic shine through from the page and are embodied in these words and ideas through a thought process, synthesis, and intellectual sensibility that are cultivated and maintained by Hip Hop DJ culture. And at its worst, hopefully the book maintains a stance presented to us by Havoc of Mobb Deep and the Alchemist in the song "Maintain (Fuck How You Feel)." In trying to describe how his longevity in Hip Hop music can be derived from creativity, Havoc says, "Push the envelope like the knob on the mixer"; worst-case scenario, *K for the Way* proves the attempt at pushing the envelope may be valiant but may also be a location that needs wrinkles ironed out in a practice session after the live event.

There is a question that still may remain here: Why DJ Rhetoric? Let's think back to James G. Spady and Joseph D. Eure's seminal 1991 text *Nation Conscious Rap*. In analyzing the emergence of Hip Hop culture, Spady writes, "The fact that a mass national cultural movement has grown organically out of disparate Black communities is a musical phenomenon worthy of further exploration" (Spady and Eure 414). Couple this sentiment with the Houston Baker mantra of 1993, with Hip Hop culture needing to be an integral part of an educator's wheelhouse if they are invested in K–12. Extend this idea to college education, specifically college writing, and we can clearly see that an exploration of DJ Rhetoric can help college students (re)imagine and (re)envision how they approach writing. By exploring DJ Rhetoric, college writers deeply invested in Hip Hop culture can see how the cultural knowledge and capital they bring with them is invaluable to their success in academia via writing and rhetoric. Thus, taking some time to understand how the DJ maneuvers the intricate details of writing and storytelling through distinctive discursive patterns is most worthy of inquiry and analysis. We have done this work for the emcee. We have also done this work with the graf writers, b-boys, and b-girls. I contend we take it back to the essence and do this work with the cornerstone of the culture: the DJ. To do such work, it must be done on the DJ's terms. So while we acknowledge this text as an embodiment of DJ discursive practices, let's also recognize that DJ sets rarely conform to a prescriptive formula. Thus, *K for the Way* won't always conform . . . and that's the point. Think of this book as an open-source textual-party-rockin' moment. Is it trade? Is it academic? Yeah and nah bro . . .

These embodied practices and aesthetic sensibilities are the elements that constitute the basis of what Comp3.0 might look like.

"Yo, Wrap It Up, Bee!?!": Concluding to Get to the Point of It All

On July 2, 1996—the same day Nas released *It Was Written*, multiplatinum Hip Hop group De La Soul (RIP Trugoy the Dove aka Plug 2) released their fourth full-length album *Stakes Is High*. The first album they recorded without longtime collaborator and producer (and DJ) Prince Paul, De La constructs a project which makes poignant commentary on the state of Hip Hop culture, specifically the shift in lyrics from consciousness to "gangster rap"—which, in their definition, focused on violence, drug distribution and usage—and the "baller" or "player" lifestyle,—which functioned on spending exorbitant amounts of money on material items to portray a lavish lifestyle usually above the spender's (and the average listener's) means. While the climate of the Hip Hop music industry seemed to be rapidly changing, in that moment De La Soul made it clear throughout the lyrics of this album that their music had not and would not change; the insightfulness they presented on this album came at a time when their record sales had steadily declined since and despite the multiplatinum crossover success of their debut album *3 Feet High and Rising*. Thus, when De La Soul entitled this album *Stakes Is High*, they were not only referencing their own positionality in the business of Hip Hop music but also the state of affairs in Hip Hop culture that was quickly moving away from its foundation based in originality, Afrocentrism, Black pride, and empowerment. A critically acclaimed classic album, *Stakes Is High* was responsible for some key Hip Hop moments, including introducing the mighty Mos Def (now known as Yasiin Bey) to a larger listening platform. Moreover, on the first single, "Stakes Is High," they featured the work of rising producer Jay Dee (also known as J Dilla—RIP). A musical historian and sample curator, Dilla created the Jazz-inspired "Stakes Is High" beat by chopping, sampling, and replaying an excerpt of Ahmad Jamal's "Jamal Plays Jamal." Before he passed away in February 2006, Dilla would be recognized as an upper-echelon producer and emcee. While Dilla was known primarily as a production genius, few knew of his origins as a DJ in his youth with Frank of Frank N Dank (Charnas, *Dilla Time*; Liu and Anderson). While Dilla came from a family steeped in musical knowledge, I wonder if I were to ask Dilla—like so many of the DJs in *K for the Way*—if he would make the argument that his processes as a DJ were instrumental and influential in his production success. Essentially, the Dilla-produced track "Stakes Is High" serves as a perfect sonic backdrop for the subject discussed in the song by De La Soul, at a time where the stakes were indeed high in the culture of Hip Hop as we knew it.

The stakes are also high in regard to this research. In constructing an argument for a DJ Rhetoric, Pedagogy, and Literacy, it involves capturing a specific "DJ Lineage" as well as identifying the roots of the DJs who have and continue to serve as mentors and role models, icons, and architects to Hip Hop DJ culture. Some of these DJs have lineages dating back to a time void of this culture we call "Hip Hop." So it becomes even more critical to reel in these historical lineages, and center Hip Hop squarely back into its roots in the Black tradition that borrows from various African-American cultural and social practices that are inherently political. Furthermore, this process centers around constructing an argument for a DJ Rhetoric and Pedagogy that encompasses the modes, practices, and discourse of what the Hip Hop DJ does: from turntablism, writing, and composing via sampling and music production, to bending and manipulating technology to serve those purposes until the technology is created specifically for the aforementioned purposes.

I am compelled to complete such high-stakes research as a DJ/scholar. And DJ comes first in this pair because since I can remember, I have been brought up surrounded by DJs, music, records, and Hip Hop. I learned how to be a researcher from studying the sounds, grooves, and breaks (both vocals and beats) of records, as well as diggin' to find the origins of those sounds, grooves, and breaks (both vocals and beats). I learned how to write from my friend Pee and other emcees . . . lyricists . . . from rewinding countless tapes and records, listening to lyricists on vinyl and cassette to understand flow and construction, to later sitting in the studio, observing some of the best rappers who have done it do it—from start to finish. I learned how to listen from Hav, Uncle Dea (RIP), Leo (RIP), and others—from finding the sound and pause-tape looping it, to finding the sound and turntable looping it . . . and even to finding the record that had the sound in the first place. I emerged from this journey as a DJ/scholar to give back to students who were cut from this same cloth. This community of students has been at times overlooked by English Studies in moments where the discipline has made no effort to relate to the textual lineage that influenced these bright, highly motivated students for them to understand what writing, orating, and critical thinking could look like. As a perfect example, just think back to the student writer who evoked the DJ in that journal article with which this chapter opened . . .

One night during a recording session for legendary Hip Hop group Mobb Deep, Havoc looked at Prodigy and said, "Yo—Todd *really* loves this Hip Hop shit, yo! He loves it more than we do, for real!" We all kinda looked at each other after that, as the gravity of the statement sunk in for everyone in the room. Reflecting on that comment now, it presents a vital point—this research comes from the premise that Hip Hop was birthed on: I do this for the love of the culture and hopefully for some student in a college or grad school course who could use some validation, or a way to figure out how to marry the culture we love with the content we study.

No doubt, the stakes are high in this research. And be clear: I'm ecstatic to have embarked on this journey. I would've done these DJ interviews no matter what. I would've wanted to speak to these people and pick their brains to understand my own Hip Hop lineage and family tree no matter what. Because I have BreakBeat Lou's records in my crates. Because Clark Kent mentored some of my all-time favorite DJs. Because Lord Finesse and Large Pro (Large Professor), Mr. Walt and Evil Dee, Mr. Len and Prince Paul crafted some of my all-time favorite beats, tracks, and albums. Because Kool Bob Love (Bobbito) and Eclipse, Matthew Africa (RIP), and Sucio Smash educated me from some of the illest underground locations known to man. Because Ca$h Money and Jazzy Jeff, Rhettmatic and Revolution, Spinderella and Shortee, Pam the Funkstress (RIP) and Kuttin Kandi helped open doors for Rob Swift and Boogie Blind, Moppy and Damage, Timbuck2 (RIP) and Illvibe, Shorty Wop and Tyra from

Saigon, Reborn and Killa-Jewel. Because I studied Spinna and Mark Farina mixes. Because Red Alert schooled me on this Hip Hop thing as a youngin! This is part of my own DNA and lineage. So this full-length offering helps me to make sense of my journey and share it with everyone involved. It's been what I've lived, eaten, and breathed way before living, eating, and breathing were in style, feel me?

Let me invite you to embark on a sonic and literary research ride orchestrated by two turntables, a mixer, and the vast and rich historical landscape that comes with it.

Welcome to *K for the Way* . . .

You know what this is? This is the sound of a caterpillar turning into a butterfly!

Sean Price at Rock The Bells 2012, New Jersey. He says this when his DJ starts playing Catalyst's "Uzuri" off the *Perception* album. This is the original sample for The Fab 5's classic collaboration entitled "Leflaur Leflah Eshkoshka."

2

"ITCHIN' FOR A SCRATCH"

Pushin' toward a DJ Rhetoric on the 1s and 2s

. . . the prophet /
sincere since the saga begun / started with nada / listening to "Nautilus" drum . . .

Fashawn + Alchemist, "Po for President," *FASH-ionably Late*, Mass Appeal
Records, 2014.

. . . for example, one of my favorite Hip Hop projects from 2014 is
Fashawn's collaborative EP with producer the Alchemist,
entitled *FASH-ionably Late*.
The first song on the EP is "Po for President," where Fashawn gives
gritty street-bravado-laced rhymes about being an underdog
who finds his way to the top of his lyrical game . . . in describing
his humble beginnings, Fashawn evokes a classic jazz song but also
a Hip Hop sample staple from Bob James.
Hearing Fashawn reference "Nautilus" immediately brought me back
to one of my most treasured Hip Hop listening moments,
which comes from an early 1990s cut from
Jeru da Damaja's album *The Sun Rises in the East*
entitled "My Mind Spray" . . .

https://doi.org/10.7330/9781646424849.c002

As I was learning the formalities of the English language, what most inspired my creative abilities in writing was my love of Hip Hop music and culture. Growing up in Queensbridge and Ravenswood Housing Projects, I was surrounded by rappers, b-boys and b-girls, writers (aka graf artists), DJs, and producers. While I quietly tried to become, and met some success in junior high school as, a rapper, I knew my cousin was a *really* dope rapper, so I ultimately wouldn't be able to go that route. Somehow, I found my way into becoming a DJ, even though when I look back on it now, all the necessary elements and ingredients were in place to get me there. The first album I ever asked for was an 8-track of Michael Jackson's *Off the Wall*. My first album on vinyl was Whodini's *Back in Black*, and for some reason "Funky Beat"—an ode to Whodini's DJ Grandmaster Dee—stuck in my head from the first time I heard it. The first record I'd really scratch on was the introductory bells on Bobby Brown's "Don't Be Cruel." I can remember the day my homegirl Felicia stood outside on the bench in front of my building and listened to the speaker I put right in the second-floor apartment window so my cousin and I could scratch the same break in the record to see who rocked the best.

My cousin continued to write rhymes, while I continued to record radio mix shows and buy records every single weekend with my allowance. I studied those tapes like scholars consume literary works and journal articles. I'd scratch records on the low on the record player connected to the AM/FM tuner, cassette, and 8-track decks. I'd already been buying up albums on cassette tape since my Sunday School days. I'd tell my mom I might stay for church but I'd leave shortly after Sunday School ended and break north to hit up the music store in QP's flea market on Queens Plaza, which the world now knows as a location called Long Island City Flea (thanks to Lara Spencer and *Flea Market Flip*). Everyone in my junior high school class knew I was the dude who'd have the dopest album that came out that week. I also followed in my cousin's footsteps by learning to loop song breaks on a double cassette tape deck. As a rapper, he always needed new beats. So when he got tired of waiting on other producers to supply him with fresh instrumentals, he learned his own early rudimentary sampling technique . . . and I was right there to pick up on it. He'd let a song play on the left-side tape, and then time where the break started. Then he'd hit the pause button on the right-side tape, which was ready to record, and let the break rock. The trick and technic required tapping the pause button in the right spot to keep the tempo of the looped segment consistent. I got to a point where I'd make beats with two different breaks from different songs. Counting out four to eight bars, I timed my pause-button-taps properly. These were integral elements to my acquisition of DJ Rhetoric and Pedagogy: the cultural and musical seeds—landmarks, rituals, and processes that helped to groom who I'd grow into as a DJ.

When I finally made that I-95 North trip to St. George's School in Newport, Rhode Island, the one thing that truly amazed me was the radio station WSGS. They had turntables in there . . . I could lock the door, close the window blinds, and really practice while no one was paying attention. Having access to that space prompted me to go hard at buying records both at school and at home. When QP's closed, there were record stores on Steinway Street, and there was one I'd go to in Flushing, just off Main Street. By senior year, I'd even made trips to Beat Street in downtown Brooklyn before a mosse of like fifteen dudes tried to rob my man Ricketts and me that one day. I was that kid who was equipped with a Walkman, Sony headphones bigger than the average-sized earmuffs, extra AA batteries, and records tucked under my wing. And when the movie _Juice_ came out, fohgettaboutit! I already had the khaki-tan certified jacket that GeeQ (Omar Epps) had. Even though I was suspicious of GeeQ's scratching in the movie (I'd later realize he wasn't really scratching in the movie at all), those scenes with him practicing, making party tapes in his bedroom, and the DJ Battle rounds further convinced me DJing was the direction I'd travel. That's when I realized the radio station wasn't enough. I needed my own turntables. So senior year in high school during Christmas vacation, I pooled what little bit of money I had together and hit a pawn shop for two turntables. They were Technics, they were belt drives, and they looked the same, so I bought them. But when I got them to my Uncle Dea, who was always known as the DJ in my family alongside my other Uncle Todd, I realized just how real it was when it took him taking _both_ of those turntables apart just to construct one that worked fully. Luckily, I lived in the hood, the world of a thousand hustles and schemes . . . my man Maurice from the first floor had a turntable he would sell me for dumb cheap when he found out I was looking for one. It was a direct drive that had no counterweight for the tonearm . . . but nothing that three AAA batteries and some tape couldn't fix. My "South-Bronx-1977-Blackout-Bequeathment" came when I made a stealth-mode move and _borrowed_ the Radio Shack Realistic mixer out of the radio station because they weren't using it, making me fully equipped. My man Leo, who was a chef in the school kitchen, bought records for me during the school year in Providence from Skippy Whites as well as a record store my homie Marcus Todd worked in because I couldn't really go too far off campus.

This is where my journey would truly start. Uncle Dea and Leo were the first to help cultivate my own DJ rhetorical practices in high school, but only after I took some things upon myself and engaged in the introductory aspects of a DJ learning curve.

My initial DJ landmark was when Uncle Dea listened to the first few mixtapes I made. He wasn't really impressed until he heard the mix with the acoustic version of Prince's "7" over that white-label Kenny Dope breakbeat. That's when he nodded his head and said, "That shit right there is *FUNKY* nephew!" He hit stop on the tape and said: "You think you can do that mix again? Then c'mon—let's make this tape together." After that tape, Uncle Dea would not only help me sharpen my skills, but he would also put me onto record spots like Rock and Soul (when they were across the street from Macy's), Disc-O-Rama, and Vinylmania. Once he opened the door to the location that served as my vinyl stacks, archives, and bookstores, I was on my way . . .

I realized then that part of being successful with DJing is studying music: analyzing different sounds and parts of records, songs, and albums—and the art of creating new music within the parameters of the songs you've been given. This had been the work of Hip Hop DJs and producers, the essence and root of the "makin' something outta nufin" philosophy. And at one point, this was also a core debate of the culture: were producers "looping" or (re)creating, merely sampling toward what academics would call "collage" or "pastiche" (Miller; Rice, "The 1963 Hip-Hop Machine"), or were they configuring toward new sonic landscapes that required the supreme science of destroying and deconstructing to rebuild in infinite synced (re)configurations?

I learned a lot about the subtleties of Hip Hop sonics by constantly listening to albums, beats, and breaks; listening to other DJs scratch on albums, beats, and breaks; scratching records; making double cassette mixtapes and pause-button beat tapes. I began to see the prominent Hip Hop artists of my day (who ironically came from QB) telling tremendous stories in the span of four minutes or less. While most rappers may not have been "formally" trained, they had picked up on the aspects and elements of creative writing, poetry, and poetics (Bradley). And I always made the argument that the best poets of my youth were rappers, simple and plain; as emcees they used all the literary techniques of storytelling, cadence, alliteration, rhyme schemes, and various others, in myriad of overt and subliminal tactics to get their point(s) across in rhyme (Jocson; Low).

Upon graduating from St. George's, I was the only one of twelve in my graduating class accepted to Williams College in northwestern Massachusetts. I arrived on campus at Williams, and after a few people heard I was a DJ, they sent me to DJ Scott, who back then was *the* DJ on campus. All-weekend night-life ran through Scott, who is still one of my best friends. "Show and Prove" has always been a Hip Hop motto (compliments of the Nation of Gods and Earths), so Scott invited me over to his apartment off campus to play some records and see what I could do. After hearing me rock for about thirty minutes, he told me I had a really good ear and that my sequencing and selection were on point. Next thing he did was put me on to the way the whole DJ science on campus functioned—from the politics of campus clubs, entries, and dorms, to the business and the financial aspects of paperwork, receipts, and the infamous 1099. Scott also let me rock with him at his parties, to help me understand different elements of scratching and how to rock on a 1200 from a visceral hands-on perspective. Those lessons were critical and necessary for me, because the transition between belt-drive and direct-drive turntables can be rocky if you don't fully comprehend the rudimentary physics of how a 1200 functions. Because of the magnet underneath the platter that connects to a high-torque motor, the Technics 1200 turntable has the ability to maintain its speed while you hold a record in place with a slipmat. With my antiquated belt-drive and one direct-drive turntables, I had acclimated my process of mixing to actually "pushing" the record into place (and thus, on[to] beat). I learned how the adjustment with the record player worked based on the rubber band that maintained the platter speed on one side and how to finesse my fingertip "push" with just enough power to match the speed of the low-torque motor on the other side. With my starter kit DJ set, I made *everything* out of nothing. Once I moved to the industry standard 1200s, that process immediately evolved.

While Scott guided me through this transition, I got a chance to rock a couple parties on campus by myself. Within about a month, a friend named Mecha, who served as culture coordinator of the Black Student Union, approached me about DJing parties for the BSU. We made a deal that I'd do a number of parties for the U and get a lump sum payment upfront; that check allowed me to shoot out to Troy Audio just outside of Albany, and purchase my first pair of Technic 1200s. This was the next critical step in my understanding of DJ Rhetoric.

I also arrived in the Berkshires speaking "the thun language." No one understood what I meant when I'd say the words "sun" or "thun" or "kitko." They thought I was a tad bit crazy, until a crew of people came back from a road trip to NYC on a brisk Saturday evening that fall semester. They ran into a party

I was DJing and geeked over how Funkmaster Flex was playing "Shook Ones Pt II" on HOT 97 like it was going outta style. That's when the *Juvenile Hell* poster on my dorm room wall started to make sense to people. By the end of that next week, people's language started switching, and I realized just where I sat in terms of Hip Hop influences and this phenomenon called "language shift." It would truly be a timely scenario, given the fact that I had officially graduated from two mismatched turntables, to rocking two matching Technic 1200s. With the industry standard equipment, I was now in a place where I was prepared to truly learn how to speak in the DJ Literacy that those around me and those to whom I'd always listened to conversed. It also allowed me to make sense of what sponsorship actually looked like.

The Role of "Put-On" Politics

The idea of sponsors was first introduced to me by Carmen Kynard. I was telling her how I planned on presenting at the Conference on College Composition and Communication (better known as CCCCs or 4Cs) and the gist of my talk had to do with interviewing DJs. Early on I was telling Carmen about how at certain moments in my writing, if I wanted to clarify or even brainstorm a nerdy Hip Hop DJ moment, I could always call Mr. Len and talk through it with him. Not only is Len a crazy DJ, producer, and musician, but he's also a real thinker and reader, so we'd have these deep intellectual conversations. When I told Carmen that Len had always been supportive of my work, she said, "That's hot! It reminds me of how in my work, we have these people called 'sponsors' who kinda serve in that same capacity that Len serves in for you." She went onto describe how sponsors are pretty much similar to those organic intellectuals (Gramsci) and cultural meaning-makers, who help to usher your progression and growth within that culture. Sponsors on the DJ level can sometimes serve as people who put other DJs on, in apprentice-fashion. For example, Funkmaster Flex used to carry record crates for Chuck Chillout. It was here that I realized that Uncle Dea, Leo, Marcus, and Scott had all served as my DJ sponsors in the early days. They were all part of my acquisition of critical components of DJ Literacy and DJ rhetorical practices.

Having a clear sense of sponsorship helped me carve out what meaningful research could look like. Up until these conversations with Carmen, a lot of my graduate professors in Comp/Rhet were either giving me very traditionalist (and very racist) work that not only didn't relate to me but also pretty much ridiculed me. I was being told my work really and truly didn't have a place in English Studies, and especially *not* in Comp/Rhet, unless I forced it to conscribe to the given traditionalist ideologies. So these moments with Carmen were helpful, and by the time I had gotten into a class called Theories of Literacy, I really didn't know what to do with myself. It was here where I met people via articles and books like Brian Street and Eric Pleasant, Elaine "Dr. E" Richardson, Morris Young, H. Samy Alim, and S. J. Meacham and "Crossroads Theory." The connection I was starting to see with New Literacy Studies made sense to me, because it approached understanding literacy from a place that embraced meaningful knowledge about language and literacy acquisition from outside the box. It allowed me to grab from different places and sources and be in the mix as I made those connections. And that was my life in a nutshell—from undergrad through my master's and doctoral programs—and throughout all the years of being a DJ. I've said this quite a few times to people, and I'm not really sure that anyone truly understood it when I said it. Thus, I think it's worth mentioning and memorializing here:

This moment I've described called "Theories of Literacy" saved my academic life.

New Literacy Studies struck a path that led my thinking on how the idea of sponsorship works within English Studies or even across different areas of academia as a whole. And we can see this work in a few places. Let's take a second to step into the mix . . .

Finding the Funky Break in the Song Called Sponsorship

In Gail Okawa's article "Diving for Pearls: Mentoring as Cultural and Activist Practice among Academics of Color," she looks at the mentoring contributions of Drs. Geneva Smitherman and Victor Villanueva. What comes out of this set of interviews with mentees of these two distinguished professors and researcher/scholars is that "mentoring must become an activist practice in this context; it is critical to the survival and success of graduate students and junior faculty of color in the academic culture, especially in fields like English that attempt to perpetuate the discourse of that culture, and especially at predominately white institutions, which seem, and in some ways are, uninviting and unfriendly to those who have been historically underrepresented or absent" (Okawa 509). But where the idea of mentoring begins to look more like a sponsorship of sorts, is in Dr. G's definition, when she elaborates and says, "Mentoring is a kind of nurturing whereby the mentor helps/motivates the mentee to construct a vision of possibilities beyond the present moment" (512). Here Okawa captures Dr. G in a moment that truly reflects the idea of sponsorship in the DJ community, that moves beyond just a mentorship. For example, DJs like Mr. Len, Rich Medina, Spinna, and BreakBeat Lou have all understood the value and importance of the research I was conducting about the DJ. Their goal(s) had nothing to do with showing me how to become a better DJ (which would be more of a mentor/apprentice relationship, similar to Funk Master Flex and Chuck Chillout) but had to do with ushering me into the culture and walking me through elements of their practice as DJs so I could—in looking at a much larger and broader picture—envision what a DJ Rhetoric could look like in a process where a DJ demonstrates a specific type of cultural and sonic literacy.

We can also see this formation and movement to understand sponsorship within a culture discussed by Eric Pleasant. In his article "Literacy Sponsors and Learning: An Ethnography of Punk Literacy in mid-1980s Waco," Pleasant uses writing from Deborah Brandt to begin to frame his idea of sponsorship: "Sponsors range from family, friends, and teachers to setting, family background, socioeconomic standing, and exposure to ideas. All forms of sponsorship direct us and influence our literacy development. Literacy itself influences the direction of further development. Sponsorship and literacy become the proverbial 'snowball' within which we develop; its shape over time is dictated by the layers of learning, background, and exposure inside" (Brandt 139). This idea of sponsorship becomes an important distinction to make and identify because while I have experienced quite the multicultural assortment of DJs within my research, an examination of their initial questionnaires will dictate that all roads point to Rome. The "Rome" I refer to is a location in which the Hip Hop DJ originates; this location is one that has much to do with socioeconomic factors but, quite frankly, it truly has everything to do with a diasporic phenomenon unfolding in New York City. A quick perusal of most DJs' mentors, role models, and idols leads us back to Black figures prominent in both Hip Hop and DJ culture . . . and if we look at these models in the form of a textual lineage, they lead back to the three founding DJ fathers: Kool Herc, Grandmaster Flash, and Afrika Bambaataa. All three of these figures are Black, or of the African diaspora. With Herc and Flash having roots in the Caribbean, sponsorship within DJ culture (mainly from the perspective of Hip Hop) functions based on a premise that the original DJs in the culture were of the African diaspora, spinning sounds in Black inner-city landscapes. Thus, mentors and sponsors were mostly Black and, oftentimes, women (Stoever), in the early stages of Hip Hop. This idea is encapsulated in an interview with emcee Yasiin Bey (you may also know him as the Mighty Mos Def) in Ice T's documentary *Something from Nothing: The Art of Rap*. When asked about his thoughts on Hip Hop music and culture, Bey states, "One of the things that I feel about Hip Hop—and I quote all the time—is from Q-Tip, when he goes: 'rap is not pop / if you call it that then stop!' [Rap] didn't start out as a popular culture movement. It didn't even have pop culture ambitions. It's a folk art. It's folk music, it's a tribal experience" (Bey). Bey helps us put this moment in DJ culture into perspective: there appears to be resistance to the humble folk beginnings of Hip Hop, which comes from the seeming necessity to rebuke the folk traditions of the DJ in order to be legitimized and accepted within the mainstream of "high art" or even the mainstream of the musical and intellectual branches of the academy. And the "folk" and "tribal" monikers that Bey uses here are meant to identify, establish, and even reify Hip Hop music's origins as located in New York City's urban underclass and as rooted in Black musical and cultural legacy.

Marcyliena Morgan also helps to flesh out this connection in her book *The Real Hiphop: Battling for Knowledge, Power, and Respect in the LA Underground*. Morgan surveys Hip Hop's cultural history as intrinsically ingrained in African-American culture as well as the African and Caribbean diaspora. Morgan identifies the DJ as more than a figure who may play different records; instead, she notes, "In African American communities DJs are not minor players in urban social and political development; rather, they have been at the core of cultural and political movements" (Morgan, *The Real Hiphop* 51–52). One can envision Morgan's description of the DJ's role as being a sponsor to both African-American and, then later, Hip Hop culture all at once: "Hip-hop DJs inherited the role of playing music that reflected the beat and the mindset of a generation as well as the responsibility of providing a voice and information within a system of oppression and misrepresentation . . . the DJ traditions merged so that not only did one get a rocking sound system, but also word (worldwide) about 'the system' and 'the man'" (52–53). The idea Morgan presents here shows the role of the Hip Hop DJ expanding beyond the simple function of rocking parties or radio airwaves with your favorite jams. The DJ becomes a reporter with sonic sources (both public and private), or even a sociopolitical tour guide with a funky fresh roadmap of beats, rhymes, and the safe haven(s) and pitfall(s) of daily life.

Jared A. Ball also utilizes elements of Hip Hop DJ Rhetoric and discourse in his book *I Mix What I Like: A Mixtape Manifesto*. Ball continues Morgan's idea of the DJ as integral meaning-maker and cultural sponsor, as he acknowledges and reflects on "the mixtape" as a source of Emancipatory Journalism: a form of media and communication disbursement that revolves around decolonizing practices. Furthermore, in explaining the importance of the mixtape in regard to fighting back against a colonial stronghold of modern media, he states:

> Both the mixtape and EJ [Emancipatory Journalism] have origins in the irreverence of anti-colonial struggle. That is, the mixtape, initially created by DJs searching for a way to disseminate their art without sanction from a mainstream corporate industry, allowed for the kinds of communication ultimately threatening to power. When Brucie B, Jazzy Joyce, DJ Hollywood, then later Ron G and Kid Capri took their artfulness to their communities by recording sessions and parties and making special custom mixes, all without institutions of state power backing them, the act itself spoke to the very tradition of unsanctioned communication that is so often seen as dangerous. It was—and is—an anti-authoritarian act, one that recalls the act of newly "freed" nations developing their own presses and traditions of journalism more suited to their national development . . . the act of creating a mixture of music and sounds (again, without sanction or permission) not necessarily intended by the initial artist, or—as is the case with Ron G—creating an entirely new genre of music, is ultimately (and potentially) no different from consciously deciding that new forms of media and journalism are required to popularize the movements seeking immediate material uplift and widespread social change. (Ball 122)

Ball continues Morgan's insights in this moment, using the rhetorical practices of the DJ, and mainly the discourse of the "mixtape," as a tool to analyze sites of anticolonial endeavors within mass media and culture. Looking at both the mixtape and pirate radio (run by DJs) shows Ball's interest in and connection to the importance of the DJ and how this discourse has been underappreciated in contemporary times among many intellectual circles and conversations. The DJ was once at the center of the popular discourse and media dissemination: a strategic type of power the DJ held (and still holds) that is threatening to the status quo of mass media. Ball presents the idea of the rap music mixtape as

> rap music's original mass medium—which has gone from the underground distribution network used by DJs to spread house (or street) party mixes to a corporate-driven, track-listed "exclusive" prerelease mechanism stripped of any originality in purpose, function, or content. However, unlike other popular forms of mass media today, the mixtape remains among the most viable spaces

for the practice of emancipatory journalism and inclusion of dissident music or cultural expression. (Ball 16)

It is important to note the mixtape discourse Ball identifies is an integral part of DJ Rhetoric: the modes, methodologies, and discursive elements of the DJ. Essentially, he uses the discourse of the mixtape as emancipatory, as the mixtape functions on the premise of DJs and artists being able to operate without the permission of the corporate-driven label, even though the featured artists and DJs may be signed to major-label deals (which typically do *not* favor the artist whatsoever) and using music that may have something to do with a contractual relationship with a label. This idea is best epitomized by Q-Tip of A Tribe Called Quest in "Check the Rhime"; here, Tip gives us the historical "Industry Rule #4080: record company people are shaaaaaady" (Q-Tip). So until the recent emergence of the label contract structure known as "the 360 Deal" (where a label claims part of all of an artist's earning power), the mixtape inevitably functioned as a revenue stream for artists and DJs that completely bypassed the financial branch of the label. It is a pushback as well as a push *back* toward the folk-art mindset presented by Bey.

Similarly, in his book *Capturing Sound: How Technology Has Changed Music*, Mark Katz connects Hip Hop turntablism and DJ battles to the African-American traditions of "playin' the dozens" as well as the "cutting contests" in Jazz music, and places the act of turntablism in context with Black rhetorical strategies and sentiments that are inherently politically and culturally based. Thus, we find DJ Rhetoric and competencies in DJ Literacy springing forth from a Black tradition, similar to many of the musical forms present in both contemporary as well as historical American society. It follows that while some scholars who write on the DJ say they'd rather not be essentialist in talking about racial parameters in the origins of the Hip Hop DJ, I'm more than happy to do so in a way that is not exclusionary. I break it down like this: to be an essentialist in this regard means to rock with the root of the word—the "essence." And the essence of the Hip Hop DJ resides with Black music, culture, traditions, and, thereby, African-American rhetorical practices; within each lies an African diasporic hybridity but also a distinctness to African-American artistic as well as sociocultural and political sensibilities that cannot be ignored or even (re)written in Hip Hop's best moments but then highlighted in darker instances. My qualm has always been that there is the desire to label Hip Hop as "global culture" when we want to sing the culture's praises but that then we see the degradation involved with labeling Hip Hop as "Black culture" when an unsavory occurrence or series of circumstances pop off. Having it both ways simply doesn't work here.

The Connection between Blackness and DJ Rhetoric

So why even address sponsors? Because in order to fully engage in a conversation—whether intellectual, pedestrian or otherwise—that discusses what DJ Rhetoric might look like, one has to think about the cultural and textual lineage of sponsors and mentors within Hip Hop DJ culture, and what it means to be fundamentally "literate" within Hip Hop DJ culture, as well as what possibilities literacy within the culture has. For this, a few definitions must be spelled out. First is the idea of textual lineage from Alfred W. Tatum; when formulating new and innovative ways to (re)engage African-American adolescent males in reading, writing, and aspects of literacy, Tatum describes the idea of a textual lineage this way: "Similar to lineages in genealogical studies, [textual lineage] is made up of texts (both literary and nonliterary) that are instrumental in one's human development because of the meaning and significance one has garnered from them" (Tatum xiv). In this moment, we can expand on Tatum's idea of textual lineage and push toward the notion of sonic lineage: a list or series of sonic sources that share the same sentiment but that, in some cases, are an earlier source that predicates the existence of the newer source (Craig, "Stacks"; Polson).

For example, one of my favorite Hip Hop projects from 2014 is Fashawn's collaborative EP with producer the Alchemist, entitled *FASH-ionably Late*. The first song on the EP is "Po for President," where Fashawn gives gritty street-bravado-laced rhymes about being an underdog who finds his way to the top of his lyrical game. When describing his demeanor, Fashawn says, "The dominant one / your timing is done / when I vomit / on top of the drum / your noggin get numb / the prophet / sincere since the saga begun / started with nada / listening to Nautilus drum" (Fashawn in Fashawn + Alchemist). In describing his humble beginnings, Fashawn evokes a classic Jazz song but also a Hip Hop sample staple from Bob James. Hearing Fashawn reference "Nautilus" immediately brought me back to one of my most treasured Hip Hop listening moments, which comes from an early 1990s cut from Jeru da Damaja's album *The Sun Rises in the East* entitled "My Mind Spray." The sample used by DJ Premier clearly summons the sentiment Jeru is trying to convey in rhyme, using his lyrical prowess to compare his mental dexterity to the brute force of a firearm; Jeru does this, however, while quoting himself from another song, when he says, "Your 9 spray / my mind spray"

(Jeru, "Come Clean"). Most Hip Hop aficionados—and many Jazz heads for that matter—will immediately recognize the song Premier sampled: Bob James's "Nautilus." Listening to Fashawn conjure up "Nautilus" in 2014 brings me to Jeru da Damaja in 1994. But "Nautilus" is also used in a series of my favorite Hip Hop records; two specific songs that come to mind are Nice & Smooth's "No Delayin'" from 1989 and Pete Rock and C.L. Smooth's "The Sun Won't Come Out" in 1994. But "Nautilus" has also been used by Slick Rick ("Children's Story" in 1988), Run-DMC ("Beats to the Rhyme" in 1988), Eric B. & Rakim ("Follow the Leader" in 1988 and "Let the Rhythm Hit 'Em" in 1990), and Main Source ("Live at the Barbeque" in 1991). I share this example to show how the sonic lineage of Fashawn's song "Po for President" can lead us to Bob James's "Nautilus" and the bevvy of Hip Hop songs that sample him. So twenty-something-year-olds listening to Fashawn might find their way to Bob James in the same way the twenty-something-year-old version of me found Bob James via Jeru, Nice and Smooth, and Pete Rock and C.L. Smooth. Hence, sonic lineage is similar to Tatum's conception of textual lineage but directly connected with the auditory via sound and song. Tatum's ideas resonate clearly when I connect my sonic lineage to the tapes I made of Mr. Magic and Marley Marl's "Rap Attack" or Marley and Pete Rock's *In Control* shows on WBLS, Chuck Chillout and Red Alert's shows on KISS-FM, *Off the Wall*, *Back in Black*, *Don't Be Cruel*, *By All Means Necessary*, *People's Instinctive Travels*, *Video Music Box*, *Yo! MTV Raps*, and many, many more. Any Hip Hop DJ committed to the craft can run through this list both quickly and effortlessly; they will also admit (like I will here), that for every one "text" listed, there are *at least five* more unlisted yet equally vital to and interchangeable within their sonic lineage.

Again, DJ Rhetoric is premised on the ways in which a DJ decides to express oneself and communicate that expression among members within and outside of DJ culture via turntables and the sounds they create with their arsenal/archive/collection of music, and thus has everything to do with the sonic quality of the choices they make. So DJ Rhetoric and sonic lineage go hand in hand. Essentially, it's about how that DJ works and interacts "in the mix" with other pre-fixed songs, or even in the mix by completely (re)configuring pre-fixed songs (DJs Ron G, Hot Day, Cutmaster Melquan, and those summertime blend tapes come to mind for me). Many of the people I have spoken with are members of DJ culture, organic intellectuals that make meaning both within and outside of the specific culture . . . but not all of them are *sponsors* to the same culture, or even mentors within it. This conversation is key in identifying integral elements of our conversation around DJ Rhetoric, textual, and sonic lineage.

Everyone Needs a Hug: DJ Sponsorship in Theory

While working on my dissertation, I caught wind of the fact that Christie Z-Pabon was selling a mixer: a Rane TTM 57SL. Fully equipped with a built-in Serato interface, this Rane mixer also had the capability to rock Video Serato. Because I had been floating this idea around of using Video Serato for my dissertation defense, I was already in the market for this mixer. However, I was going to have to buy the Rane 62, as the 57 was discontinued. So when I saw Christie's for sale message on Facebook, I immediately hit her up.

There were a number of reasons I copped the mixer from Christie. The main reason was she was selling it to help fund the 2012 DMC USA team's travel and stay in London for the DMC World Championships. At that point, since my academic research as well as my dissertation focused on DJs, I felt compelled to support the cause. The second reason for me was pretty economical; I honestly thought this would be one of the last mixers that I'd buy. The previous time I had bought a mixer (aside from the tiny Numark I use when I travel with the Vestax Handytrax to academic conferences) was when I bought my Vestax mixer, the PMC-26. When I copped it in like '96 or '97, it was roughly $700 or $800. However, I still have that same mixer to this day; it's treated me well and rocked out religiously. One of my peoples from college said, "Todd, that is one lesson you taught me: spend the money on a high-end mixer, because it's a worthy investment." The 57 wasn't cheap. It wasn't a cheap mixer brand new; getting it used was a break, but I would be spending some paper. So it really was an investment for me. And I honestly didn't want to spend the extra $500-plus it would've cost for the 62 at that time. Now don't get me wrong—some people thought I should buy a new mixer, as this one was used and had no warranty. But Christie explained how the mixer was used in the past three DMC US DJ competitions; with that in mind, there was some sentimentality and history that came along with this piece of equipment. Initially, I agreed with some folks in that turntablists straight beat mixers up . . . I mean, they are, after all, doing all sorts of tricks and routines. Ask anybody about how many slider knobs DJ Precision has sent flying across a stage or the room . . .

On the one hand, here was this used mixer—used by turntablists nonetheless—that wasn't really cheap. On the other hand, because of Christie's Rane sponsorship, when we spoke about it and my concern with it not having a warranty, she agreed to have the mixer sent to Rane so they could give it a once-over before I purchased it. They also agreed to give me the Video Serato download, which meant another couple hundred dollars in savings. And just before Christie left for the DMC World, she was waiting on the mixer to come back from Rane. Finally she said, "Todd—I know the mixer is good. And Rane treats me well, they're one of my best sponsors. But here's what I'll do: if anything happens to your mixer, as long as you get it to me, I will make sure that I get it to Rane, have them check and fix it, and then get it back to you." This was all I needed to hear; I was ready to shoot uptown right then and give Christie the paper for it. But since it was still in transit from Rane, I had to wait a couple more weeks.

When I went to meet up with Christie in Harlem, I parked my truck and eagerly waited. I saw her leave the building, walking toward me carrying the box. She gave it to me, and as she was talking to one of her neighbors, I couldn't help but straight open the box like a child on Christmas morning. I saw it was sealed with postage still on it. As I broke it open, the first thing I saw was a pink slip. I looked and sure enough, it was the invoice from Rane, describing what they looked at, what they tweaked, and what they replaced altogether. After talking to her neighbor, Christie turned to me, and I handed her the pink slip. Her comments were simple: "I wanted to keep it sealed so you could be the first one to open it when it came back from Rane." She proceeded to walk through the mixer with me: the redline series with new slider knobs all around. Then she flipped it over and said, "That's our DMC USA sticker right there. And then the 'DMC' handwritten on the back. Fabel wrote that, not me—so it's kinda his autograph. And that's it right there, you should be all set with the new addition to your family. Enjoy!" Now to some people, this isn't a surprise at all, myself included. But to those who don't know Christie, her full name is Christie Z-Pabon. Some people know her as the wife of Popmaster Fabel—longtime member of the legendary Rock Steady Crew. However, New York City DJ culture knows Christie as the person who organizes the DMC USA competitions, orchestrates the *Tools of War Grassroots Hip Hop Newsletter*, and is responsible for the Crotona Park Jams in the Bronx as well as Diggers' Delight in St. Nicholas Park in Harlem. Christie is also known for her strong opinions as well as the work she does within New York City DJ and Hip Hop culture. And finally, she is a trustworthy person, full of integrity and honor, and fully committed to all things involved with the DJ. So in essence, buying a mixer from Christie is probably one of the safest bets you could make, especially on anything Rane.

I interviewed Christie to include her perspective on the DJ in my dissertation. But Christie was also instrumental in regard to plugging me in with other

DJs to interview. The highlight was when I received a phone call one day on my cell, which started pretty cryptic but wound up being one of the most memorable moments in my research process:

> "Hello"
> "Hello, I'm looking for Todd."
> "This is Todd, who is this?"
> "Is this Todd Craig?"
> "Yes, it is? Now who exactly is this???"
> "This is KOOL DJ Red Alert, and I was calling you in regards to the email Christie sent me about your research. I like the sound of what you're doing and I'd like to be involved."

(Now picture me pulling the phone from my ear and looking at it like "yo—are you effin' kidding me??? Is KOOOOOOOOL DJ Red Alert calling *me* on MY phone right now??? YEEEEEEEEEEEEEEEEEEEAH!!!")

In the months after interviewing Christie, she became a sponsor for me while I completed my dissertation. She reached out to a number of people; not only did Christie advocate for my work, but she circulated it amongst her network of DJs. The networking she did on my behalf to help me progress with my dissertation research and my interaction with DJs could only be considered as a certain type of sponsorship. So why not buy a mixer from a sponsor that you know and trust?

DJ Sponsorship in Action

Ultimately, the way I was able to move throughout New York City DJ culture was primarily through an organic type of sponsorship. While it did start off with a few people I knew, it was their affiliations that helped me make connections and inroads with other DJs, which in turn led to connections and inroads with other DJs. And of course, I always had a personal "DJ Interview Wish List" that I kept in the stash; some of those people I can honestly say I was able to interview . . . and it was indeed an honor and a humbling experience to talk to women and men who influenced who I am and how I think as a DJ/scholar. So it started as me talking to people like Mr. Len, Rich Medina, Illvibe Collective, and Mas Yamagata over at Barefoot Distribution. Those dudes alone opened the doors for me to interview other critical sponsors. J over at Cornerstone, a company devoted to the promotion and lifestyle choices linked with the DJ (as their trademarked motto is "the DJ IS the Cornerstone"), connected me with DJs including Statik Selektah, Spinderella, and an arsenal of other folks. Mas put me in touch with an array of major players: Rhettmatic (World Famous Beat Junkies), Jazzy Jeff, M.O.S., and DJ Spinna—who is not only one of the most genuine people on the planet Earth but is also the dude who put me in touch with Clark Kent, Marley Marl, and other important DJs. Both Mas and J triangulated my J Period connect, in the same way BreakBeat Lou and Lord Finesse triangulated my interview with Boogie Blind. And as time went on, talking to Lord Finesse after making it through my senior year in high school listening to the *Funky Technician* album brought things full circle for me. Then, DJ Ultraviolet (who's known in Philly as DJ UV) put me onto Large Professor. Talking to Large Pro after studying his music, production, and lyrics and knowing his influence on my cousin's music career was colossal in that it began to help me connect the dots with my Hip Hop DJ/sonic lineage. In the same way DJ Ambush put me on with DJ Shorty Wop—Estelle's tour DJ—DJ A.Vee connected me with Prince Paul, Freddie Foxxx connected me with Lord Finesse, LJ Smith connected me to DJ Nabs via Spinderella, and Skeme Richards put me on with BreakBeat Lou. And BreakBeat Lou still—to this day—will hit me on the humble like "Yo Todd, what's good brother? Just checking in on you, how's the family?" Understand that I've done numerous interviews, so there's really a million and one stories about how all these interviews were orchestrated. I've been really lucky to make some genuine connections and relationships with people, and that has made my research truly fulfilling. Remember, I told you this is work I'd want to do regardless. And to me, it will always be what separates my academic job from this life work I've been fortunate enough to be able to do.

Chef Curry with That DJ Rhetoric Pot

If we look at my earlier interpolation of Kynard's definition of rhetoric, which has a textual lineage based in Black protest rhetoric and movements and New Literacy Studies, coupled with Tatum's notion of textual lineage and Pleasant's idea of sponsorship, we can clearly see the making of DJ Rhetoric: the recipe involves a cup of the social and cultural practices of the DJ (pre-, mid- and post-sonic work: what we hear), an additional cup of sponsorship, anywhere from one-half to one full cup of mentoring, and finally two cups' worth of skill development, acquisition, and innate talent. Because at the end of the day, one can have all those things but not be talented as a DJ, so the formula still doesn't work out. Thus, sponsors in DJ culture also become the rhetorical fact checkers—the ones who make sure that as a DJ, you've cheffed up the recipe properly. After all, you can have all the Le Creuset cookware in the world, but that ain't gon' make yo' food taste right . . . similarly, a Mac laptop, Serato mixer, and 500 GB hard drive full of music don't mean you gon' know how to rock a party. What becomes critically important is an acknowledgment as well as an understanding of the rhetorical savvy embedded in DJ culture: the study of Hip Hop music coupled with a broad listening of music generally; an awareness of how DJs function with two turntables and a mixer; both an interest in and investigation of how technology interfaces, and thereby affects, the functionality of DJ practices; a clear and vested interest in the study of who's who in the DJ community; finally, the initial woodshed moments of practice and acquisition of rudimentary and advanced DJ skills. I contend that these primary elements begin one's journey into DJ Rhetoric. Mentorship and sponsorship may emerge along the way but might also happen after these initial stages. Furthermore, everyone's journey might be different, but the ingredients to this process will always be discernable and integral to the narrative of any Hip Hop DJ.

In using these elements to define and construct a framework for DJ Rhetoric, we must also nod our heads and pay homage to the fact that in Hip Hop, it is the DJ that—whether advertently or inadvertently—controls, dictates, and/or sits at the forefront of each of these specific moments. In H. Samy Alim's seminal text *Roc the Mic Right: The Language of Hip Hop Culture*, where he linguistically constructs a model for and then situates the importance of Hip Hop Nation Language (HHNL), he goes directly to the source (or "the essence") when thinking about how the language works: the influential MCs within Hip Hop music and culture. What Alim also does is clearly makes the inherent connection when talking about HHNL and its relationship to Black Language (BL):

> The relationship between HHNL and BL is a familial one. Since Hip Hop's culture creators are members of the broader Black American community, the language that they use most often when communicating with each other is BL. HHNL can be seen as the *submerged area* (Brathwaite 1984: 13) of BL that is used within the HHN, particularly during Hip Hop-centered cultural activities, but also during other playful, creative, artistic, and intimate settings. This conception of HHNL is broad enough to include the language of Rap lyrics, album interludes, Hip Hop stage performances, and Hip Hop conversational discourse. Black Americans are on the cutting edge of the sociolinguistic situation in the US (as evidenced by the preponderance of recent sociolinguistic research). HHNL, thus, is the cutting edge of the cutting edge. (Alim 74)

Interesting, then by default, is the DJ becomes the focal slicing point of the cutting edge's cutting edge. For example, storytelling in Hip Hop truly stems from the DJ giving the MC an opportunity to speak into the mic piece. If not for this moment, the MC doesn't emerge as poet and storyteller. Remember in the last chapter, when Clark Kent encapsulates this concept by saying, "You ain't hear about no rappers before you heard about DJs . . . DJs *are* the cornerstone of Hip Hop" (DJ Clark Kent). The DJ has been the shaman who has manipulated the breaks in order to let the poppers pop and let the breakers break; again, without the DJ enacting a break-filled sonic call-and-response in surveying the crowd to contort the rhythm of the break, the poppers, lockers, and breakers do not become the dancing phenomena that we see, and, instead, they might have a historical trajectory vastly different from what we see now as a present-day, everyday "household-name" status. BreakBeat Lou talked about how the graffiti artists he knew who painted in the yards would always have a radio with them, because the music was the sonic muse and inspiration for the visual art. And that music was supplied by none other than who . . . ? The DJ. BreakBeat Lou really broke it down when he stated, "Us being rhythmic people as a whole, without the rhythm, you have very little to be driven by . . . everything was connected through the music . . . if the DJ came out with no mic, [the MC] stayed quiet, cuz they ain't gonna hear you . . . the DJ was the focal point" (BreakBeat Lou). Without the producer mentality of the DJ, we don't see the same composing of songs based on the manipulation of breaks (which could truly be considered the original source of sampling), so again, the MC finds him- or herself without a sonic landscape by which to rhyme. Everyday banter, and thus linguistic directives, for Hip Hop were always communicated in songs, and the banter was a transactional process—a call-and-response of sorts—between the artists and the streets. But the DJs make and break those influential records that begin to dictate the language of the culture. Thus, DJ Rhetoric leads not only to a certain form of DJ Literacy but to a certain form of Hip Hop Language and Literacy (Alim, *Roc the Mic Right*; Richardson, *Hiphop Literacies*) as well. It is here that one could make the argument that HHNL is a submerged area of DJ Rhetoric and Literacy, which is a submerged area of Black Language and rhetoric and African-American literacy.

Because DJ Rhetoric Indeed Sits on the Black-Hand Side

Equally, part of the work that is necessary and integral to the formation of DJ Rhetoric is to firmly place the DJ in its cultural, social, and racial roots, which stem from a very Black tradition. It is equally imperative to look at the textual and sonic lineages of the majority of DJs interviewed for this project. For many of the female DJs, women-chief-rockers behind the 1s and 2s, their role models and/or mentors (or what we might categorize as "sponsors") were DJ Spinderella (Salt-N-Pepa), Pam the Funkstress (The Coup), and Kuttin Kandi (the 5th Platoon). While Kuttin Kandi is Filipino—and it is important to recognize the Filipino contribution to turntablism in DJ culture, especially on the West Coast (Wang)—both Spinderella and Pam the Funkstress are African-American women. Many males looked up to some of the pioneers in the culture who are included in my initial research study: KOOL DJ Red Alert, Clark Kent, BreakBeat Lou, Lord Finesse, Large Professor, and Jazzy Jeff. As we move through this list and through the textual and sonic lineage of mentors and sponsors on this list, we find that KOOL DJ Red Alert was influenced by Bam, and Clark Kent was influenced by Larry Levan—a popular club DJ who was responsible for playing disco and house music. But again, as "all roads lead to Rome," Rome—in this context—becomes a very Black center. We cannot continue to have conversations about the DJ without centering the DJ in an African diaspora that centers Black music, culture, and discourse. And it is when we do this centering that an integral point emerges: in the same way Hip Hop is rooted in the Black community, so too is the language, discursive practices, and techniques of the Hip Hop DJ. This line of thought could be perceived as essentialist in its connecting Hip Hop to racial parameters. Yet shouldn't we also be equally concerned when we see Hip Hop categorized as "global popular culture" or even "smart business acumen" when the music and culture seem to benefit other communities, but at the same time characterized with the negative connotations that relegate that same "global popular culture" to being "a Black thing" that others might not understand? This question sits at the heart of my earlier qualm, and this is the very energy both Morgan and Ball tap into; as we move into Hip Hop culture turning fifty years old, it becomes increasingly crucial to properly document the past half-century. Ball identifies the contemporary notoriety and financial viability of the Hip Hop mixtape. But equally important to keeping this awareness in popular culture, we cannot lose sight of the very history, rooted in anticolonial business practices for up-and-coming artists (both DJs and MCs), and a rhetorical practice created and enacted by the DJ, who served as a lighthouse and beacon for African-American and Black culture throughout decades across various geographic landscapes and locations, a grassroots and folk set of maneuverings and stylings birthed and entrenched by, with, and for Black people in America. The intrinsically undeniable relationship between Hip Hop / DJ Rhetoric and its roots in Black culture—and fields like Comp/Rhet and its attempts at marginalization, erasure, or even exclusion (or more harshly put, the Comp/Rhet version of a Hip Hop sociocultural ethnic cleansing)—cannot be ignored or dismissed in any way. This erasure is similar to the exclusion of marginalized voices writing and researching Hip Hop in Comp/Rhet spaces that I identified in the prior chapter and experienced in my doctoral program. Although this predominately white institution, ironically enough, is located in an urban enclave for Blacks, it hides that connection—even in its own street address. It is the same erasure and exclusion Dr. G highlights and disrupts in her mentoring strategies. It is also similar to the gatekeeping of *New York Times Book Review* writers identified by Adam Mansbach in his article "On Lit Hop" (cited in Chang, *Total Chaos*). And borrowing directly from Hip Hop, it's like that interview when early in his career, a young artist by the name of Vanilla Ice denied that the beat for "Ice Ice Baby" was a sample of Queen and David Bowie's "Under Pressure." *Everyone* knew what it was. Let us not forget these egregious errors of our past as we begin to understand our now in order to direct a more inclusive and factual future.

Perhaps a balance can be struck here by reflecting on the scholarship of Imani Perry. In her book *Prophets of the Hood: Politics and Poetics in Hip Hop*, she makes clear distinctions between Hip Hop culture becoming a global enterprise while also recognizing the origin and roots of Hip Hop for establishing critically important historical implications:

> Hip hop music is black American music. Even with its hybridity: the consistent contributions from nonblack artists, and the borrowings from cultural forms of other communities, it is nevertheless black American music. It is constituted as such because of four central characteristics: (1) its primary language is African American Vernacular English (AAVE); (2) it has a political location in society distinctly ascribed to black people, music, and cultural forms; (3) it is derived from black American oral culture; and (4) it is derived from black American musical traditions . . . why, then, is it so troubling to define something as black? Color consciousness that allows for an understanding of both the political implications of the category of race and the cultural forms that have emerged under that category is useful and progressive, and certainly not essentialist. (Perry 10–11)

As Perry has stated, I'd rather be an essentialist and root my culture where it belongs than watch my Blues, my Jazz, and ultimately, my Hip Hop be taken away. It's not to say that other cultures haven't been involved in Hip Hop from the start, nor is it saying that other cultures have not contributed highly to the modes, techniques, and processes that we know as Hip Hop–oriented. But even those true-blue Hip Hop heads will tell you—it all comes from a very Black planet. And to be able to move forward, we need to acknowledge that . . . even if it means that acknowledgment (re)writes how you envision contemporary American popular culture as we know it.

This idea is clearly expressed on the podcast *The People's Party with Talib Kweli*. In his interview with Hip Hop artist Rapsody, Kweli asks her to make sense of the phrase "Culture Over Everything," specifically as it relates to a pro-Black mindset. A critical point that comes out of this particular part of the interview is how both Kweli and Rapsody situate the roots of Hip Hop culture in connecting it to Black culture:

> TALIB KWELI (TK): You are unapologetically, staunchly, pro-Black.
>
> RAPSODY: Oh, to the core.
>
> TK: To the core. At the same time as you're being so pro-Black, you have a phrase "Culture Over Everything."
>
> RAPSODY: Yes.
>
> TK: And in Hip Hop culture, it's not just Black people, obviously. It started with Black and Brown people, and anyone in the culture has to recognize that, right?
>
> RAPSODY: Right, Black and Brown, disenfranchised and poor.
>
> TK: That's right. Everybody in the culture has to recognize that. Explain for people who might not know, people who might get offended by the phrase "pro-Black," how pro-Blackness fits into a "Hip Hop culture over everything" mind frame and why that's not anti-white.
>
> RAPSODY: It's not anti-white because it's about loving yourself and your culture. Loving yourself does not mean we hate you, especially in a country where we're taught to not love ourselves, how we look . . . it's important for us to remind ourselves that "I'm me, I love me." Everything that you show and depict of me is false . . . it's ours, just to get ownership back of what was stripped away and what's always tried to be turned into a false narrative of who we are.
>
> (Talib Kweli and Rapsody, qtd. in Kweli)

There are two critical points that come out of this excerpt of the interview. First, Talib Kweli clearly defines the roots of Hip Hop culture as acutely created by "Black and Brown" people; the critical aspect they agree on is every and anyone "in the culture has to recognize that" (Kweli). But moving forward, the second critical point is that Rapsody adds on to Kweli and how he has situated Hip Hop culture within the Black community but then describes the elements of pro-Blackness with regard to her "Culture Over Everything" phrase as that which allows Black people to embrace their cultural legacy in this country, while not succumbing to the barrage of negative images that are spread about them. But where Rapsody starts her thinking is most paramount: "It's not anti-white because it's about loving yourself and your culture. Loving yourself does not mean we hate you" (Rapsody, qtd. in Kweli). This idea coincides with her song "Nina," where Rapsody aims for the same sentiment of self-love that is devoid of any hatred. She says, "Spread love / the Brooklyn way or like Marmalade / no matter if you street-street, or more like the promenade / we gotta come together like the corn and the dookie braids / for the present and future days, I say what I gotta say" (Rapsody). This not only taps into aspects of the pathology of Black people in America, but it simply asks that a space be made for connecting a culture that is currently global popular culture to the people who were the architects of it.

This idea is also encapsulated on the album *The Allegory* by Royce Da 5'9". On the song entitled "Perspective," Royce captures Eminem discussing various ideas involving racial and cultural standings and identifications in Hip Hop as well as popular music in America. Eminem says,

> So now you got little white kids growing up with Black idols, and you got Black kids growing up with white idols. It's just this whole mixing pot. Nothing has brought more races and more people from all different walks of life together than Hip Hop. No music has done that—I don't think anything has done that—as much as Hip Hop has. So, in the same token, I can understand the frustration being that, you know, damn near every form of music—period—was created by Black people.

While this statement does a great job depicting some of the racialized roots of Hip Hop music, the irony is that as a Black scholar, I may be categorized as "an essentialist" for saying this; yet I am conscious of the fact that Eminem's words on this topic will be looked at as "timely," or even as "appropriate"— though we are essentially saying the same exact thing. Further into the skit, Eminem does mention the fact that if he were on the other side of this dichotomy, he would be able to understand how a person who is a victim of such treatment might have "a chip on their shoulder" (Eminem). Introducing Eminem to be in conversation with me—and with us—here is both critical and strategic. How we understand this dichotomy, and how we move forward from it, becomes paramount in this moment. Ask Rapsody, and she'll call it "Culture Over Everything." Ask Nipsey Hussle, he would have called it "The Marathon" (Rapsody qtd. in Kweli). In the words of lyrical tactician Pharaohe Monch ("Let My People Go"), it's "undisputable logic [that's] blastin' through ya speaker now." Or to bring us back full circle, we can return to Q-Tip via Yasiin Bey, when he highlights the quote "Rap is not pop / if you call it that then stop!" (A Tribe Called Quest, "Check the Rhime" qtd. in *Something from Nothing*).

The Technic 1200 Roots of the "K for the Way" Tree of Life

For me, this book has a variety of textual lineage roots that range from Morris Young's idea of how literacy narratives can begin to help us construct a citizenship rhetoric (Young), to Dr. E's connections within Hip Hop literacy to the larger diaspora of African-American literacies (Richardson, *African American Literacies*), and then back to scholars like Pleasant, Meacham, Street, and even Scott Richard Lyons and his concept of rhetorical sovereignty (Lyons). Furthermore, we see a number of scholars address the aesthetic value and critical importance of lyrical production and poetics (Bradley; Perry), and the connection of Hip Hop music to its ancestors in other African-American and African musical traditions (Baker; Coleman; T. Harris; Keyes; Rabaka; Spady; Weheliye; Welbeck), as well as ideas pertaining to DJ musical notation practices (Miyakawa; Smith). Thus, the stories I tell across these chapters are key to the formation and fruition of DJ Rhetoric and Literacy for me. I place the DJ in the context of New Literacy Studies because my own personal narrative affects the way I approach my acquisition and synthesis of Hip Hop DJ culture. At the nexus of my first childhood memories of my uncles DJing coupled with the 98.7 to 107.5 chunky-silver-dial-spun Hip Hop Literacy, the "right hand-left hand" mentality from Medina's TEDxPhilly talk, and Kamaal's early DJ sessions sits a critical site of rhetoric and literacy, where the importance of the memoir, narrative, and storytelling can lend to assessing the question presented in the previous chapter: Who gets to tell our story? In this moment, I contend the aspects of my own literacy acquisition around DJ Rhetoric and Pedagogy are just as critical—and add an additional epistemological layer—to the mix known as this book. Thus, the stories that encapsulate my own upbringing in Hip Hop DJ culture help to make a different type of meaning when seated alongside scholarly texts on

Hip Hop and interview data. As we delve deeper into the idea of a distinctive DJ Rhetoric and Pedagogy, the landscape will encompass a set of theoretical terrains that examine Hip Hop scholarship, DJ interviews, personal narrative, and Hip Hop folklore. If we viewed the idea of scholarship and memoir as being two sides of a coin, it might look similar to what Imani Perry describes as "the division between the respectable and funky stuff" (Perry 4). If the academic texts connect to Perry's Motown, then these narratives exist as its Stax counterpart.

Bill Brewster and Frank Broughton's book *last night a dj saved my life: the history of the disc jockey* is a historical survey of the DJ and helps us to further flesh out these ideas. Entitling the DJ "the lord of the dance" (Brewster and Broughton 6), Brewster and Broughton extend back, examining and linking the history of the DJ to earlier religious rituals, and then move forward into and then past Hip Hop (in this text, Hip Hop DJs inhabit two chapters: the only other DJ genre to do this in their text is Disco). Thus, it is helpful in pointing to the roots and lineage from which the Hip Hop DJ emerges. Between Herc's concept of playing the breaks, Flash's technicality in creating methods such as "The Quick Mix," "punch phrasing" (inserting one song into another song via the scratch), and body tricks (which we later see as a turntablist staple in DJ battles); and Bambaataa's obscure ear and collection of records (which were a combination of Rock, Jazz, Blues, Electro, and various other sources Bam would receive from various record pools), Hip Hop is birthed and constructed on the backs and in the musical minds of the DJ. These DJs, though, have mentors and idols that are their predecessors; those folks, live in a world that is void of this thing we now know as "Hip Hop." However, it is this same set of DJs who function with the Black and African diasporic practice of "making something outta nothing" and "makin' a way outta no way": phrases and philosophies that can be found amongst Black folklore and traced back throughout the history of the culture.

For my research, a similar textual and sonic lineage for the Hip Hop DJ begins from a location that encompasses a few key individuals: Clark Kent, KOOL DJ Red Alert, Spinderella, and BreakBeat Lou. I find it is important to look at these four cultural practitioners, as they follow along with the premise that "all roads lead to Rome." The almighty and original DJ trifecta, which also serves as the historical hierarchy of Hip Hop, consists of Kool Herc, Afrika Bambaataa, and Grandmaster Flash. And as Hip Hop moves forward, all things flow from here. So I made an active decision not to address this piece of Hip Hop's lineage. *K for the Way* aims to move to a layer after this pretty undisputed

Hip Hop factoid, thus aiming the focal point toward a different part of the Hip Hop DJs lineage and family tree.

Clark Kent was that young kid who was rocking at age eleven alongside Grandmaster Flowers, who gave DJ Flash the name "Grandmaster" (Clark Kent). His legacy sits with Grandmaster Flowers and Larry Levan, among others. KOOL DJ Red Alert was an early member of the Universal Zulu Nation, recruited by Bam via Red's cousin—the Original Jazzy Jay. Red Alert also gets the "KOOL" moniker in his name after a convo he had with Kool Herc, where he pays homage and asks for permission *before* he started rockin' the name (KOOL DJ Red Alert). Spinderella is one of the first female DJs that we see in the spotlight, rockin' alongside Salt-N-Pepa during the days where *every* rap group had a DJ—it was protocol, prerequisite . . . as they used to say in the old-school Charles Barkley Right Guard commercials, "Anything less would be uncivilized." Spinderella (and shortly after her, Pam the Funkstress), would ignite the fire for various female DJs to rock in a testosterone-heavy, ego-driven, overly masculine Hip Hop industry. They would not only rock but truly get it in. Finally, BreakBeat Lou along with his partner Breakbeat Lenny (RIP), would collaborate to produce one of the most important musical compilation series to Hip Hop: *Ultimate Breaks and Beats* (UBB). It was BreakBeat Lou who catapulted the movement of collecting all those necessary records from which Hip Hop DJs and producers pulled their party breaks and *loved* to sample. (Re)configuring and (re)imagining how they might be mixed with the Hip Hop DJ and producer in mind, BreakBeat Lou and UBB was one of the first projects that placed all those foundational songs on one album and then curated a series of those albums. UBB vinyl was like the equivalent of a limited Quickstrike Air Jordan retro sneaker release from back in the day . . . everyone was on it. Whether you were a DJ, producer, turntablist, or a music aficionado, if your concern was Hip Hop, you were up on the Octopus. And Lou's science is critical. Just think: folklore has it that in California, a young producer named Dr. Dre meets a young rapper named Easy E in a record store . . . looking for what, you might ask? An *Ultimate Breaks and Beats* album (BreakBeat Lou). If you are familiar with the old-school Hip Hop song "It Takes Two" by Rob Base and DJ E-Z Rock, know that BreakBeat Lou was responsible for that record; listen closely, and you'll realize they sampled a song that was a version of Lou's mix—a distinctive (re)arrangement that *only* appeared on a UBB album. I think I can safely say the rest is absolute history . . . and Lou sits at that epicenter.

It is at this convergence—where we see definitions of sponsorship, rhetoric, and literacy—where we can begin to have an informative and critical conversation as to the importance of the DJ's connection to African-American rhetoric and literacy, as well as the DJ's role in the formation of Hip Hop literacy. It is a vital aspect of the story, and not a trivial notion to be omitted, excerpted, and/or gatekept by Comp/Rhet, or even English Studies. Finally, the elements of this convergence clearly usher the path toward a DJ Rhetoric and Literacy.

. . . Spread love / the Brooklyn way or like Marmalade /
no matter if you street-street, or more like the promenade /
we gotta come together like the corn and the dookie braids /
for the present and future days, I say what I gotta say . . .

I'm from the back woods where Nina would /
sing about the life we should / lead / a new dawn, another deed/
I try to do some good /
I felt more damned than Mississippi was / they deny Nina in Philadelphia/
And still we persevere like all the 400 years / of our own blood /
Africa /
old Panthers lookin' back like 'who gon' come up after us . . . ?'

Rapsody, "Nina," *Eve*, Jamla Records, 2019.

. . . Rapsody adds on to Kweli and how he has situated Hip Hop culture
within the Black community, but then describes the elements of
pro-Blackness with regard to her "Culture Over Everything" phrase
as that which allows Black people to embrace their
cultural legacy in this country, while not succumbing to the
barrage of negative images that are spread about them.
But where Rapsody starts her thinking is most paramount:
"It's not anti-white because it's about loving yourself and your culture.
Loving yourself does not mean we hate you" (Rapsody).
This idea coincides with her song "Nina," where Rapsody
aims for the same sentiment of self-love
that is devoid of any hatred . . .

3

JACKIN' FOR BEATS V2.0

The Intertextuality (Re)Mix

. . . I project my voice so it's right in the crowd / There's a sign at the door:
'No Bitin' Allowed!' / And if you didn't read it, I suggest you do so /
or you'll be stranded, just like Caruso /
Sleep if ya wanna, ga'head, get some shut-eye /
A man broke his jaw tryin' to say what I / say on the microphone /
you shoulda left it alone /
just for the record, let it be known . . .

Marley Marl featuring Masta Ace, Craig G, Kool G Rap and Big Daddy Kane, "The
Symphony," *In Control: Volume 1*, Co-Chillin / Warner Bros. Records, 1988.

. . . it was clear to me in both moments that somebody was bitin' styles and
tryin' to pass it off as his or her own . . . ah, the foulness of it all.
Somewhere along the line,
people straight forgot that classic Masta Ace line
from that classic posse cut entitled "The Symphony"
(which, of course, appeared on the legendary DJ Marley Marl's album
In Control: Volume 1) . . . it only makes me think about the ways in which
originality and borrowing have changed based on technology,
the internet, and a whole slew of other forces.
Masta Ace stated it clearly in 1988.
Thirty-four years later, it seems the game done gon' and changed, word . . .

https://doi.org/10.7330/9781646424849.c003

"And you know how I do / put the beef behind me to put your soul behind you like De La": The Breeze in the Air That Makes Me Think about This Joint . . .

Picture this: a number of years ago, you're standing at the launch party of the second edition of your first novel. You're with your peoples who are in attendance. Mr. Len, who's doing a special guest spot for your launch, is killin' his set at Club APT so ill, that when you're standing outside with two of your peoples, resident DJ Rich Medina opens the door to go to the DJ booth and says, "Yo Len, I just wanted to say FUCK YOU sun . . . cuz you're KILLIN' it right now!!!" You speak to Len two days after the party and he tells you an interesting anecdote about how he had gotten a call the next afternoon, as there was a radio personality who was playing the same songs from his set that sounded quite reminiscent of the exact same set order. You've already gotten the word from the day before that the Twitter buzz was *crazy* from that night . . . word on the wire was it was the party of the night. And all you can think is "so Twitter's buzzin' ALL night, but you ain't gon say that's my sun, sun? Yeah, aight . . ."

Skip stage to a more recent moment: you're at an academic conference, serving in the capacity of panel chair. Because you've been doing some strong critical work in Hip Hop and Writing Studies, you put a panel together of some younger up-and-coming scholars to help give them some light. Not too many of the scholars in your field before you helped in this way. In moments when certain established scholars had a chance to support you, they would actually bail on the panel, hours before it would start, without leaving you an opportunity to even concoct a Plan B. So in your attempt to "pay it forward," you pull a younger crew together and, as panel chair, help to give them a platform. The first presentation goes smoothly, but when the second presentation gets going, you stop dead in your tracks as you're taking notes . . . you realize the second presentation sounds way too familiar. As a matter of fact, it sounds almost identical to the ideas you expressed as a panel presenter and then published as a journal article years before. You listen intently, you hang on to every word, and you wait for it. But it never comes. The presenter rattles off the names of scholar after scholar. Yet by the end of the presentation, this presenter hasn't cited your name nor your work at all. And you're completely aware that there is such a thing as the ecstasy of influence. You also know that this right here . . . *ain't* it!

Both of these moments forced me to recognize there was something in the air, a funny type of cool breeze blowin' through the trees that forced me to focus on the fact that this sound was in the air. It was clear to me in both moments that somebody was bitin' styles and tryin' to pass it off as his or her own . . . ah, the foulness of it all. Somewhere along the line, people straight forgot that classic Masta Ace line from that classic posse cut entitled "The Symphony" (which, of course, appeared on the legendary DJ Marley Marl's album *In Control: Volume 1*): "I project my voice so it's right in the crowd / There's a sign at the door: 'No Bitin' Allowed!' / And if you didn't read it, I suggest you do so / or you'll be stranded, just like Caruso / Sleep if ya wanna, ga'head, get some shut-eye / A man broke his jaw tryin' to say what I / say on the microphone / you shoulda left it alone / just for the record, let it be known" (Marley Marl featuring Masta Ace). It only makes me think about the ways in which originality and borrowing have changed based on technology, the internet, and a whole slew of other forces. Masta Ace stated it clearly in 1988. Thirty-four years later, it seems the game done gon' and changed, word. So I sat down to catch the sentiment on the page before the wind flipped New England, and started to blow in another way—a different direction, density, and temperature.

"You know the outcome, when your pedigree is Martin-Malcolm—Don't appreciate you, but when you dead, they study ALL your albums": The Entryway into Sonic Homage

I can recall sitting in Baxter Dining Hall on a Sunday morning during spring semester eating brunch. It seemed like the typical Sunday: late morning start after a late-night party the night before. But the regularity of the day would quickly dissipate. One of my peoples at the time came into the dining hall and was like "Yo Todd, ya man BIG is dead." It was the mid-1990s, the East Coast–West Coast drama piece was quite real, as evidenced by what we knew at the time being Tupac's death. I looked at him with the serious stare "Yo, sun, don't joke like that. That shit ain't funny!" His response was one I'll never forget: "I'm not joking, I'm dead serious" were the words coming out his mouth as his hand motioned from the air down onto the table. Right there, on the front cover of the *New York Post* was a headline showing The Notorious B.I.G. had been shot and killed. The whole thing seemed surreal, especially given he was just about to drop an album. Needless to say, when the album dropped, I made sure I copped double copies of the double album. From that moment on, my double copies of *Life After Death* on vinyl became paramount to each of the parties I was rocking. For me, the record on that album that was most significant was the "BIG Interlude."

I remember stretching that record out at parties; it felt so smart for Biggie to make it an interlude, since his version only flipped the hook. The sonic quality of the beat is so strong: the cymbals and the drums are huge and resounding on that record. But it always reminded me of years before, and how my DJ set construction at live events would work. At almost every one of my parties, I would rock a classic Hip Hop set. What's critical to this time period is this is the time of the DJ pre-Serato. Preparing for a four-hour function meant going through my crates and pulling two flight cases' worth of singles and full-length albums on vinyl. And if you saw me at the party on campus with record bags, you knew I had just come back from record shopping in New York, so I probably had a set of bottle rockets—or what I'd call "heatrocks"—which meant that night you'd catch the pulse of New York Hip Hop in western Massachusetts. But those two flight cases were important, because while the rhetorical act of constructing a DJ set is spontaneous and most often predicated on the interaction of call-and-response with the crowd, the curation of pulling records before the party was (and still is) a cerebral and calculated act. And regardless of whether I played it or not, one of the records I'd always have on deck for my old-school set was "PSK" by Schoolly D. It was an undeniable record when it came out, and still is an undeniable party-rocker, a tune that truly stood the test of time sonically. I always thought Schoolly D killed that song. His flow was dope and innovative, no one was really rhyming like that just quite yet, the beat was hard-hitting, and the vibrations from the overly reverbed TR-909 drum through the speaker woofers will still rattle your chest cavity.

Almost twenty years later, I'd start my tenure-track gig wanting to buy decorative letters to put "PSK" in my office. Not being from Philly, I was never really in tune with what PSK was, other than the fact that Schoolly explained it in the hook. My wife was like "You sure you want to do that? PSK—Park Side Killers?" Needless to say, I didn't put the PSK letters up. But it never changed my relationship with either of those records. And I've always loved the way Biggie was able to thread the needle for me to a dope moment back to my childhood radio-listening days, where one's ability to be adept with the tuning dial was critical.

Skip stage to today, and one of the dudes I see in Hip Hop who exemplifies this move is French Montana. Of course, French works with Diddy—we all know Puff "invented the remix"—but he is also known for the production ear that brings certain older records back into a second coming. We see this very clearly with French Montana. Throughout his career, a number of his big records have been those that reach back to the classic Hip Hop tracks of decades past. What makes French's maneuvering so dope is that with each producer he works with, the tracks for each song becomes a keenly astute interpolation of the record before it.

"One Time, Two Time, Three Time, Four Time . . .": New Source, New Essence, Same Hip Hop

During summer 2011, French invaded the radio airwaves with one of his biggest breakthrough records—"Shot Caller"—where French and Charlie Rock take turns rhyming back and forth over the Lords of the Underground (LOTUG) classic "Funky Child." On this record, they use the signature introduction of the LOTUG beat that MC Do It All speaks over before the record starts. The luminously lush and sprawling horn hits the high note that is unmistakable; anyone whose ear is deft to identifying classic Hip Hop tunes knows the horns are sampled straight from the Lords of the Underground. However, producers Marley Marl and K-Def, crate-digging specialists in their own right, unearthed that sample from the song "A Theme for L.A.'s Team" that appeared on the soundtrack for the movie *The Fish That Saved Pittsburgh* by the Thomas Bell Orchestra. While many might remember the basketball-inspired movie of the late 1970s that, at the time, was considered a cinematic flop, no one questioned the sonic dexterity of the soundtrack and score, created by Thomas Bell (RIP). Thom Bell is best known for his musical involvement with the creation of what we now know as "The Sound of Philadelphia." Working with musical greats such as Kenny Gamble, Leon Huff, and Daryl Hall, Bell would produce and arrange for numerous Soul groups including the Delfonics, the O'Jays, the Stylistics, the Spinners, and other artists like Johnny Mathis and Elton John.

While "A Theme for L.A.'s Team" uncovered the source for a classic Hip Hop gem, the soundtrack would spawn the source records for other timeless Hip Hop songs. For example, a quick listen to "Moses Theme" will immediately bring an avid Hip Hop listener to Ma$e's classic posse cut "24 Hours to Live," which featured Black Rob (RIP), the L.O.X., and DMX (RIP). It wouldn't stop there, though, as *The Fish That Saved Pittsburgh* was an album used by artists including Method Man, Redman, and Saukrates; Killer Mike; Wale and J. Cole; Lupe Fiasco; Bryson Tiller; and the Young Gunz. Less than ten years after the soundtrack's release, we can find DJ Marley Marl working with MC Shan on a song called "The Bridge"; the well-known record that pays homage to Shan and Marley's home of Queensbridge Houses was part of Marley Marl's production legacy, as he'd work with MC Shan, Roxanne Shante, and the Juice Crew (Big

Daddy Kane, Master Ace, Craig G, Biz Markie, Kool G. Rap, and TJ Swan). What brings this point full circle is Marley's first records would be released on a label called Pop Art Music . . . a recording label based in Philadelphia. So it almost makes sense that six years after his Pop Art smash "The Bridge," we could find Marley Marl excavating Thom Bell's song for his own Hip Hop samplings. And the NYC-to-Philly connection would run rampant in the early days of Hip Hop, with Marley Marl and K-Def revisiting this connection with LOTUG in 1993.

French has created several examples of this interpolation-inspired sampling of Hip Hop songs. Within a year of releasing "Shot Caller," French would play wingman for Coke Boy crew affiliate, rapper Chinx Drugz (RIP), rhyming on a song called "I'm a Coke Boy." On this song, we find producer Harry Fraud snatching the introduction of Royal Flush's breakthrough single "Worldwide" from 1997. The following year, Montana made a splash with the song "Freaks" featuring a rising Young Money spitter named Nicki Minaj. While French's iteration of "Freaks" was geared toward the club and a party vibe, it held true to the Caribbean mashup idea as it utilized Likkle Vicious from his song "Freaks" overlaid onto the Bam Bam riddim best known from Dancehall records like Chaka Demus & Pliers's "Murder She Wrote" and Cutty Ranks's "A Who Seh Me Dun" that dominated Reggae, Dancehall, and even the Hip Hop radio and club scenes in 1993. Finally, French teamed up with both Chinx Drugz and Noreaga (cohost of the podcast *Drink Champs* and member of Hip Hop group Capone-N-Noreaga [C-N-N]) for the hardcore banger entitled "Off the Rip." On this street anthem, French goes to Rampage the Last Boy Scout (Busta Rhymes's Flipmode Squad Lieutenant) and his classic lead-off single "Wild for the Night" off his 1997 album *Scout's Honor . . . By Way of Blood*. The sonic clarity of the syncopated solitary piano by way of Zulema's 1972 song "American Fruit, African Roots," coupled with N.O.R.E. on deck to lend his signature vocal from the hook off the CNN street banger "Bloody Money," epitomizes the gritty nature and essence for what "Off the Rip" aimed to capture. Again, borrowing from yet another set of premier Hip Hop gems but being sure to add on, tweak, and re-create the sonics in the beat allows for it to be a nod to the predecessor yet a clear look to the present and future.

What French Montana does in all these songs is evoke a specific type of feeling, a certain sense of historian-esque nostalgia rarely enacted in Hip Hop. Yet this is not just a move toward the past for "the past's sake." This definitely isn't that "your music is trash now—back when I was your age, people made real music" sentiment that can sometimes permeate recording situations, linger amidst conversations between different generations within the Hip Hop nation, or even cloud the landscape and muddy the waters of what current Hip

Hop can and should sound like. Nah, this is a different choice. I'm convinced that part of this choice comes with his label situation with Bad Boy Records and Puff Daddy, and Diddy's uncanny choices in the records he goes back in the crates to dig for and exhume. But there is another part of this equation that is truly exciting for me and should be for the culture. As Hip Hop music and culture are almost half a century old, we have arrived at a place where Hip Hop can actually sample itself. Instead of finding various other records from countless genres to sample from, we are in a place where Hip Hop has existed for so long that some producers are making and creating original Hip Hop compositions (see Frank Dukes and Kingsway Music Library, or Deringer and Griselda). At the same time, though, you can "dig in the crates" and unearth Hip Hop gems worthy of (re)mix, (re)introduction, and (re)interpretation. And this digging in the crates process can also unveil the wonderfully intricate and complex lineage that we can find in locations (from NYC to Philly), in production connections (with Marley Marl sitting in the epicenter of this specific sampling citation), and in connecting our pasts, presents, and everchanging futures.

Now That We're Here, Why Are We Here? Continuing the Construction of a DJ-Based Citation Critique

In the previous chapter, I described how New Literacy Studies struck a path that led me to thinking about the idea of sponsorship and how it works itself out within English Studies, Writing Studies, and Hip Hop scholarship. For this chapter, I began pulling from myriad places to think through how DJ Rhetoric and Literacy moves from theory and into practice. The concept of this chapter, "Jackin' for Beats v2.0: The Intertextuality (Re)Mix," stems from a few sources. First and foremost, it is important to understand the history of Hip Hop sampling has been referred to throughout various academic texts as a borrowing, an innovative type of new media composition that is constantly working in the vein of archiving, quoting, and citing—paying homage to all those "sources" that come before and through it.

Alongside the research that positions Hip Hop sampling as a textual borrowing, a second conceptual framework guides my idea of "Jackin' for Beats v2.0: The Intertextuality (Re)Mix." This framework emanates from Sarah Wakefield's article "Using Music Sampling to Teach Research Skills," in which she explains that "music sampling provides a metaphor for skillful incorporation of quotations . . . discussing, or better yet, playing a sampled song demonstrates to the class how quoted research should be used. The outside material ought to enhance *their* statements and arguments, flowing smoothly rather than standing out" (Wakefield 358–359). Wakefield begins a student-centered conversation by highlighting the example of P. Diddy and his choices in sampling throughout his music career. The third piece of this conceptual framework sits with Alastair Pennycook in his work dealing with plagiarism, its connections to Western ideologies with regard to composing, and the relationship between authorship, ownership, and knowledge. In his essay "Borrowing Others' Words: Text, Ownership, Memory, and Plagiarism," he promotes an alternative view of intertextuality over the archaic black-and-white term "plagiarism." Pennycook presents an interesting situation in terms of academic citation with a layered quote in which he reads an essay by Morgan citing Ann Raimes, who quotes Henry Giroux. When he reads the Raimes piece, he sees that Raimes claims she is citing Lester Faigley, who's citing Giroux. When he finds the Faigley source, he sees that Faigley seems to be paraphrasing Giroux; what becomes noteworthy in this conundrum is when he finds the actual Giroux text as referenced by Faigley in his bibliography:

> The phrase "theoretical depth and methodological refinement" does not appear in the Giroux book on the page that Faigley references: (or at least in the copy I looked at). And so, as these words and ideas circulate around the academic community, it becomes unclear quite what their origins are. And does it matter . . . within contemporary academic writing practices, with layers of citations, e-mail, cutting and pasting, and so on, the adherence to supposed norms of authoriality are becoming increasingly hazy. (Pennycook 216)

This moment demonstrates a necessity for envisioning texts and citation methods in ways that model an everchanging landscape in English Studies, specifically how we as practitioners approach citation methods and strategies within a twenty-first-century writing landscape. Simply put, technology has changed the outlook on citation and paraphrasing; how do we as English scholars begin to help our students envision this issue in a different way—one that reflects the newly arrived advent of digital technology and cyberspace that complicates the former parameters of "the teaching of writing?"

Based on the intersection of these three conceptual frameworks, I aim in this chapter to explore new ways to frame citation, quoting, and plagiarism—all of which can impact English Composition classrooms—by investigating the Hip Hop DJ's treatment of sampling. This exploration can, at once, foster a new type of conversation, one that jettisons some of the archaic constrains of plagiarism as a "black and white" phenomenon but can also lay part of the groundwork for constructing key elements of DJ Rhetoric and Literacy. Pennycook so eloquently demonstrates an idea that appears in the movie *The Pursuit of Happyness*. In the film, the protagonist, Chris Gardner (Will Smith), says how in the Declaration of Independence, "Thomas Jefferson calls the English 'the disturbers of our harmony.'" It interestingly demonstrates Pennycook's theories on plagiarism: a Western ideology that constrains, constricts, and inhibits students' abilities to find their own voice in writing as "plagiarism" becomes the disturber of their writing harmonies. With these layered concepts in mind, this chapter samples these three conceptual frameworks, using Pennycook to further Wakefield's conversation about research skills and Hip Hop sampling.

Since it has been further documented that the Hip Hop DJ has been at the historical forefront and burgeoning of Hip Hop sampling, this writing theoretically functions how the Hip Hop DJ both utilizes and critiques sampling. DJ Rhetoric and Literacy through the lens of the Hip Hop DJ allows us to look at this quandary in a way that is different and innovative. Pennycook's idea of transgressive versus nontransgressive intertextuality has been quite the radical challenge to literature and composition scholars stuck in the engendered and traditional ideologies of plagiarism. However, this complex and organic understanding of intertextuality has been fully manipulated and exploited by the Hip Hop DJ, especially in categorizing music within three rhetorical tropes: "biters," "jackers," and, finally, "transformers." Because the central argument of this chapter revolves around these three fluid categories, it is evident that the Hip Hop DJ's lens promotes Pennycook's understanding of intertextuality in twenty-first-century literacies in ways in which the twentieth-century notion of plagiarism simply does not and will not work. Complicating the black-and-white of plagiarism to open up a conversation within new media technologies' creation of the gray areas presents a more fruitful understanding of citation, paraphrasing, and quoting for a community of writers. In order to do this, we need to do a lil work—take this upcoming section as a sample of the samplings.

D.I.T.C. = Diggin' in the Crates or Demarcatin' Intelligent Textual Considerations

To begin, the first thing that must be done is recognize sampling as a viable means of composition. A quick tour through a series of academic works will bring us to some important scholars who have already defined the sample. So instead of re-creating the wheel, I'll simple sample them.

In his 1991 article "The Fine Art of Rap," Richard Shusterman forges through a convincing and witty argument positioning the emergence of rap music not only as a powerful postmodern form of cultural poetry (with its roots deeply planted in an African-American underclass) but also as fine art. When identifying the role of the Hip Hop DJ in the section "Appropriative Sampling," he shows an early understanding of how "the music derives from selecting and combining parts of prerecorded songs to produce a 'new' soundtrack. This soundtrack, produced by the DJ on a multiple turntable, constitutes the musical background for the rap lyrics [which] in turn are frequently devoted . . . to praising the DJ's inimitable virtuosity in sampling and synthesizing the appropriated music" (Shusterman 614). Two years later in his seminal text, *Black Studies, Rap, and the Academy*, Houston Baker not only works toward defining the Hip Hop sample but also places the Hip Hop DJ in the center of that discourse. Baker shows how Hip Hop DJs would abandon any particular song if they felt that only twenty or so seconds contained the worthwhile music. So with two turntables, two copies of the same record, and some really quick hands, Hip Hop DJs began to sample, or loop, that twenty-second beat live. As the technology grew, so did the sampling technique, including various soundbites and riffs—which demonstrated a unique type of archiving and referencing:

> The result was an indefinitely extendable, varied, reflexively signifying hip-hop sonics-indeed, a deft sounding of postmodernism. The techniques of rap were not simply ones of selective extension and modification. They also included massive archiving. Black sound (African drums, bebop melodies, James Brown shouts, jazz improvs, Ellington riffs, blues innuendos, doo-wop croons, reggae words, calypso rhythms) were gathered into a reservoir of threads that DJs wove into intriguing tapestries of anxiety and influence. (Baker 88–89)

A year later, Andrew Bartlett helps to flesh out the definition of sampling, labeling it as a new form of digital collaboration that entails a dialogue between various pieces of musical soundbites and representations that become overlaid to create a sole "text": "Sampling in hip hop is not collaboration in any familiar sense of that term. It is a high-tech and highly selective archiving, bringing into dialogue by virtue of even the most slight representation . . . with digital sampling, expropriated material is (often minutely and momentarily) recognizable, yet placed so that it often sounds radically anomalous, especially when the sampled material is overlapped or 'layered'" (Bartlett 647–650).

Nelson George documents the duality in dueling opinions of early Hip Hop sampling practices. In his chapter entitled "Sample This" from his book *Hip Hop America*, he balances both sides of the opinion scales of sampling by examining Mtume's (RIP) stern objections to Hip Hop's "use of sampling as a substitute for musical composition" (George 90). The outcome of Mtume's radio show rant would be Stetsasonic's "Talkin' All That Jazz"—both an overt and covert signifyin' sonic response to what Daddy-O might call Mtume's initial shortsightedness around sampling practices. Before the Philadelphia-based legendary Roots crew came into existence, Stetsasonic served as the original self-proclaimed Hip Hop band and used a sample from Lonnie Liston Smith's "Expansions" to both expand and expound on the archival awareness ever-present in Hip Hop sampling aesthetics. George uses this narrative moment around sampling to ponder how African-American musicianship has consistently used technology to break with current norms and how those initially criticized breaks would later become the sonic norm; ironically, one of those breaks involved an early 1970s Miles Davis, whose percussionist was a younger musician named Mtume. George discusses the obstacles and objections that many listeners had for Miles Davis's shift away from acoustic instruments in the 1970s, as well as Muddy Waters's, Chuck Berry's, and Monk Montgomery's shift toward electronic instruments, which extended to both Quincy Jones's and Stevie Wonder's sonic expansion through the advent of technology in instrumentation. George pinpoints ideas around sampling best when he states:

> Before hip hop, producers would use sampling to disguise the absence of a live instrument. If a horn was needed or a particular keyboard line was missing, a pop producer might sample it from another record, trying to camouflage its artificiality in the process. However, a hip hop producer, whose sonic aesthetic was molded by the use of break beats from old records pulled from dirty crates, wasn't embarrassed to be using somebody else's sounds. Recontextualizing someone else's sounds was, after all, how hip hop started . . . sampling's flexibility not only gave hip hop–bred music makers the tools to create tracks that were in the hip hop tradition, but also allowed them to extend that tradition. For them the depth and complexity of sounds achievable on a creatively sampled record has made live instrumentation seem, at best, an adjunct to record making. Records were no longer recordings of instruments being played—they had become a collection of previously performed and found sounds. (George 92–93)

George expands the idea of sampling in his assessment of both the artistic workings of sampling practices (he samples Greg Tate [RIP] in a moment where Tate evokes the artist Romare Beardon) but also in spotlighting the highly racialized conundrum of Hip Hop sampling. He identifies how Hip Hop artists, upon widening their reach to sample other genres successfully, are sued in an effort to smear an artist, and thus diminish the reach of the current, and future artists (this happened with De La Soul, Public Enemy, and most notably, Biz Markie [RIP] and his song "Alone Again"). In this moment, George is able to again highlight the irony of the diminishment and demonization of Hip Hop sampling practices for African-Americans yet the celebratory "innovation" that sampling brings to other musical genres:

> The most audacious uses of sampling in the '90s have not come from hip hop proper but from acts directly influenced by hip hop aesthetics (the Beastie Boys, Beck, Tricky, Forest for the Trees) and from those for whom hip hop is but one key point of reference (Prodigy, the Chemical Brothers). The gulf between instruments and sampling, bridged by hip hop, is now a given in progressive dance music around the world. Hip hop moved sampling technology to a central place in record making. (95)

Jeff Rice brings us full circle to a more contemporary definition of sampling, as the "hip-hop process of saving snippets of prerecorded music and sound into a computer memory. These sounds become cut from their original source and pasted into a new composition" (Rice, "The 1963 Hip-Hop Machine" 454). These sources can be vast: from music, TV shows, speeches, and even video games—all of which are used methodologically to construct a new work based on recontextualized sources or citations (458). Rice later presents a critical point that deserves our attention in his book *The Rhetoric of Cool*. In the chapter "Appropriation," he states:

> The mere mention of sampling as a research method tells me to explore hip-hop's usage of digital sampling (inspired by the role DJs play in hip-hop) in order to learn more about how this practice informs rhetoric . . . crying plagiarism has done little to teach writing how appropriation works for various purposes . . . to cry theft is to refuse to recognize the mix's role in new media-based expression and how that role may destabilize rhetorical and pedagogical expectations . . . to teach the mix through appropriation, we have to reject the disciplinary fixation on theft (represented in the general fear of plagiarism—whether that fear is posed as an economic one or a pedagogical one) and recognize that appropriation as mix signifies more than just borrowing texts . . . we become as mixed and appropriated as the compositions we write. (67–69)

With this in mind, sampling not only functions as a worthy source of information for composing, but it also lends to a transactional practice, a back-and-forth interplay between sampling as "text constructing" and the identity of the Hip Hop DJ who "mixes," writes, or constructs that text. There is a sonic lineage in the formation of the sampled text; that sonic "text" thus stands as a testament of the musical influences that both precede it and live with it con-temporarily. This idea is embodied in French Montana's song "Shot Caller": it traces a path from producer Harry Fraud, to Montana signing with Puff Daddy and Bad Boy Records, to the sample's history with Lords of the Un-derground, producer pioneer Marley Marl, and the Hip Hop geography that spans from Queens, New York, to Philadelphia, Pennsylvania. As a form of "new media-based expression," the intricacies of twenty-first-century under-standings of the sample cannot be useful in a twentieth-century context called plagiarism. Rice shows how this lending and borrowing of texts in the sample can be a critical location for students to see intertextuality at work.

Rice's thinking is also embodied on the page and enacted in poetic form by interdisciplinary artist robert karimi in his poem "how I found my inner DJ." (qtd. in Chang, *Total Chaos*). Using footnotes as the method to document the "source texts," karimi composes this piece in DJ fashion by combining snip-pets of various texts, sounds, and comments from a variety of other DJs, art-ists, writers, and poets. In the piece, he identifies "sampled consciousness." He continues, "It's an old idea with one of Hip Hop's gifts, the sample, serving as a point of departure. Every generation engages in this quest to establish self (and culture) in order to find one's relation to the universe and the universe's relation to one" (222), and he explains his thinking more fully in the footnote, when he expresses the difference between the ideas of sample, sampled, and sampling. In this moment, karimi identifies the importance of sampling as the act of using a part of a larger context in order to infer toward and include the larger context into a current mindset or a contemporary happening. Thus, his entire piece pulls sections from a number of larger moments to describe and document his philosophies on the "now" of his ruminations on exploring his inner DJ and the presence of other voices and moments within that time-space continuum.

Finally, after allowing the academic musings, I took it to the source to make sure I included the culture I'm writing about: Hip Hop. So I called my man Mr. Len: Hip Hop DJ and producer whose worked with artists from Company Flow (as a founding member and DJ) to Jean Grae, Prince Paul to Pharoahe Monch, and countless others. When I told Len I was writing this chapter, we went into one of many frequent extensive conversations about the Hip Hop DJ and sampling. Len put it simply: "Yeah mayn—the DJ was the one who sampled WAY before the producer. That comes from Kool Herc. The true Hip Hop DJs sampled based on the name 'DJ'—cuz they Jockeyed the Disc and rode the beat. They would ride that two or three second riff, and stretched it into minutes . . . live!" (Mr. Len)

What all of these academic and DJ scholars do is not only help us understand the idea of the sample but place the Hip Hop DJ at the forefront of sampling origins and conversations as a new type of "composer." They also push us toward looking at sampling as a creative way to engage students in the process of composing. In all these texts we find the sample being used as (re)creation toward the aim of composing but also archiving—the types of quotation and citation sourcing we ask our composition students to do in their writing. These scholars also highlight the importance of the advent of the sample as composition and, with that, Hip Hop culture and pedagogy's "whatever" mentality. This mentality, in turn, bumps back against a sometimes oppressive and outdated academy that sees composing and writing in simple "black and white" terms: mainly—"either you write it *our* way or it's wrong . . . you wrote it yourself, or you had to steal it, and NOW you in trouble, sun . . . on God!!!"

Next, we must recognize that just as sampling comes to the table with a rich legacy, so too do the roots of Pennycook's understanding of transgressive-versus-nontransgressive intertextuality. Around the same time the landscape is being established for the Hip Hop sample, there's another set of records playing from another set of crates in relation to the Hip Hop DJ's "citation critique" contextual framework. Pennycook's notion of intertextuality extends from a movement in recontextualizing, reinterpreting, and reenvisioning plagiarism; throughout the 1990s, the scholar who avidly carried this torch was Rebecca Moore Howard. Her overwhelming concern involves reconsidering and revising the notion of the word "plagiarism": from probing students' intentions when deliberating over the individual cases of "patchwriting as academic dishonesty" to completely abandoning the word "plagiarism" because of its negatively engendered and punitive etymology.

In her article "Sexuality, Textuality: The Cultural Work of Plagiarism," Howard lays out a comprehensive history on the legacy of the word (and all that travels with it): "[Plagiarism] is derived from the Latin term for kidnapping, a term whose meaning the Roman poet Martial extended to include not only the stealing of slaves but also textual appropriation" (Howard 479). Howard also illuminates the argument that the engendered and negatively marred term "plagiarism"—along with all its historical and cultural metaphors, meanings, and connotations—requires us more so to abandon the term than to actually try to reconfigure its etymology:

> Gender, weakness, collaboration, disease, adultery, rape, heterosexuality, and property: This whole set of metaphors and associations lies behind every utterance of the word *plagiarism*, rendering fruitless our pedagogical efforts to

teach useful textual strategies and to adjudicate this plagiarism thing . . . the
term *plagiarism*, denoting a heterogeneous variety of textual activities, is doing
cultural work that few of us would deliberately endorse. But notwithstand-
ing attempts (my own included) to redefine that category, as long as the term
marks any sort of academic activities, rules, or events, it will continue to do the
distasteful, hierarchical work that its metaphors describe, even if some of us
eschew or reject those metaphors. (Howard 487–488)

With this in mind, plagiarism—throughout the academy—becomes a difficult
term to define, an err-filled concept to unilaterally universalize across a disciplinary committee that handles such cases, and an ideal that simply can't be
"washed clean and worn again"; Moore clearly advocates for an extensive "Spring
Cleaning" and a new wardrobe in addressing the concept of "plagiarism."

After cementing her argument in regard to plagiarism, Howard moves forward by offering solutions that might jumpstart the conversation for writers,
scholars, English Studies, and the academy at large. She constructs a working draft for a new "academic honesty" collegiate policy (see "Plagiarism,
Authorships, and the Academic Death Penalty"), taking into account student
motives in cases that could involve various degrees of plagiarism that remove
the negative and highly engendered stigma placed on the word. In this document, she deciphers potential student decisions in patchwriting (a source
of inquiry for Pennycook in describing certain aspects of intertextuality). As
well, Howard writes intertextually—using the scholars from various writing
disciplines that have come both before and with her (thus, "a sample of the
samplings")—to construct a comprehensive argument for viewing the word
"plagiarism" with all its negative metaphors and engendered binary attitudes,
and why the prevalent discussion of the word is a Western ideological contor-
tion that should be done away with completely.

Howard introduces a new framework for intellectual and pedagogical conversation about what's necessary in the twenty-first century for an emerging
set of student writers based on all that's come before and through this necessary shift. Detailing the large circumference of landscape—spanning over
three centuries—involved with an academic and literary conversation on plagiarism becomes Pennycook's intellectual playground in his attempts to set the
boundaries on the field where intertextuality can breathe and play. Essentially,
the product of Howard's sampling of plagiarism blazes trails for Pennycook's
intertextuality sounds.

Because these scholars have advocated for a different view of composing,
it makes sense that this leads us to Pennycook's analysis, which requires us

to complicate mere "plagiarism" for the idea of intertextuality, where the connection between texts, authorship, and knowledge are continuously (re)writing each other. The issue isn't as simple as "stealing" and theft but, instead, degrees of recycled thoughts and writing to the point where the intertextuality becomes "transgressive": a violation of the one and/or many sources that may have contributed to the words, ideas, or composition a student may present as his or her own.

As we think about "stealing" and theft, an important contemporary text should be included. In the book *Rhymin' and Stealin': Musical Borrowing in Hip-Hop*, Justin Williams pushes toward a different type of intertextuality that specifically takes into account Hip Hop music, culture, and sampling practices. He identifies lyrical and visual arrangement exhibited by specific Hip Hop artists to elucidate his (re)imagining of terms within the Hip Hop sampling paradigm:

> I find it more productive, however, to create a distinction between musical borrowing and digital sampling as a special case of musical borrowing. In contrast, I have chosen to use the terms *autosonic quotation* and *allosonic quotation*, from Serge Lacasse, to differentiate between sampled and nonsampled quotations, respectively. Autosonic quotation is quotation of a recording by digitally sampling it (digital or analogue), as opposed to allosonic quotation, which quotes the previous material by way of rerecording or performing it live (like a quote in jazz performance), rather than sampling from the original recording. (Williams 3)

Following along similar thinking with Nelson George, Williams is also tuned into how Hip Hop continues a tradition and legacy of Black music: "Intertextuality in hip-hop culture always lies at the crossroads between technology and history, between African and African American artistic traditions and newer technologies like digital sampling that allow practitioners to extend older traditions in new and varied ways" (5). Williams isolates a particular type of intertextuality, mainly through the idea of "textual signaling" and "non-textual signaling." For Williams, sampling in Hip Hop serves as a special type of borrowing that members of the Hip Hop nation may or may not immediately recognize. Where Williams's concern becomes helpful in this framework is how he envisions the parameters of textual signaling: "Hip-hop music largely celebrates its intertextualities and references, and knowledgeable listeners will no doubt understand certain references even when the borrowing is not textually signaled . . . and again, this will vary among listeners: some will know the exact song, some will recognize a genre, and some will realize that it could reference a number of elements, as hip-hop is often a multivocal discourse" (12–15). Williams's concept of "textual signaling" in Hip Hop functions similarly to Pennycook's notions of what becomes transgressive or nontransgressive. What remains critical to an understanding of intertextuality in Hip Hop is how members within and outside of the Hip Hop community may know or not know, may discuss, celebrate, or hide the textual signal(s) of sampling's intertextuality.

We now have a sense of the source of our samples and the records required to rock this set—now we can let a Hip Hop DJ show us what they all sound like with each other . . .

"I Hate a Rhyme-Biter's Rhyme": Workin' ON the Mix, IN the Mix

Approaching this conversation with the Hip Hop DJ's perspective of *biters, jackers,* and *transformers* in mind, we find that Pennycook's notion of intertextuality alongside Williams's ideas of textual signaling can help us to further the conversation that Wakefield presents. While she gives her students more extensive examples of P. Diddy and Vanilla Ice, this chapter utilizes the philosophies of the Hip Hop DJ to add on and continue a deeper conversation. Thus, instead of Diddy being labeled by students as an artist using "too many samples," DJ Rhetoric would speak to this situation by presenting three categories for Diddy's work: Diddy as biter; Diddy as jacker; or Diddy as transformer. After all, it is DJ Rhetoric that would speak to the ways in which the practices, modes, methods, and cultural critiques of Hip Hop music get defined and classified. So, the idea of biters, jackers, and transformers comes from a categorization the DJ has traditionally made in commenting on and critiquing music.

"Biters" would be considered artists who simply take a loop, disregarding the context the loop comes from, and potentially creating a composition that goes completely against the grain of what the original source represents. For example, walking on a crowded college campus, a student named Murv stops me and says, "Hey, that's a cool t-shirt! Where did you get it?" I tell the student, "I got it from a website: www.dontbitemystyle.net—check it out!" A week later, Murv is seen by Lillith wearing an *identical* t-shirt. When Lillith asks Murv, "Hey, that's a cool t-shirt! Where'd you get it?," Murv's response is "Secret styles . . . I got it from an undisclosed location I found myself and I ain't tellin' you about it!" Murv has officially become a biter.

Wakefield presents an excellent example (that we revisit here from the previous chapter) of chief biter #1—Vanilla Ice. In her conversation with students, she states, "Vanilla Ice, whose 'Ice Ice Baby' includes an obvious backbeat from

'Under Pressure' (Queen/David Bowie) and who denied the similarity, also fits into a lesson where the instructor wants to discourage overreliance on quotation and promote honesty in research" (Wakefield 359). While Wakefield does a good job in highlighting this moment, another aspect of Vanilla Ice not present in her work is Ice's complete disregard of the original source in his actual "writing"—as the only time Vanilla Ice was probably "under pressure" was when he denied the sample AND when Suge Knight held him off the hotel balcony by his ankles . . . but alas, I digress.

There is a flip side to this moment in the bitin' paradigm, in that Ice acknowledging Queen and Bowie here would be admitting the sample source; if it wasn't cleared (a process by which an artist/producer gets permission from the original song composer to use the sample), Ice may have been in Biz Markie's shoes, facing a lawsuit. This example cuts deep, as it is reminiscent of how Black music has been usurped and appropriated in American culture since the dawn of American culture. To credit the rightful source, in either instance, would mean both legitimizing the importance of, and thereby rightfully compensating, the original creators of the source. And in some cases, sample clearance is expensive—a multimillion-dollar business in and of itself. And while some artists who get sample clearance requests are gracious and excited about seeing their music have a second or third life, other folks see the opportunity as a time to cash in when an emerging artist might not have a budget to support the price tag. The question that emerges: if all pricing were constant, would every artist/producer credit the creator of the sample? In some cases, there has been a mystique around unearthing the original sample source, so creating a beat without a readily recognizable sample sometimes stood as a badge of honor. In other situations, clearing the sample for *one song* might cost an artist an entire *album* budget.

On some level, there is some nuance to be further explored. However, when you're bitin', your aim is not rooted in acknowledging a sonic lineage but instead in divorcing oneself from it. Real recognize real, though—so in this case, the moniker that must get embraced is "biter." Thus, Wakefield's example shows how it is important to reference and cite properly. This can be best described by Pennycook's examination of "transgressive intertextuality" because of Ice's direct refusal of the original source in his own sonic composition.

The next category is "jackers," those who can be seen as borrowers or sharers: someone who lifts directly, but is sharing, so never denying where that piece of writing came from. For example, walking through a crowded college campus, I am stopped by Herbie, who says, "Hey man, that's a dope t-shirt! Where'd you get it?" I respond to Herbie with "a website called www.dontbitemystyle.net—you should check it out!" A week later, Herbie—wearing the same t-shirt in a different color—is approached by Murv. When Murv (our resident "biter") asks, "Yo man, where'd you get that t-shirt from?" Herbie is quick to say, "I got it from this website, www.dontbitemystyle.net. This dude I met last week put me onto it. You should check it out." While Herbie may have the same t-shirt in a different color, he doesn't deny the source of his knowledge in regard to the website, or who told him about it.

When we think of the term "jackin'" in Hip Hop culture, it simply means to "get got"; to be jacked is to be a victim of a robbery or hostile takeover of sorts. Our understanding of jackin' expanded when the concept was introduced by Ice Cube on his 1990s EP *Kill at Will* on a song called "Jackin' for Beats." The first line of the song—"Gimme that beat fool! / It's a full-time jack-move!" (Ice Cube)—clearly relates to Pennycook's notion of institutional resistance that students can possibly present in their intertextual writing. This song is also an intertextual composition, as Cube rocks over various beats that at the time were hot on the Hip Hop music radar. In this moment, both sonic lineage and Williams's idea of "textual signaling" comes into play, as Cube is banking on the shared understanding of the Hip Hop listening community to know the source of each beat he's jacked. This idea in practice dates back to DJ Kool Herc and his Caribbean influences. It is a process that demonstrates the vast legacy Hip Hop has in terms of its musical and cultural roots. Sharing comes from the Jamaican Dancehall dub plate and "riddim" mentality, where various Dancehall artists share the same beat to create multiple songs. Another contemporary example for Hip Hop would be mixtape culture, which is dominated by "freestyles": artists rhyming on other artists popular beats. The most recent display of the mixtape freestyle moment comes from The LOX vs. Dipset #VERZUZ celebration, when Jadakiss performs his 2010 freestyle to The Notorious B.I.G.'s "Who Shot Ya" instrumental. Back when it released, Jadakiss made a big splash with a long freestyle verse laced with braggadocio, gun talk, and street-corner philosophies that almost rivaled the original Biggie classic. In 2021, his live performance of the song showed just how meaningful a freestyle can be when it evokes and pays homage to the original but also extends the sonic sentiment.

Here, I present three useful examples to help students see both sides of the coin.

In 2006, Too $hort (re)engaged the national radio airwaves with "Blow the Whistle." While Jay-Z would quickly jack the beat for a freestyle remix, one of the clear punchlines comes in $hort's first verse, which immediately captures the listener right out the gate. Wasting no time, $hort rhymes: "I go on and on / can't understand how I last so long / I must have superpowers / rap two hundred twenty-five thousand hours!" (Too $hort). Ten years later, we can see something closer to jackin' on DJ Khaled's 2016 album *Major Key*, when Drake appears on the song "For Free." While Khaled's production is a different take sonically, it does have an energy and bounce reminiscent of the Too $hort record. However, it is Drake's rhymes that truly seal the deal in the flashback-throwback. In identical fashion to Too $hort, Drake starts his verse with the bars "I go on and on / can't understand how I last so long / I must have the superpowers / last two hundred twenty-three thousand hours" (Drake). In 2006, Too $hort's verse really alluded to the amount of time compiled in all of his songs on all of his albums, which he continues to rhyme about after the opening bars. However, Drake jacks those bars to discuss his sexual prowess, which, interestingly enough, is typically a subject about which Too $hort is well known for rhyming. This "jack move" as interplay becomes interesting, as Drake borrows some Too $hort bars to invigorate in them the sexuality that $hort did not originally include. Thus, Drake is citing and textually signaling Too $hort, while also repurposing the words in those specific bars to fit the purpose of his record with Khaled. Drake makes no discursive and/ or rhetorical moves to deny Too $hort's song; instead, he demonstrates his scholarly prowess in understanding Hip Hop music, history, and lyricism. Here, borrowing and sharing differ from biting because the latter source references its predecessor. This is a critical stakeholding moment in Hip Hop's cultural economy. Jackin' gone well is an astute signaling, like a solid chess move: it demonstrates strategic thinking steps ahead of schedule, in order to show a well-thought-out, overarching long-term plan of action. The plan with Drake's jackin' is a nod to historic Hip Hop plot points, to show how much of a student of the game he is. "For Free" highlights Drake's intricate awareness of "Blow the Whistle" and its importance to both historical and contemporary cultural cues. Consequently, jackin' gone wrong is a nightmare: it is based on a checkers-like strategy, which could influence an artist's perception of being knowledgeable and credible in understanding (or overstanding—depending on how you envision this concept/element) both the music and culture . . . in Hip Hop culture, it leads one to the unwanted category of bitin', described previously.

While Wakefield presents Diddy and his infamous "this is the remix . . . take dat, take dat, take dat . . . that's right!" movement, a more complex example that takes place before Diddy is MC Hammer, with his song "U Can't Touch This," which includes a loop from Rick James's classic Soul song "Superfreak." On the one hand, there is *clearly* a complete difference between Hammer's emcee composition and that of Rick James. One would think—to be blunt—that the Superfreak is indeed touchable. As well, Hammer actually thanks God in a composition where Rick James discusses very unholy topics in his text. However, MC Hammer complicates this idea, as he has credited Rick James as a cowriter of this composition (similar to how Jay-Z, Kanye West, and No I.D. credit Otis Redding on the 2011 single "Otis" off their collaborative *Watch the Throne* album). This example highlights the fine line between biting and jacking that can be used in student-centered conversations to illustrate the delicate line between transgressive and nontransgressive intertextuality.

Another, and even more complicated, example of jacking can be pulled from popular culture's shunning of a Hip Hop citation. In the Nike commercial series with Lebron James entitled "MVPuppets," the Lebron puppet is shown in the barbershop with his then-teammate Zydrunas Ilgauskas. While they go through a complicated handshake, the song that plays in the background is "The Message" by Cymande—the original source sampled by Masta Ace in his song "Me and the Biz." While Nike is working intertextually, sharing this visual concept from its 1996 commercials for the Anfernee "Penny" Hardaway sneaker campaign, this work was done after Masta Ace shot his video for "Me and the Biz" in 1990; Masta Ace acts as if Biz Markie is on the song, but he is doing a voice mimicking his fellow Juice Crew rapper. In the video, Ace is seen with a Biz Markie puppet that he works as a ventriloquist. Although Nike seems to be borrowing and sharing from itself, when it uses the Cymande song and reuses the puppet concept, it inadvertently evokes Masta Ace but never references Ace at all—neither with the Penny nor the Lebron campaigns. While this example demonstrates an "unwriting" of a Hip Hop musical legacy in the sense of leaving Masta Ace out of the conversation, it is a fruitful location and an interesting dynamic for beginning a student-centered conversation about the outcome of instances where borrowing and sharing can either work toward or malfunction around citation. This example shows a collective memory that does not cite a source and instead writes that source out of a collective history for a demographic that has kept Nike afloat for years: the Hip Hop community. So what does it mean when Hip Hop is left out of the conversation of cultural history and production but is clearly the influence that has led to a moment that would be categorized as "smart business acumen?" Is it sharing? Intertextual transgression? I leave that answer to you and your students in the classroom.

The last category is "transforming." This is a moment where intertextuality works at its best: it lends the writer a new voice through a creative usage of ideas and texts that precede it. The transformative category of sampling within Hip Hop is shown when artists are not only borrowing or sharing but when they are also using that intertextuality to transform the initial text of a song in order to create a completely new work, while still archiving and referencing the ideas from which they were originally cited. It is a transactional process, where the borrowing or sharing leads to fresh, innovative, and creative ways to express a similar idea from the sample that preceded it. So walking through the crowded college campus, I am stopped by Shawn, who says, "Nice tee, my dude! Where'd you git that?" Of course, my response is "www.dontbitemystyle .net—you should check it out." A week later, Murv stops Shawn because he has on a completely different t-shirt that Murv's never seen. When Murv—resident biter—asks Shawn the infamous question, Shawn gives a unique answer: "I saw this dude who had a Classic Material NY t-shirt on, and he told me he got it from dontbitemystyle.net. So I went to the website, and it was lit! They had all sorts of fly gear: CMNY, No Mas, Carhartt WIP. So I bought this one, cuz it was different—I haven't seen anyone wit' this one yet!" Shawn's answer epitomizes transformin'. While "jackin' as sharing/borrowing" might use a concept to further a new textual conversation, transformin' becomes an evolution of the text—an evolution students should strive toward in their journey between citing various resources and finding their own voice.

A strong example of transforming at its best is the work done on Rapsody's album *The Idea of Beautiful*. Rapsody pens an album that resonates in the vein of a modern-day version of the *Miseducation* album. Indeed, Rapsody evokes the presence and reminiscent feel of Lauryn Hill's 1998 classic solo album *The Miseducation of Lauryn Hill*. However, part of the current Hip Hop sonic climate revolves in a space succinctly defined by lyricist Royce Da 5'9" when he says, "You're just an algorithm," likening current MCs to following the equation that produces a duplication of a "successfully commercial" sonic text. So in an era of recording artists who are comfortable with sounding identical to one another, and potentially crossing into the transgressive intertextual realm of biting, Rapsody is clear about not only evoking but citing Lauryn as well. Rapsody makes two distinct references in two of the early songs on her album. And when "Believe Me" comes on, it doesn't take Rapsody sixty seconds to arrive at the line "Lauryn ain't crazy / just don't know what she been through." This line becomes a segue for the hook of the song that comes forty-five seconds later: "Believe me / frontin' nigguhs gimme heebie jeebies," a quote from Lauryn's verse on "Ready or Not," a single on the Fugees 1996 breakout album *The Score*. The work that Rapsody does in invoking Lauryn before she gets to this moment on the album is an example of transforming intertextuality at its best: she is able to utilize, evoke, and cite the source while also (re)envisioning the famous bars that Lauryn provided in her verse.

Another intricate example of this work on a global level is Prince Paul's album *A Prince Among Thieves*. When I asked Prince Paul about this album, he described it as an intertextual process: "When I sat [down to write], I wanted to parody every wild movie, or Black movie or every movie I've ever seen, and I put in my own thoughts as I wrote it" (Prince Paul). In writing the screenplay for this album, Paul demonstrates this album is on the one hand a text and on the other a transformative process that shows the intricacies of citing. In this story of Tarik (an aspiring rapper), Tarik uses the Big Daddy Kane "Young, Gifted and Black" instrumental for his demo, which he is presenting to be signed to Wu-Tang's record label. The conversation between Tarik and his best friend, Tru, starts off with Tru saying, "Yo didn't Kane use that?" Tarik responds with "Yeah, but he didn't flip it like this tho . . ." Tarik identifies Big Daddy Kane's "Young, Gifted and Black"—a song that samples Blues artist Albert King's song "I'll Play the Blues for You"—and finds Kane transformin' the sentiment of the sample, which is clearly evidenced by the juxtaposition of the song titles. But for *Prince Among Thieves*, not only does Paul use the beat and reference Kane but also Kane later appears as a character in the story the album tells. He also transforms "Steady Mobbin'" from Ice Cube's *Death Certificate* album for a song called "Steady Slobbin'." This album is significant because it functions as a complete text—telling an intricate story with each song. This album is a story (and a "text") because no one song truly stands alone: it's only when you listen to the album from beginning to end that you understand its conceptual nature and how each song in sequential order furthers the complete story of the larger "text." What Paul does is also transformative because the story revolves around the idea of a "Prince among Thieves"—an honorable character among biters and crooks. This perspective challenges the way Hip Hop albums have traditionally been composed, as a text that contains elements of research and a variety of citation methods: from sharing and borrowing, to transforming.

"What's the Happenings with the Forward Motion on Things . . .": *Pushing Intertextuality, Textual Signaling, and Citation Critique Forward*

Still, none of these categories are "permanently fixed." Artists can inhabit any one, or two, or even three simultaneously, or any combination at many points during their careers. For example, Emily Lordi identifies a moment in the conclusion of her book *Black Resonance: Iconic Women Singers and African American Literature* that interrogates the relationship(s) between Jazz and Blues singers, and the poetry that their music muses in creation. As Lordi works through detailing the sonic and textual relationship between the music of Etta James and Linda Jackson's James-inspired poetry collection *What Yellow Sounds Like*, she highlights Hip Hop's ability to (re)animate past music for new listeners: "Since the rise of recognizable samples in the 1980s, hip hop has not only given listeners new ways to hear oft-sampled Funk and Soul legends like James Brown and George Clinton but has literally *introduced* younger listeners to these artists" (Lordi 221). In describing the intertextual possibilities of Hip Hop, she examines production team Blue Sky Black Death's (BSBD's) use of an Etta James sample in lyrical powerhouse Jean Grae's song "Threats." While Lordi identifies three specific sonic movements with how BSBD samples Etta James's voice, she also pinpoints how Grae has evoked Jay-Z's lyrics from his song "Threat," which appears on *The Black Album* and was produced by longtime Jean Grae collaborator 9th Wonder. In this moment, Lordi highlights Grae's textual signaling in jackin' Jay's lyrics while simultaneously walking readers through an intricate sonic transformation between BSBD's use of an Etta James sample (while also relating the lyrical production and similarities between James and Grae). This logic leads Lordi to call for an expansion of the academic analysis and discourse around Hip Hop, by elevating Hip Hop as a distinct musical form, worthy to study and interrogate on its own terms, instead of the typical academic placement of Hip Hop "alongside" blank (insert any "recognized" intellectual genre in said blank):

> Although I have often spoken about revaluing literature in the wake of the Black Arts, current discourse on hip hop reveals a need to revalue music . . . while I understand the cultural politics that motivate this argument, I nonetheless believe that hip hop is best understood as a unique musical form . . . I support [Kelefa] Sanneh's assertion that what makes Jay-Z's art so compelling "has something to do with his odd, perpetually adolescent-sounding voice, and a lot to do with his sophisticated sense of rhythm. Sure, he's a poet—and, while we're at it, a singer and percussionist, too. But why should any of these titles be more impressive than 'rapper'?" While Sanneh is clearly aware that the answer lies in these titles' differing degrees of artistic respectability, the question productively highlights the biases and limitations of our current analytic lexicon when it comes to music and writing. (Lordi 223–224)

While Lordi deftly spotlights both jackin' and transformin', a deeper look uncovers a moment of bitin' as well, as Grae ceased her contract with Baby

Grande Records over the release of the album *The Evil Jeanius* (which contained the song "Threats") because Baby Grande allegedly created the album by using a series of Grae's vocals without her permission. It is in this intricate web of intertextualities that Lordi leads us to a fruitfully fluid example of all three tropes at play.

Tory Lanez, another Hip Hop artist who found breakout commercial success by reintroducing listeners to older soundscapes in Hip Hop culture (see Lanez's use of Brownstone's 1994 single "If You Love Me" for his 2015 single entitled "Say It"), returned to the radio airwaves in 2019 alongside T-Pain, for their song "Jerry Sprunger." While Lanez initially seems to use a loop of T-Pain's 2005 song "I'm Sprung," he appears on the song accompanied by T-Pain, using new lyrics to evoke T-Pain's original concept of being "sprung" in a newfound relationship. The intertextuality and textual signaling are evident in both the song and the music videos (with Akon and T-Pain in the original video, which then switches to T-Pain playing Akon's role, and Lanez's playing T-Pain's role in the latest iteration); while there are clearly elements of jackin' present, the newly composed lyrics are definitely transformed.

Rapsody's album *Eve* is constructed as an homage to the multifaceted complexities of the Black woman, and the 9th Wonder–produced single "Ibtihaj" finds her rhyming over a transformed version of GZA's Hip Hop classic "Liquid Swords." While the beat clearly signals its predecessor, Rapsody takes it a step further by featuring GZA on the song. To evoke the true feeling of 1990s Hip Hop sonic lineage and recollection, the listener finds D'Angelo singing the chorus to "Ibtihaj": named after Ibtihaj Muhammad—the first Muslim-American female *fencer* to wear a hijab during competition. The covert and overt textual signalings that Rapsody uses, from the song title and underlying meanings, to the sonic backdrops and inclusion of GZA, are a witty display of both jackin' and transformin'.

When Lil Wayne returned in 2018 with the highly anticipated *Carter V* album, his Swizz Beatz–produced single "Uproar" was the perfect anthem to drive the long-awaited project. A quick listen to the opening of "Uproar" will bring finely tuned ears right back to 2001 and G-Dep's song "Special Delivery" produced by EZ Elpee. The sonic signaling is crystal-clear; unfortunately, the textual signaling in the songwriting credits is nonexistent. The fact that EZ Elpee is not listed in the credits for "Uproar" or anywhere in the *Carter V* definitely gives the song a jackin'-turned-bitin' feel. After an interview in which Elpee discusses his slight disdain for the crediting snub based primarily on the principle of giving "credit where credit is due," Swizz Beatz took to Twitter and posted, "Super Shout

Out to EZ Elpee the Original Producer of Special Delivery." A quick review of the online comments shows posters going back and forth between agreeing with Elpee and defending Swizz Beatz, based on the premise that Elpee didn't "invent" the sample but merely "identified" it for public consumption. The comment that resonated most clearly for this conversation was from C'Mon, who states: "He does not own the sample, true. But Swizz recreated Elpee's version of the sample. Elpee manipulated the sample and Swizz used that manipulated version, did almost nothing to it, and they just credit the original. Not cool. Not illegal, but still not cool" (qtd. in Wallace). From the sonics of the beats, to the reinvigorated dance the "Harlem Shake"—introduced in 2001, then revisited as the "Uproar Challenge," there is no mistaking the 2018 production and its sonic lineage from seventeen years prior. This is a clear example of how a few words in the form of citation can take an excellent moment in jackin' and lean it toward bitin'.

We can also look at examples given by J. Cole on "St. Tropez"—a 2014 sonic transformation clearly inspired by Mobb Deep's 1995 classic "Give Up the Goods." Similarly, Bronx rapper Swave HMG and his song "Blue Faces" stand as a 2019 transformed iteration of the 1997 Busta Rhymes hit record "Put Your Hands Where My Eyes Can See." Armani White's 2022 song "Billie Eilish" does similar work with Noreaga's Neptune-produced 2002 single "Nothin'." Finally, we can look to Busta Rhymes's 2020 song "Outta My Mind," which features 1990s R&B sensation Bell Biv Devoe (BBD) with a reconfigured version of BBD's chart-topping smash single "Poison." Each of these occurrences presents an extension of Wakefield's conversation and a conduit by which students can begin to understand the importance of the various modes of citation. As well, this chapter functions as an intertextual composition, citing various sources to describe each category through DJ Literacy by evoking terminology that springs from DJ Rhetoric and is rooted in Hip Hop culture.

In their essay "Intertextuality in the Transcultural Contact Zone," Celia Thompson and Alastair Pennycook reach a conclusion with a very intertextual moment for describing the importance of these ideas: "It is precisely here at this point of intertextual engagement, we suggest, that Bakhtin's dialogue and battle for meaning occur, as teachers and students struggle to locate themselves in the constantly shifting transcultural contact zones that characterize today's global universities [and] as students struggle to establish ownership over and investment in the written academic texts they produce" (Thompson and Pennycook 136). Engaging in DJ Rhetoric to formulate a Hip Hop DJ critique can be valuable to helping students understand the idea of citation and referencing;

this should be done through the idea of intertextuality, as opposed to a continuous dwelling within the realm of "plagiarism"—the grand disturber of harmony. This conversation will also help students understand the nature of intertextuality and how being able to identify with the areas of bitin', jackin', and finally transformin' can allow for them to find their voice in their own writing (while sampling various sources), as well as understand the severity of issues involving transgressive intertextuality. With this foundation, we give students a new approach in thinking about how they can reference and cite information. And some of the best examples are clearly demonstrated through DJ Rhetoric. We will close with three different Hip Hop DJ anecdotes.

When asked about the significance of DJing to writing, legendary female DJ Spinderella stated very clearly, "[DJing] is a form of research" (Spinderella), which clearly connects the idea of the DJ's research legacy entitled "diggin' in the crates" to aspects of research in college writing classrooms. But when asked what advice she would give to up-and-coming DJs, she not only makes a relevant point about working with the new contemporary technology, but she also urges DJs to heed this beacon call:

> If you *really* really want to maintain, and challenge yourself and keep your integrity, and [the integrity] of DJing—the art form itself—you'll learn from the beginning. And that's just a really good feeling to say, "I'm a DJ and I learned on vinyl and I use vinyl as well." I'm proud to say that I am one of those DJs who learned from the beginning, but even if you're not and you're just starting to DJ today: challenge yourself to do those things, to learn with the origins. (DJ Spinderella)

It is here that DJ Spinderella both gives valuable lessons on the importance of research techniques and labels the range we can see between biters, jackers, and transformers. Essentially, she expresses the importance of acknowledging the new and contemporary landscape of information (she says later in the interview, "I'm knowledgeable enough to have come this far, with twenty-five years doing it, but I have to say I'm still learning"), while impressing the importance of understanding the foundation of the culture—thus there is new writing in the culture of the DJ, but it is constantly influenced by the writing and the sources that have come before it . . . sound familiar?

DJ Skeme Richards eloquently put Hip Hop culture on blast when he talked in his interview about the importance of the cultural legacy of Hip Hop, and rightfully preserving it for the upcoming generations. His statement, quite simply:

New kids aren't digging. They're playing for the now. I'm trying to play for forever. Nobody's going back to where it starts . . . nobody's digging for history like that . . . If you ask a MC—if you ask 90s MCs—who was the first person to say, "mic check one-two," they can't tell you. It was Melle Mel. But they can't tell you! Y'knowuti'msayin'? They can't tell you! (Skeme Richards)

Besides clearly seeing Skeme's passion about the state of Hip Hop's cultural history, we find he clearly places the DJ's art of "diggin'" in the paradigm of research—and then demonstrates the importance of the research and understanding a historical context to sociocultural moments. In writing, this can be likened to understanding the inherent characteristics of intertextuality and that within different pieces of writing, there may be other authors and/or scholars whose work and writing are relevant to the conversation.

Finally, an internationally known Philadelphia DJ by the name of Ca$h Money shared with me the importance of his legacy on both Hip Hop culture and on DJ culture as well, by explaining the history of the "Battle Style" turntable setup. In the interview, Ca$h describes why turntables were turned 90 degrees, set up with the tone arm at the top:

That's MY style. Grand Wizard Rasheen—the guy that I learned from—that's how he used to spin. Why he turned them that way—I guess it was to fit on the table that he had, cuz the table was mad small. When he was teaching me, I just thought that was the way to do it. I seen everybody else doing it the regular way, but I was a little sloppy. My sleeve would honestly hit the tone arm. I learned from Rasheen, and the world learned from me. So you can look at any tape from 1987 on—no one was doing that. I was the only one spinning that way. Everyone was copying off of me, and the people they were teaching, they never told them any different. So they think, "oh this is Battle Style." *Nah*—that's Ca$h Money style. I didn't know anything about putting a patent on anything like that. Who's thinking that? It was just comfortable for me . . . the setup on that "Ugly People Be Quiet" [record cover] was what everybody was trying to be, *that* setup. And what's crazy is the turntable companies, that's how they started making the turntables—with the tone arm at the top! That came from me and Grand Wizard Rasheen. (DJ Ca$h Money)

It is here with DJ Ca$h Money that we can see the entire paradigm of DJ Rhetoric enacted, focusing on biters, jackers, and transformers from Ca$h's mentor Rasheen, to the DJ champions who came after Ca$h, to the pupils those champions mentored, all the way down to the companies who began producing turntables specifically with the Hip Hop DJ in mind. And it is here that Skeme Richards shows us the importance of the DJ working intertextually, as well as the relevance and significance of the Hip Hop DJ as cultural historian:

> If you ask any of these kids now: who was the first person to turn a turntable sideways, "Philly Style"? They'll be like "I don't know, that's just the way it's supposed to be done." No—Ca$h Money started that. It's called "Battle Style" but really, it's "Philly Style." If you ask who the first person was to do a transformer [scratch], and they can't tell you, then it's like "see—you didn't do your homework. You're a DJ, but you didn't do your homework." So I believe in digging, I believe in knowing history. You don't write a book on a subject until you go back in history. If you're into art, you can't just say, "oh, I like this" but then you don't know Van Gough's history, or you don't know Picasso's history, or Andy Warhol's history. People aren't diggin' in this generation . . . but we dig. The dudes that have been doin' it, we STAY digging! (Skeme Richards)

Now can you think of a better way to express the idea of research and documentation to students? If so, ga'head and make it happen. But if not, let the DJ walk you through it.

Class is now in session . . .

Ladies and Gentlemen, we got MC Shan and Marley Marl in the house tonight. They just came from off tour, and they want to tell you a little story about where they come from . . .

You love to hear the story /again and again/
of *how it all got started* / way *back when*/
the monument is right in your face/
sit and listen for awhile to the name of the place/
The Bridge

MC Shan, "The Bridge," *Down by Law*, Co-Chillin' / Warner Bros., 1987, Vinyl/LP.

Check out the oracle bred from city housing / Nas, I arise the dead by thousands /
I remember seeing Shan / chilling near his Audi / Hollis had Run and them but I proudly /
Put a poster up of Shan and Marley / that was art kid / *You love to hear the story how it started* /
The bubbly I'm pouring wasn't popped yet / Before there was an audience to watch us /
I assure you, there was a process /
"*You love to hear the story (yeah), how it all, how it all got started*" /
How it all got started, yeah /
"You love to hear the story, how it all, how it all (**how it**) got started, got started" /
How it all got started /
"You love to hear the story (**hear the story**) / how it all got started, got started" /
Started off / Started off, started off /
How it all got started /
"Back when, back when, back when,
back when / Back when, **back when**,
back when, back when"

Nas, "Back When," *Life Is Good*, Def Jam, 2012, CD.

4

"A WHOLE LOTTA SOMETHIN' FROM NUFIN"

Racism, Revision, and Rotating Records: The
Hip Hop DJ in Composition Praxis

. . . push the envelope like the knob on the mixer . . .

Havoc and Alchemist, "Maintain (Fuck How You Feel)," *The Silent Partner*, Baby Grande Records, 2016.

> . . . hopefully the book maintains a stance presented to us
> by Havoc of Mobb Deep and the Alchemist in the song
> "Maintain (Fuck How You Feel)."
> In trying to describe how his longevity in Hip Hop music can be
> derived from creativity,
> Havoc says, "Push the envelope like the knob on the mixer" . . .
> *K for the Way* proves the attempt
> at pushing the envelope may be valiant . . .

https://doi.org/10.7330/9781646424849.c004

Imagine crossing the threshold of a room and looking for a seat. As you settle in, you look up to see two turntables and a mixer, underneath a hovering computer. Two records rotate at a constant syncopated pace. More people nestle into their seats until the flow of human traffic is complete. Finally, a figure walks up and reaches for a pair of headphones. Turning a fitted baseball cap cocked at a 35-degree angle to face straight ahead allows the headphones to be mounted. The top headphone band is adjusted to sit at a comfortable slant, enabling the device to create an angled rainbow: from left ear, curved across the back brim of the fitted hat, around and behind the right ear. A set of fingers maneuver the turntable tone arm, first lifting then positioning the needle at the beginning of the record on the turntable to the right. The hand manipulates the record back and forth, positioning the record then hitting a button to stop the record's circular motion. This process is repeated on the turntable on the left. Once this exercise is over, the figure looks up at everyone and says, "Aight, y'all ready?" You look at all the eager faces around you . . . most confused, in awe or excited to see what will happen next.

Under most circumstances, this sight might be seen in a club or a lounge, a record store, small intimate party, or even a radio station. Not today, though. On this day, the location is a first-year college writing class circa 2008. And during this particular session, it's evident the instructor of the day is the DJ . . .

Turntable Church Starring the Good Reverend Hip Hop DJ/Producer: The Premise of "Makin' Somethin' Outta Little-to-Nufin"

While there may be a precedent for bringing Hip Hop into the classroom, I'm not sure there's many prior cases of a DJ walking into an English classroom and convening "Turntable Tabernacle" (aka "chuuuuuurch" in a Snoop Dogg voice) with the "1s and 2s" (aka two turntables and a mixer). But this moment in the classroom with the DJ becomes integral to including the tastemakers in a conversation involving Hip Hop music and culture. We have already seen instances where educators use Hip Hop as "supplemental" material; the text, corresponding narrative(s), and cultural epistemologies of Hip Hop become secondary or even tertiary in that Hip Hop is only relevant when put behind an intellectual query or theoretical framework. This chapter will bump up against such models, like a push-and-pull jockeying for full-airplane-armrest positioning.

In the last chapter, we envisioned the DJ as theorist, making sense of how one might (re)imagine ideas around plagiarism and citation via textual signaling and sample practices; the goal was for the DJ—as analyst and critic—to decipher the tropes of bitin', jackin', and transformin'. The premise of this chapter is to continue such theorizing and to look at how the Hip Hop DJ and Hip Hop DJ/Producer become the intrinsic examples for first-year writing students in thinking about how they conduct revision in their writing. An important aspect of this conversation is using the Gramscian model of the organic intellectual as the instructor in the course. Ideally, this lesson does not work without the DJ at the forefront of the conversation; thus, Hip Hop culture and the DJ are not "supplemental"—they are the primary examples used to investigate revision quandaries and incite learning in the college classroom. This lesson only functions with the DJ—the cornerstone of Hip Hop culture—being the centerpiece and chief facilitator of the intellectual discourse.

For this chapter, I start with moments of discourse around Hip Hop in the classroom while interjecting various formative sections of narrative that depict the resistance to and inherent racism toward Hip Hop–centered teaching strategies. A seminal Hip Hop text serves as a psychic prologue to introduce a variety of scholarly works that can help us make sense of Hip Hop discourse in the classroom. Another groundbreaking source will help to frame and situate the Hip Hop DJ as critical in the progression of the Hip Hop producer. This paradigm will center the DJ and DJ practices in conversation with first-year college writing students in (re)imagining and (re)envisioning writing and revision at both the local and global levels. Furthermore, by including the voices of well-known Hip Hop DJ/Producers, I contend there is a unique collaborative investment in the relationship between the Hip Hop DJ/Producer and emcee/MC in creating "the remix." This relationship presents an intriguing conundrum for the ways we might envision teaching practices in college-level Composition Studies. Central to this moment is the way Hip Hop flips the script for students to absorb the idea of revision in Writing Studies—and the Hip Hop DJ sits at the center of this disrupt.

We Been Told You That We Won't Stop: A Landmark Premonition to Hip Hop in the Academy

Houston Baker's 1993 seminal text *Black Studies, Rap, and the Academy* has always struck me as a positively apocalyptic revelation that grounds this scholarly work. The author systematically constructs a concise and lucid argument for the necessity of Black Studies—and with it Hip Hop music and culture. Baker does this through a number of narratives, as well as through academic theorizing, which allows him to situate Hip Hop (or "rap") as an important moment of postmodern happening as well as an academic, cultural, and intellectual site of rich and lush history.

What Baker does best in this book is depict, historicize, and situate the four elements of Hip Hop culture. He goes into detail constructing the history of the DJ, and the DJ's roots in Disco, Rhythm & Blues (or R&B), and musical genres dating even further back. Working from the 1970s and moving through the '80s (and knocking on the door of the '90s), he first addresses the DJ and later broaches the topic of the emcee as rhetorician and modern-day poet of impoverished inner-city communities. This ordering is paramount. As he relates this history, Baker writes using this lens with a very specific position: "A reporter for London's The Mail on Sunday had gotten onto the fact that I advocated rap as an absolute prerequisite for any teacher attempting to communicate with students between the ages of twelve and twenty-five" (Baker 97). The premise holds even truer today, as Baker predicted (while talking to a group of graduate students overseas) that the future of the modern-day poet, as well as the most salient and valuable future teaching tool(s), resided in Hip Hop music and culture. In charting Hip Hop as a culture, he not only constructs a blueprint for a history but also highlights the shifts while comparing and contrasting popular culture elements of the time such as Dick Clark's *American Bandstand*, Don Cornelius's *Soul Train*, *College Bowl*, and Elvis. Within this context, Baker makes an argument for a shifting populous—one that has moved from other forms of popular culture into the underground street-swell of Hip Hop. Thirty years later, we see this prediction living and breathing, with Hip Hop existing, not as a sub- or counterculture but as popular culture across the globe.

As Baker weaves through various disciplines in the midst of situating Hip Hop, he also gives a call to arms for academics of Black Studies to use and validate Hip Hop culture. In painting Hip Hop within the backdrop of impoverished and disenfranchised youth held under the thumb of oppression and brutality (as evidenced by the Rodney King beating and subsequent acquittals), Baker says, "Black Studies engages rap at the site of the academy in order to begin a cultural studies project that may, if we are extraordinarily lucky and courageous, get us on our feet again, out of the immediate reach of swinging batons we did not simply think we saw, but actually did see with the clarity of a national disaster" (Baker 103). Baker ends this text with a call to the Black

Studies community of his time to forward both the notion of Black Studies and the importance of the legacy of Hip Hop music and culture that intrinsically and organically comes with it. Placing his writing in a contemporary context, we find it is crystal clear that Baker's psychic premonitions about Hip Hop in 1993 were indeed true. Within thirty years, Hip Hop stands as mainstream, global popular culture. Thus, it makes complete sense that Hip Hop would be seen as one of many possible teaching tools in twenty-first-century academic environments.

Now There's Enough of Us Talkin' About Us: Hip Hop Scholarship in Action

A number of books and articles can help us visualize Hip Hop as a salient and viable teaching tool in a variety of disciplines. For example, Marc Lamont Hill and Emery Petchauer's 2013 essay collection *Schooling Hip-Hop: Expanding Hip-Hop Based Education across the Curriculum* chronicles the viability of Hip Hop culture as a teaching tool, aesthetic, and pedagogical lens of inquiry. Chapters run the gamut of content areas from English Composition to the sciences, at both the secondary and university levels. Collectively, these writings present a distinctive contemporary roadmap for how we envision aesthetics, curricula, worldviews, pedagogies, and educational practices situating Hip Hop as the focal centerpiece and intellectual springboard. In *Hip Hop's Li'l Sistas Speak: Negotiating Hip Hop Identities and Politics in the New South*, Hip Hop and Urban Education scholar Bettina Love (2012) demonstrates the importance of framing the investment that the young middle and high school girls in her ethnographic study have in understanding their world in relation to Hip Hop and with Hip Hop as a principle sociocultural lens necessary for contemporary cultural analysis. The philosophy that educators be particularly in tune with the level of Hip Hop engagement students ascribe to their sociocultural and political worldviews, and consequently the classroom, is also integral to this chapter.

These scholars—along with Deborah Sánchez, Jabari Mahiri, H. Samy Alim, Elaine Richardson, James Braxton Peterson, Chris Emdin, and others—are committed to looking at how we can envision Hip Hop pedagogy enacted in the classroom in visceral and tangible ways that place Hip Hop as the primary source and theoretical framework. This philosophical and pedagogical effort can empower students and allow them to use the cultural capital and Hip Hop currency (or what we sometimes refer to as the fifth element of the culture—the idea of "overstanding") in a way that validates their academic existence. A number of scholars and educators have also created curriculum and educational projects in the classroom that function in the spirit of Hip Hop culture.

Because Producers Make Beats: Texts That Explore the DJ/Producer

Because we will be talking about the work that DJ/Producers do with reference to student revision, it is also important to mention the scholarship of Joseph Schloss. Schloss is one of the first people to have explicit conversations with Hip Hop producers (some of whom are actually DJs) to include their voices in the intellectual landscape of the academy. As he states in his seminal text *Making Beats: The Art of Sample-Based Hip-Hop*: "Although deejays continued to make music with turntables when performing live, most also developed other strategies for use in the studio, and these eventually came to include the use of digital sampling. As these studio methodologies gained popularity, the deejays who used them became known as producers" (Schloss 2). Schloss is adamant about solidifying the basis of Hip Hop music production through the legacy bequeathed by the DJ (Schloss) and aspects of DJ Rhetoric and Literacy (Craig, "'Tell Virgil Write BRICK'"). Thus, a natural progression for many DJs is entering the realm of production, or "beat-making." This connection to a specific sequence in Hip Hop's cultural narrative becomes crucial to how we see the work of particular DJ/Producers: "Producers see deejaying as an essential element of hip-hop production, to the extent that elements of the practice are often read as symbols of an individual's commitment to hip-hop history and communal identity" (Schloss 25).

For the Hip Hop DJ, the sine qua non is the order of things: both the chronology and the acquisition of a particular skill set devoted to and invested in the tenants of Hip Hop cultural practices (Petchauer, "Starting with Style"). What becomes vital is the progression the DJ makes to producer and not the progression the producer (or the musician or the rapper, for that matter) makes into becoming a DJ. It's the difference between dudes like DJ Premier, Statik Selektah, DJ Pete Rock, DJ Jazzy Jeff, DJ Revolution, and various other producers who can't speak to a production foundation based and rooted in DJ Rhetoric and Literacy. Here lies the significance of the order of things. It's the "organic capital" Victor Rios identifies that makes the difference: the creative response to blocked opportunities and criminalization the DJ brings to the table. DJs initially embraced the mantra of Hip Hop and made "something out of nothing." Their "nothing" was two turntables, and later, a mixer. Their rhetorical savvy emerges from writing meaning out of these seemingly disparate objects that come together to make what we know today as popular American *and* global culture . . . because Hip Hop is just that!

For the purposes of this chapter, the highlighted producers engage in a Hip Hop cultural investment that recognizes the DJ—and thus the cultural and literacy practices of the craft—as paramount. With this focus in mind, we find almost all of the producers mentioned are Hip Hop DJ/Producers because the premise is the Hip Hop DJ/Producer's work will become an example that is both stellar and innovative for students to make sense of revision practices in the composition classroom.

"But Nufin's Been Somethin' for a Minute": Where the Landscape and Practice Converge

So far, we have journeyed through the opening moments of an impending educational DJ set, examined scholarship invested in Hip Hop as a primary pedagogical lens and teaching tool, and situated the label of the Hip Hop DJ/Producer. We can now move to a writing assignment and the moments in which students begin to explore the idea of revision practices.

While this assignment revolves around Hip Hop as the overriding vehicle for scholarship, the context of the assignment, ironically enough, emerges from a very anti–Hip Hop space that should actually be pro–Hip Hop. The institutional setting is one that purports to cater to a very diverse student population and prides itself on a mission that aims to serve the "disadvantaged." Sitting in a metropolitan area formative to the early stages of Hip Hop music, this institution makes the choice to claim the greater township in its address instead of claiming the smaller town in which it is located; to claim the actual town might deter the enrollment of more affluent students, as some might consider the town "seedy" or even "dangerous." Thus, the institution immediately negates its "mission" by rejecting the very location in which it sits.

Understanding the landscape this assignment emanates from is important. It was created within an academic terrain that not only devalued the lives and experiences of students of color but also worked overtly to undermine and sabotage all pedagogy and philosophy involving Hip Hop music and culture; the anti–Hip Hop sentiments serve as the undertow of anti-Black and racist currents in this intellectual environment. In "Teaching While Black: Witnessing and Countering Disciplinary Whiteness, Racial Violence, and University Race-Management," Carmen Kynard elucidates the blatant racial underpinnings that professors and students of color experience on many college campuses. After detailing numerous racist narratives stemming from both undergraduate and graduate school settings, Kynard states, "The responses that I have described are quite typical in the classrooms of black and Latina female professors, especially when your course centers the scholarship of folk of color and issues of race" (Kynard, "Teaching While Black" 5). Kynard's statement reverberates with a moment I experienced in an academic space, when one prominent professor asked, "Why Hip Hop, Todd? Why not Rock-n-Roll? I mean, the only Hip Hop that made sense to me was Public Enemy." This was also a landscape where his colleague, another prominent professor on the same campus, saw a rapper at a national conference and continued to cite this rapper any chance he got to have a conversation with me, since I was "the Hip Hop guy." Unfortunately, he continued to refer to the rapper by the name of Kwalib Teli . . . clearly, he meant Talib Kweli. These white men's comfort with overtly and covertly refuting Hip Hop as "scholarly" on the one hand, but then misspelling and mispronouncing names of prominent emcees on the other, shows a blatant sense of entitlement and privilege, and a disrespect for Hip Hop culture. Furthermore, only citing Public Enemy without acknowledging over a decade of inherently radical and subversive counternarratives presented in Hip Hop music is problematic. I'm sure if they asked Kwalib Teli, he would be more than happy to explain that Public Enemy was not the sole influence in a collaboration called Black Star. Also, arguing that Public Enemy isn't concerned with "race" but "class" is an old-school racist strategy in the academy: the classic "shell game" misdirection.

Yet these same professors wielded power in key administrative positions that allowed them to make choices both for and about a substantially large student of color population. This was the pervasive mindset of the majority of instructors in this space. While this was one of the most racist academic centers I have ever experienced, this is fodder for another article or book chapter, as the depth and breadth of this moment cannot be addressed fully here. It is critical to highlight this juncture, though, as this was the academic space in which I was forced to dwell. It is here that the "whole lotta something" of my "nufin" comes out of . . .

The idea for the writing assignment was initially presented to me by the white "Public Enemy Only" professor. When I asked if I could use it as a catalyst for (re)envisioning a writing assignment, he replied, "Todd, that's not even my idea. I can't even remember where I got it from, I just stole it somewhere along the line in my teaching." So while I would like to properly cite the source,

I can't; my Blackness, however, does not afford me the same luxury of blatant theft by said professor (because this goes far beyond mere "appropriation" and/or "biting" [Craig, "'Jackin' for Beats'"]). The closest remnant I could find of this "theft" was a book chapter written by Wendy Bishop in 2002 entitled "Steal This Assignment: The Radical Revision"; it is important to note that if the assignment was stolen from here, it was done without giving credit to the source. Now when I asked, the PE-Only-Prof led me in a direction other than Wendy Bishop, using her more as a side-note than an actual source. It follows that the root of this assignment comes from what I am calling "site unknown." However, this assignment does (re)think moments that can be found in Nancy Sommers's article entitled "Revision Strategies of Student Writers and Experienced Adult Writers" (1980).

The premise of the writing assignment is simple. Toward the end of the semester, I ask students to choose any of the major essays they have written for our class. Once they have identified an essay, I ask them to revisit the essay, identifying three to five sentences that serve as the core or the premise. The next step feels drastic for students: I ask them to keep those three to five sentences, delete the rest, and use the chosen sentences as the focal point of their new writing. Thus, the goal in this "Radical Revision" is truly to (re)think and (re)contextualize an essay with a particular direction in mind.

Clearly a level of anxiety emanates from students that can be summarized in one question I have typically heard in various iterations: "How the hell you gon' tell me after I put blood, sweat and tears into this six-page banger, that now I gotta find three to five sentences and cut the rest??? Is you stupid?" My immediate response is "Touché, young scribe, touché!" And after a few laughs, we zone back in to focus our energies. At this point, the way I facilitate the conversation around revision stems from Hip Hop music, culture, and the work the Hip Hop DJ/Producer does in revision, specifically in regard to DJ practices as well as the collaborative engagement and interaction with the emcee.

The Beats, the Rhymes, and the World That's Yours: Diggin' in the Crates for Sonic Revision Records

What remains constant in my pedagogy is that I advocate for students to (re)think aspects of composing by using the Hip Hop DJ as the quintessential example of an innovative twenty-first-century new media reader and writer. The Hip Hop DJ (and in this case, the DJ/Producer) creates a sonic landscape that fosters an interactive relationship with the emcee in the remix that gives birth to a (re)envisioned methodology for revision practices in writing. The DJ/Producer allows for the emcee to remix (and thus, revise) through finding new "centers" in a sonic composition (in this case, lyrics as text). We can make correlations here between "radically revised" sonic landscapes in Hip Hop music (incorporating both the instrumental and the written word) and writing landscapes in composition incorporating aspects of textual production. The two examples I will use to show this point are A Tribe Called Quest's original and remixed versions of the song "Bonita Applebum," and Nas's original and remixed versions of the song "The World is Yours." In these particular cases of "remix as revision," the impetus for revision doesn't necessarily emerge from the emcee but comes to the emcee from the DJ/Producer.

Cut to the Academy: The Jewel in the Muck Called Revision
aka "New Rules": Remixing Sommers's Strategies

To begin thinking through this paradigm properly, I start with the premise that there are several points of contention stemming from Sommers's article. The sense and subsequent labeling of "novice" versus "adult/experienced" writers discount and discredit the vast array of cultural capital students bring to the writing classroom in their philosophical and cultural backpacks. The question I always ask is "Does an instructor have the knowledge to access and use the backpack that students carry?" This is a critical question that we, as educators, should constantly contemplate. However, in this moment, using this Sommers's piece fueled some signifyin' and straight-talkin' back to the racist viewpoints presented toward Hip Hop in the classroom of the academic space in which I found myself. That being said, we can find some value in the four revision operations presented by Sommers: deletion, substitution, addition, and reordering (Sommers 380). However, since Sommers never imagined how the Hip Hop DJ might influence these strategies, what might DJ Rhetoric lend to this respective composing situation? With this question in mind, I use Sommers as a launching pad to (re)imagine these revision strategies from the DJ's perspective.

Since the DJ was the original producer by way of being the original sampler (because of the ways that DJs extended the breaks, courtesy of Grandmaster Flash, who first methodically "looped" the breaks), looking at revision practices through the lens of the DJ as producer makes all the sense in the world. The first strategy emulates addition: we'll call it "adding on." In reflecting on Flash's "Clock Theory" and extending the break, it requires a new perspective: mainly,

Flash ushers in the critical innovation of DJs actually touching the records they are playing. This reflects the same kind of revolution and innovation that comes with word processing and being able to move (and/or "touch") large chunks of text. The DJ allows us to see the "add-on" as a new way of building more written material in the act of revision.

The second strategy, deletion, can be categorized as "the cut away." In many DJ sets, there's always a moment when a DJ reimagines the song simply by shortening it. This "cut away" strategy is different from the contemporary DJ technique of playing sixty seconds or less of any sequence of records. Instead, the "cut away" strategy is employed by DJs who might see a song originally recorded with three verses and two to three choruses, and instead play the first two verses, the chorus in between, and then "cut away" to the next song, essentially deleting the third verse of the song.

The third strategy, substitution, we'll call "the flip." The Hip Hop DJ has always been heavily invested in the creative process of reimagining traditional sonic structures and deeply steeped in the practice of playing with music in seemingly unorthodox ways. The Hip Hop DJ evolves from extending the break to live restructuring: using an instrumental or an acapella to rewrite the text or "context" of a song. "The flip" reflects the DJ's uncanny ability to see that the vocals of one song (let's call it song A) would sound incredible over the instrumental of another song (which we'll call song B). Thus, "flipping" the beat and vocals can evoke a completely new sonic sentiment. This was a practice that was presented by DJs such as Hot Day and Ron G, and lives today with Mel Starr and Ted Smooth amongst others.

The last strategy, reordering, can be reconceived as "the swap." Once the practice of touching the record is proliferated, it simply allows DJs the open door to reprogram songs on the fly, moving various parts of the same songs into a different sonic sequence. For example, many people are familiar with the 1990s Hip Hop classic "All About the Benjamins" remix featuring Puff Daddy, Jadakiss, Sheek Louch, Lil Kim, and The Notorious B.I.G. However, in a live setting, a DJ trying to excite the crowd might consider a solid swap, which could entail playing Lil Kim's verse of "Benjamins" first (instead of fourth), then going back to the beginning of the song. Another example that DJs have used is playing the bridge to the Fugees "Killing Me Softly" before starting the song from the beginning. Lauryn Hill's crooning across the bridge of the Fugees classic cover of Roberta Flack is always an audience magnet and immediate dancefloor flooder. Swapping the order of parts of a song can also evoke a revised attitude, altered from an initial way of seeing, hearing, and reading a sonic text. All of these operations reimagined from the lens of the DJ can inspire students' experiences with revision in creative ways.

Part of Sommers's argument is what students lack in their writing backpacks is the ability to resee an essay (or text) as opposed to just conducting a lexical game of "musical word chairs." Part of my assignment construction is based upon Sommers's premise that "revising confuses the beginning and end, the agent and vehicle; it confuses, in order to find, the line of argument . . . these revision strategies are a process of more than communication; they are part of the process of discovering meaning altogether" (Sommers 384–385). Using Sommers's revision strategies through the lens of DJ Rhetoric serves the goal of rediscovering—or even uncovering—new meaning altogether. Thus, these "New Rules" in DJ revision strategies serve as the tools to help in completing radical revision on either a local or global level. Coupled with the four revision operations, this newly envisaged premise can be helpful in moving forward when contextualized in a different light. While the songs I use from A Tribe Called Quest and Nas were recorded earlier in their music careers, they most strongly demonstrate the progression of their experiences as lyricists, well trained in the art of writing and revising.

The Remix as Sonic Revision: The DJ/Producer's Role in the Writing

A Tribe Called Quest's leading vocalist and producer, Q-Tip, makes this writing shift and radical revision on the group's first album, *People's Instinctive Travels and the Paths of Rhythm*, with the classic song "Bonita Applebum." If we look at the lyrics as text, Q-Tip uses all four of the DJ revision strategies. In the shift from the "original" version of the text to the "radically revised" text, Q-Tip uses "the cut away" by losing the entire text of the original song except for its center. He is also able to employ "the flip" by switching in different concepts that push forward his argument in the song in a different way. Q-Tip "adds on" with the implementation of a new structure in the text; finally, "the swap" appears as he articulates the narrative within the original text in a new way.

This is a brief synopsis of Q-Tip's work as a writer/lyricist. However, we must look at how this progression evolves. I argue that this radical revision is illuminated for Q-Tip in his work as a producer; the radical revision of the song lyrics is an extension of the sonic landscape both (re)envisioned and (re)presented by the beat. What Q-Tip does as a DJ/Producer is reminiscent of a concept from Jeff Rice's "The 1963 Hip-Hop Machine":

[James] Brown, like many of the artists of Blue Note records, appealed to DJs experimenting with sampling practices in the 1970s, '80s, and '90s . . . supplying contemporary hip-hop with the basis of a new method of composition: empowering through sampling . . . just as DJs often search for breaks and cuts in the music that reveal patterns, so, too, does the student writer look for a pattern as a way to unite these moments into a new alternative argument and critique. (Rice, "1963" 463–465)

Thus, Q-Tip makes a move as a DJ/Producer through what he samples by connecting that sample to the pattern his original composition presented. In speaking lyrically about a woman of his desires, Q-Tip moves from the sonic landscape offered by sampling RAMP's song "Daylight" to a sample from the Isley Brothers, "Between the Sheets"; this sonic change prompts a different rhetorical response from Q-Tip—one that is "radically revised." But this sample changes the landscape by focusing the center of the beat in a legacy that illuminates the same idea Q-Tip originally intended. While the "center" of the song remains the same, the execution in writing is drastically different, "radically revised." In this moment, Q-Tip's narrative progresses from a shy young boy who is trying to woo a young girl's interest (in the original album version) to a much more confident young man, who has grown both physically and mentally—with a newfound determination to win the young woman over (in the "Hootie Mix"). This radical revision functions at the global level, as the only thing textually and sonically remaining is the name of Q-Tip's desired counterpart: a young woman he calls Bonita Applebum.

Students immediately gravitate to this moment, as it has tapped into the cultural capital with which they arrive in class. First and foremost, it illuminates revision viscerally and turns it into a tangible practice. The concept of a "global revision" becomes very evident in hearing both songs. However, not only is the idea of revision made clear, but this also gives rise to other processes in writing. When this was presented in class, one student mentioned the distinct similarity between the drum sample of the original version of "Bonita Applebum" (1990), citing that "they"—A Tribe Called Quest—took the drums from Lauryn Hill's song "Lost Ones" (1998). However, a quick discography check will demonstrate that the Fugees were actually the "borrowers" on their song "Killing Me Softly" (1996). This exchange immediately presents a segue into conversations about sonic lineage, intertextuality, and citation practices from the last chapter. But it is important to note Sommers doesn't incite this level of discourse for students—the Hip Hop DJ does.

And Carry on Tradition: The Collaborative Journey in Sonic Remix Revision

Q-Tip then lends this experience in practice to up-and-coming rapper Nas on his first album, *Illmatic*. Using the same strategies, Q-Tip works with Nas as DJ/Producer and helps Nas move from his original text "The World is Yours" to classic remixed revision "The World Is Yours (Tip Mix)" (Nas). Q-Tip helps Nas envision revision strategies on a local level but using all of the DJ revision strategies in the hook and the second verse of his song/text. Essentially what Nas does is shift his original work with DJ/Producer Pete Rock—envisioned from the blimp in the movie *Scarface*—to a revised work orchestrated by Q-Tip, who provides Nas with a (re)envisioned sonic landscape by which to (re)see and (re)enter his original text. Nas engages with a variety of the revision strategies on a local level. For example, Nas shows the cut away, as he only keeps the "center" of the hook with the words "the world is yours." He also employs the flip in changing sentences and lines within the text. He strategically adds on by supplementing the text with new ways of explaining the center of his argument. The notion of adding on in his verse finds Nas moving from a more abstract vision of inner-city life in the original version to honing in specifically on a critique of the Rudolph Giuliani mayoral administration of New York City. In this remix, Nas gives his sociopolitical commentary on the state of how Black youth are seen in New York urban environments. Finally, Nas demonstrates the swap by switching elements of the remixed text within the same structure he used in the original version.

The variation in these two songs is a bit more subtle. Still, the revision aspects are more tangible and even palatable for students, as they truly meet students where they frequently congregate: the landscape of Hip Hop. The example from Nas helps students to experience how rhetorical choices in language can truly evoke emotions in the most simplistic of ways. After all, is there any mistaking the sentiment of Nas explicating that "Giuliani is 6-6-6" (Nas, "The World Is Yours (Remix)")? In this example, Nas's writing presents more elusive changes that enhance and evoke more sophisticated claims and meaning-making. Again, students are able to engage in this work fully through Nas, Pete Rock, and Q-Tip . . . and not primarily through Sommers.

In addition, we see here how the sonic landscape of the DJ/Producer provides the impetus for how the emcee approaches revision. Here we can clearly see the historical order and importance of the DJ first, followed by the emcee, unfolding culturally and in praxis. Furthermore, we can clearly see how the initial investment of the DJ/Producer is the action that fosters the emcee's direction in revision: both locally and globally.

From "Trapped in the '90s" to the Twenty-First Century and Beyond: Contemporary Examples of the Sonic Situation

While I have used some examples deemed "Hip Hop classics," one can look at various other time periods in Hip Hop music to find similar examples executed in different ways. For example, in the early 2000s, Curtis "50 Cent" Jackson used the Ice Cube's "Jackin' for Beats" mentality as he hopped on every hot rapper's instrumental to create his own sonic compositions. In these moments, 50 stuck to "the flip" script but literally stripped the original artist's vocals in order to add his own. And because 50 is such a talented lyricist and songwriter, many times his "freestyles" were better than the original songs and overshadowed the original artists' radio airplay. We later see this same mentality carried out by Hip Hop artist Drake, as he engaged in a run of serving as the featured guest artist on various remixes.

Brooklyn's own M.O.P. (Mash Out Posse) employed the same techniques in the original version of their hit single "Ante Up." Upon the moment of the remix, M.O.P. recruited remix-verse specialist Busta Rhymes and Terror Squad emcee Remy Ma to facilitate a more global remix lyrically, even though the musical production remained constant.

These revision strategies are also evident when Jay-Z and Jay Electronica highjack the Drake freestyle featuring Soulja Boy entitled "We Made It" (2014). Truly employing aspects of cutting away and adding on, they completely reconfigure the content and context of the original composition. Similarly, Dej Loaf's single "Try Me" (2014) received myriad official and unofficial remixes producing the localized revision approach from a number of artists including The LOX, Young Jeezy, T.I., Ty Dolla $ign, and Remy Ma.

The strategic revisionist/remix treatment can be seen between the Kendrick Lamar single "i" versus the live version he includes on his 2015 album *To Pimp a Butterfly* that is immediately followed by the "N-E-G-U-S freestyle." Lamar can also be seen on the Jidenna song "Classic Man," where the revision sits somewhere in the middle of an example of revision on a local versus a global level lyrically. Finally, these revisionist practices appear in the summer anthem by Fat Joe and Remy Ma "All the Way Up." While Joe and Remy lace the original with two hard-hitting verses, the remix comes in reconfiguring the song with a Jay-Z appearance. Again, this particular remix shows signs of global revision, as all the verses have changed. Still, the locale remains constant as they all rhyme to the original beat from the record before without Jay.

The Implications of Remix and Revision Practices in Turntable Rotation

As most often in my own research and scholarship, the conversation must start and end with the DJ. It is the only way the conversation makes sense. This work stems from the DJ because it is the DJ who uses all of these practices live within his or her work: the DJ transcends Sommers's argument in that "the spoken word cannot be revised" (Sommers 379). Once Flash put the act of touching the record into play, the DJ has consistently been able to revise spoken/auditory words live through a complex composition containing myriad sampling of various texts. Thus, the Hip Hop DJ has the ability to "speak" (through records and production) while simultaneously revising. While speech cannot be revised, a DJ can create a new and innovative rhetorical situation by "speaking" the story of these progressions simultaneously: by sequentially playing all of the aforementioned songs to show the legacy and the progression of how these songs/texts work in interplay, speaking with, to, and about each other. This type of work refers to Rice's "whatever" moment in Hip Hop pedagogy and composition. It is a language that is essentially indescribable, a concept that cannot easily be explained by words—instead it exists within space, time, and sound. It also exists within Hip Hop culture . . . not traditional English Composition Studies. This theoretical framework also lends itself to a unique understanding and positioning in regard to the relationship between the DJ/Producer and emcee in writing and remixing.

If the DJ/Producer is creating a sonic landscape for a remix/revision, the DJ/Producer is already culturally invested in a particularly deliberate sonic outcome. So the auditory terrain created is already socially and culturally invested, and steeped in a distinct tradition that holds the emcee in mind and is acutely in tune with the social and cultural capital—and thereby literacy—the emcee comes to the table with. If we see the value and potential in using this relationship, it immediately presents a pedagogical conundrum for the field of Writing Studies.

DJ/Producers are extremely invested in a particular type of process—the outcome is not necessarily the objective but the process and how it is constructed and fostered, nurtured, and nourished. DJ/Producers are willing to engage in a creatively collaborative journey with the emcee toward an unknown sonic outcome. But both are willing to exchange and interplay with one another in this journey to eventually arrive at a sonic destination. However, one can argue that this same journey does not present itself in Composition classrooms, because the writing instructors are not typically vested in the same Hip Hop cultural capital students bring in their backpacks to the writing classroom. This idea is expressed by Bronwen Low's article "The Tale of the Talent Night Rap: Hip-Hop Culture in Schools and the Challenge of Interpretation," when she highlights the relationship between student Gerard and his principal, around Gerard's talent show rap performance being cut short (Low). Gerard's principal seems to have no authentic investment in Hip Hop music or culture. This idea begs a series of questions, though: When are students presented with someone who is intuitively invested in learning and writing outcomes that are steeped in students' cultural capital? When do students get to see professors from traditional Composition and Rhetoric spaces that are acutely in tune with the cultural capital—and thereby literacy—they come to the table with?

A Sample of Scratching Samplers: The DJ's Voice in this DJ Talk

There are a bevy of DJs who follow the progression that Schloss highlights in being a DJ before a producer. DJs like Ayres and Eleven (The Rub); Mr. Len, Rhettmatic, and Prince Paul (Dirty Disco Squares); Lord Finesse (D.I.T.C.); Mr. Walt and Evil Dee (Da Beatminerz); Neil Armstrong; Tyra from Saigon; Killa-Jewel; Shortee; Clark Kent; and BreakBeat Lou (UBB) will all attest to the fact that they are much better producers specifically because they began their musical careers in Hip Hop culture as DJs. These sentiments are most clearly articulated and echoed by the DJs I will highlight in this section: Statik Selektah (ShowOff), DJ Bear-One (Control Freaks), and Large Professor. These voices also become paramount because for far too long the academy has talked about "Hip Hop" without speaking both to and with "Hip Hop." In order to engage in theory and practice centered around the Hip Hop DJ/Producer, we must include their voices in our pedagogically and radically revised mix.

When talking about what prompted him to be a DJ, Statik Selektah clearly recalls the moment. He says, "DJ Premier! Hearing him Thanksgiving, November of 1995 on Hot 97" (Statik Selektah). He started DJing when he was thirteen years old on a radio station that was next door to his high school—a spot in New Hampshire some of you might know called Phillips Academy. And even though Statik Selektah is a producer, he'll tell you his production stemmed from his initial love of DJ culture and work as a DJ.

As an organic intellectual, researcher, and student of the DJ and production game, Statik advises any aspiring DJs to listen to routines from QBert and Craze, and the turntablists who use the turntables as actual instruments. When it comes to his own production work, Statik clearly says, "A lot of my beats are based around cuts. Everything I do is based around me starting as a DJ. Whether I'm chopping up a sample, or the way I'm mixing a record. It's all because of the DJ element, it's the foundation to my music—period" (Statik Selektah). In this moment, Statik Selektah attributes his production talents to his origins as a DJ; the ways he envisions constructing a sonic landscape are intrinsically tied to his earlier work as a DJ. Thus, the DJ/Producer's techniques and strategies become a great example for writing students to (re)invent and (re)shape the way(s) in which they engage with writing and revision strategies.

DJ Bear-One was growing up in Virginia when he first saw the movie *Wildstyle*, so he attributes his initial exposure to DJ culture to "seeing Flash, seeing Kool Herc, seeing Jam Master Jay" (DJ Bear-One). As he learned and entrenched himself in DJ culture, he became a DJ, then a producer and engineer; in the midst of this activity, he worked with a number of different record labels, but he immediately identifies his focus and love as "DJing and producing, which I feel goes hand in hand" (DJ Bear-One). He pinpoints his foundation as a DJ as the key component in his production career. Since his first production placement from Hip Hop artist Cormega, Bear-One has produced for artists including Money Making Jam Boys (Black Thought, Dice Raw, Truck North, and STS), The Planets, Junior Reid, Wale, Jim Jones (Dipset), and a variety of other musicians.

When it comes to production, DJ Bear-One relies heavily on his DJ knowledge of digging for records: "Digging is basically being a scientist of records. When we say 'dig' . . . we search for obscure records. A record could be about three minutes long, but in the first minute and a half, we find the break, the funky part" (DJ Bear-One). This is the classic science of most producers, but again, he leans heavily on the cultural capital he acquired from being a DJ first. When thinking about the relationship between the DJ/Producer and emcee in collaboration and creating sonic texts, he states, "I feel like it's an equal thing . . . [as a DJ] I can collage words to put sentences together" (DJ Bear-One). When it comes to his progression and craft:

> It's all about DJing. DJing allowed me to [understand] timing and selection—knowing records. And not just Hip Hop records. Knowing Soul, World, Reggae, Rock, Jazz [records]. So by knowing those records, when I got

an ASR—a popular sampling keyboard from the mid-90s—I already had the records. When it was time to make the beats, I already had the timing, I already knew how to blend. Machines now, you can throw something into a software and it can chop it up for you. But back then, you didn't have a WAV form you could look at. So it was a gradual progression, from DJ to producer to engineer, but it all stemmed from DJing. (DJ Bear-One)

By collaging words and putting sentences together live as a DJ/Producer, Bear-One clearly speaks to transcending Sommers's argument about the unrevisable "spoken word." For Bear-One, the act of "diggin'" in the crates for records is what establishes his knowledge pool for his production. If we envision "diggin'" for writing students as an act of research—actively searching, investigating, and sifting through various sources of knowledge—it makes sense that their writing would be enhanced and that their ability to (re)configure through revision would be strengthened as well, given the fact their original writing is steeped in a particular type of intellectual investment. A radical revision in this sense would allow for students to (re)formulate and (re)structure the research in which they have already engaged.

One of the most foundational Hip Hop DJ/Producers to the culture and sound-shaping of Hip Hop music in the 1990s is a figure named Large Professor. Large Professor (aka Large Pro aka Extra P), a DJ since 1984, cites his catalyst for entering Hip Hop culture as natural because "growing up in Hip Hop, it [was] all around you" (Large Professor). And Large Professor was all around . . . a self-identified DJ/Producer, he has had an extensive career. But what differentiates Large Pro from the crowd is he is a DJ, a producer, and an emcee. While he has produced for Nas, A Tribe Called Quest, Non Phixion, Boot Camp Clik, Slick Rick, Common, Mobb Deep, and Eric B. & Rakim, he has also appeared as an emcee first with the group Main Source, then as a solo artist with features alongside artists such as Nas, A Tribe Called Quest, Busta Rhymes, Cormega, Kool G Rap, Organized Konfusion, Marco Polo, and myriad others.

Large Pro saw early on the connection between the DJ and the producer: "When the production aspect came into play with people like Marley Marl, you heard some of the records that dudes was DJing and cutting up at one time; now they started to use those sounds with sampling. So from there, it was just about building on with the technology—drums machines, DJing and everything" (Large Professor). Actively participating in a trifecta of Hip Hop music, the chronology starts with his love of DJing; that same love serves as the cornerstone for his music production. Large Pro says:

Me being a DJ helped me being an MC. When you're writing songs, it's better to have the music there. So it's like "aight, this is what this song is saying. This is what this beat is telling me." So BOOM—lemme write to that. So I think the DJing helped me with the writing . . . I was a DJ first, then I started writing. I loved the English language. I'd drift off in class and have time on my hands, and I'd just start writing rhymes. After that is when the production element came in. (Large Professor)

In this moment, Large Pro acknowledges the integral nature of this ordering: being a DJ first, then an emcee, then a producer. Understanding the intricacies within the sonic landscape helps to foster and nurture the collaborative quality in songwriting and penning words. Again, this relationship becomes one that could revolutionize the way(s) we (re)envision and (re)invest our teaching pedagogies and philosophies around ideas of writing and revision. However, this theoretical framework must include the voices of the organic intellectuals who demonstrate both the cultural capital and investment we see in our student writers. Thus, the conversation is incomplete without the centerpiece of Hip Hop culture: the DJ.

"Pooool Up!!!": The Science of the Remix Revisionist Set in Full

Looking at these elements from the lens of the DJ can provide new and "radical" ways for students to think about how they approach elements of revision, on local and global levels. The skills, practices, and techniques of the Hip Hop DJ/Producer not only show student writers a way to (re)see their work within revision but also help writers to revise on both a local and global level through example, mainly by the "radical revision" of the musical landscape revised by DJ as producer.

Reflecting on the academic space I mentioned earlier in the chapter, which functioned on many "racist tendencies," I'm not sure why those professors would actively sabotage a viable classroom moment that Hip Hop was centered in, especially given the student population and demographic the institution served. It is clear there are a number of issues at play for both of these dudes. All I can do is ask the questions . . . and continue to pronounce rappers' and DJs' names correctly. I know they'll never answer them, and it's all good. I'll just keep doin' what I do, letting Hip Hop music and culture be the pedagogical vehicle that creates a safe and student-centered rhetorical landscape in my writing classes. And identifying the organically collaborative revisionist/remix relationship between the Hip Hop DJ/Producer and emcee as theoretic and pedagogical writing example that is innovative and viable could lead to (re)seeing and (re)envisioning the ways we, as instructors and educators, approach the level of investment we bring to students' literacy lives both inside and outside the classroom, but specifically in Writing Studies.

Never seen before or heard in this fashion / convert the work to magic /
bury a beat six-feet / pour dirt in the casket /
hard to imitate / I'm cut from a certain fabric . . .

Hit-Boy x The Alchemist, "Slipping Into Darkness," *YouTube*, 10 Mar. 2023,
https://www.youtube.com/watch?v=IqeK6BIS_pQ.

5

"SISTA GIRL ROCK"

Women of Color and Hip Hop Deejaying as Raced/
Gendered Knowledge and Language

. . . It's so hard to fake when everything I do is real /
Money and a doggie bag, I ain't missin' no meals /
Don't move on me wrong, I need to save my energy /
"Everybody family"—leave it to the industry /
Kill all that noise / We ain't talkin' that way /
We ain't movin' like that / No way, no way /
Kill all that noise / Only positive vibes / I don't pay it no mind /
I don't pay it no mind /
Every day like my birthday / Bring the cake in /
Bring the cake in / Bring the cake in /
I feel good, I feel great / Man, I feel amazing /
Man, I feel amazing /
Man, I feel amazing /
Everyday celebrate, not just on occasion / On occasion / Not just on occasion /
I feel good, I feel great / man, I feel amazing / Feel amazing /
Man, I feel amazing . . . raise your glasses up . . .

Mary J. Blige featuring DJ Khaled, "Amazing,"
Good Morning Gorgeous, 300 / Mary Jane, 2022.

https://doi.org/10.7330/9781646424849.c005

"Dedication": The Purple Pam Prelude

When I thought about identifying a song that tapped into this moment, "Amazing" by Mary J. Blige featuring DJ Khaled quickly came to mind. With its club-smash party-rockin' vibe, it brought me right into good feelings about one of the chief party-rockin' DJs: Purple Pam aka Pam the Funkstress. In trying to capture the importance of positive vibes and celebratory moments, Mary J. gives us yet another musical selection that touches the soul and resonates with women and men alike: "Kill all that noise / only positive vibes / I don't pay it no mind / I don't pay it no mind / Every day like my birthday / bring the cake in / bring the cake in / bring the cake in / I feel good, I feel great / Man, I feel amazing / Man, I feel amazing / Man, I feel amazing / Everyday celebrate, not just on occasion" (Blige). When Mary croons, "Raises your glasses up, party party," it felt like the proper tribute to a powerhouse DJ but also like the type of record Pam would rock at a party.

In November 2011, I began a conversation with Pam the Funkstress (via DJ Shred One) about doing an interview to be included in my dissertation research. I emailed Pam on the 2nd—she hit me right back by the 3rd. From there, we discussed the details, and by December 6, 2011, we had completed the process. I truly appreciated having a conversation about DJing with Pam the Funkstress, as I had been an East Coast kid who listened to The Coup and had some of their records in my own vinyl arsenal. We spoke about four and a half years before she would take a trip to talk to Prince about becoming his DJ, and before she would be dubbed "Purple Pam" by the musical icon himself (Hartlaub).

In July 2017, a version of this chapter was cowritten with Carmen Kynard and published in London-based journal *Changing English: Studies in Culture and Education*. Next thing I knew, summer break was done, the start of the academic year had taken over, and I was swamped with the typical collegiate responsibilities. By the time I was able to reconnect with the DJs included here, Pam had already made her way to continuing her DJ work with Prince in the next plane of life. I was excited about discussing the importance of Pam's legacy in the Hip Hop DJ world in my research back then, and I was even more excited to highlight her legacy in the article years later. So as I approach this moment, it felt really proper to let Pam's legacy continue on here in *K for the Way*. Thank you, Pam: for your time, your energy, and your positive vibes in helping a young kid from the 'hood find his way to the other side of a doctoral degree, and a text that speaks to DJ Rhetoric and Literacy: two moments of discourse you absolutely mastered . . .

"Sista Girl Rock": Women of Color and Hip Hop Deejaying
as Raced/Gendered Knowledge and Language

    Todd Craig and Carmen Kynard

In the last chapter, we examined the concept of "radical revision" alongside Q-Tip, Nas, and Pete Rock, as well as DJs Statik Selektah, Bear-One, and Large Professor. These conversations allowed us to explore the work of the DJ and DJ/Producer in tandem with the MC in creating a platform for engaging the revision process for first-year writing students, on both local and global levels. This chapter focuses on the seldom-discussed role of women DJs/deejays as producers and Hip Hop cultural sponsors, sound theorists, and rhetorical innovators. Because women deejays have important stories to tell about knowledge, technologies, and gendered lives in the twenty-first century, this chapter uses the term "Sista Girl Rock" after the cultural phenomenon and movement of "Black Girls Rock." Thus, "Sista Girl Rock" situates women deejays as a new source of inspiration and example for not only the deejay's communicative competence and cultural centrality in Hip Hop culture and, thereby, today's global music and aesthetics (Miller; Reighley; Schloss; Wang) but also the masterful (re)mix of gendered, racist hierarchies that would otherwise impede women's visibility, impact, and social imaginations in racist and masculinist contexts that attempt to deny our full humanity.

    This chapter's inquiry into the lives and worlds of women deejays intimately rests with six women—DJs Spinderella, Pam the Funkstress, Kuttin Kandi, Shorty Wop, Reborn, and Natasha Diggs—who stand on the cutting edge of Hip Hop deejay culture. These six deejays vary in age and status in the industry and, collectively, span at almost forty years of Hip Hop music and DJ cultural production. But even more specifically, they offer us Hip Hop DJ culture from women's lenses in a landscape that has been overly controlled and surveyed by male DJs. Whether a DJ for an all-women Hip Hop group, the DJ of a "Hip Hop revolutionary group," a pioneering woman turntablist in a scratch DJ crew, or just bad-ass #BlackGirlMagic DJ women who have demonstrated that gender is a guise that—if leaned upon too much—can get you scratched in a battle (literally), these six women are torchbearers for Hip Hop's necessity for the presence of "girl power" that counterbalances what can sometimes be unhealthy levels of testosterone-infused patriarchy and misogyny. These women will also tell you they have been influenced by the other women in this interview pool. Thus, there is an organically cultivated and sustained synergy between these women as they exemplify what Hip Hop DJ culture can and should be. The work these women have done both individually and collectively further speaks to the ways that educators, researchers, and students—Hip Hop heads and otherwise—can begin to (re)think and (re)envision the modes and practices of communication that have affected social change for racially marginalized communities. Their practices can and should dictate theories and bodies of knowledge about the intersections of gender, race, knowledge, and rhetoric (Campbell; Pough).

A very rich tradition of Hip Hop scholarship at the nexus of Black Studies theorizes Hip Hop productions as central Black cultural artifacts. Earlier texts like Tricia Rose's *Black Noise: Rap Music and Black Culture in Contemporary America*, Nelson George's *Hip Hop America*, and Michael Eric Dyson's *From God to Gangsta Rap* have laid important foundations. However, Gwendolyn Pough's *Check It While I Wreck It: Black Womanhood, Hip-Hop Culture, and the Public Sphere* offers a seismic shift in pushing us past a seemingly endless analysis of sexism and misogyny in men's rap lyrics as the focus of cultural critique in Hip Hop Studies. Instead, Pough has propelled us to focus on the narratives of women in Hip Hop, which she argues are central to the workings of the culture. This chapter attempts to vibrate on a similar frequency as Pough in thinking about the narratives of women Hip Hop deejays.

There is also a different rhetorical approach here: the very creative and genre-bending nature of what these women deejays do on a daily basis—as soundsmiths, sonic technicians, and gendered subjects in misogynist systems—compels a push past the usual academic boundaries that dictate how their stories are presented, especially when such institutions have done very little to value and sustain Hip Hop culture and/or the kind of BIPOC women who are centered here. This chapter is grounded in the interviews of the six women deejays, deliberately situating their stories first, with the deejays' words framing each section, as opposed to the usual academic expectation that a tedious delineation of methods and an extant literature review come before a discussion of the actual *subjects* of the research. This chapter is also highly cognizant of a now long-standing and well-warranted distrust of academics, which many of the deejays here forthrightly express, when those academics appropriate Hip Hop culture through publication and promotion, though these so-called experts are far removed from the everyday cultural production of Hip Hop. Thus, these deejays' critiques of the academy not only embolden this chapter but require that it is styled differently.

This text opens with an interview with DJ Spinderella, now an icon who gained notoriety as the deejay for the group, Salt-N-Pepa, as a high school student in 1987. Spinderella has been a deejay for over thirty years and is a veteran and stalwart in Hip Hop culture; Spinderella continues to rock parties, weddings, clubs, and private events. Her experiences inspire us to think about gender, deejay skills, and Hip Hop through what Black feminists call an intersectional lens. Based on the gendered notions around deejay skills that the interviewees help us see, we examine the particular technological ethos and expertise these women represent. Following through on this discussion of ethos presents another central, rhetorical strategy of the deejays in focus: the role of storytelling. Ultimately, this chapter attempts to frame what we call Hip Hop feminist methodologies as a kind of final sound-check for staging the everyday work and lives of Hip Hop's most esteemed cultural producers and the relevance of women Hip Hop deejays to English/Aesthetic/Literacy Studies today.

"Oh Hell Yeah . . . I Had to Work Twice as Hard": "Being Skilled" in Gender and Hip Hop

"You have to fight for it." ~Pam the Funkstress
"Don't let nobody try to play you." ~ Shorty Wop
"There are thousands of women who spin." ~Reborn
"There's a lot of women deejays out there and we're rockin'
   it. It's a beautiful feeling." ~Spinderella

This series of interviews begins with a foundational presence in Hip Hop deejay culture, Spinderella. In 1987, Dee Roper (AKA Spinderella) was a sixteen-year-old high-school student who was selected from an open audition to travel as Salt-N-Pepa's deejay. Her longevity as a deejay represents a set of critical, intersectional challenges for recovering the unique work of women deejays in Hip Hop. As a woman, as a Black woman, as a deejay, as a Hip Hopper, and as a teenager from a working-class Black vernacular culture, Spinderella's story sits at a crossroads where her particular knowledge and resistance are usually marginalized or altogether erased. We use intersectionality theory and its political origins in Black feminism to challenge this erasure (Alexander-Floyd; Bilge 2013; Cooper; Crenshaw "Demarginalizing," "Mapping," "From Private Violence"). The convergence of whitestream feminism, a patriarchal music / Hip Hop industry, a Western preoccupation with lyrics/MCing over deejays/sonic-technicians, white racist disbelief in the genius of Black vernacular culture, and the (early) marginalization and (later) hyperconsumption of Hip Hop all seem to unite in a distinct and concerted front that masks the creative, political, and intellectual work women like DJ Spinderella do. Spinderella's lightning-quick and deeply embodied response in her interview session that "oh hell yeah" (the words quoted as the title to this section) she had to work at least twice as hard as the men attests to this concerted front that we are suggesting operates in masking the unique contributions of women deejays in Hip Hop.

Although Spinderella gained early notice and notoriety as the deejay for Salt-N-Pepa, she traces her origins as a Hip Hop deejay to her father, especially to his expansive vinyl collection of Funk and Soul. Upon entry to high school, she traveled with her boyfriend, who was a deejay at the time, to all of his sets and learned deejay technique, carried records, and became skilled at digging through crates. Later, as a sixteen-year-old auditioning for the role of deejay with Salt-N-Pepa, she came with an early skill set, a library of music, a distinct sonic lineage, and a connection to what we can call the sonic origins of Hip Hop. She has always worked as a deejay, even while she was touring with Salt-N-Pepa, playing events like weddings, club parties, corporate events, and bar/bat mitzvahs. Today, she has a large community of deejay friends as well as a college-age daughter with whom she shares music. Thus, the combination of family, neighborhood, and Hip Hop community has remained at the core of her Hip Hop identity, where she sees herself as someone who is still learning and continuously working on her craft. As just a sixteen-year-old girl on tour as a concert deejay in the 1980s, Spinderella learned her skills in contexts that often did not include other women deejays. She stresses that she was not the first woman Hip Hop deejay, only that they were not made visible in her early years when Jam Master Jay—Queens, New York–native and world-renowned DJ for the Hip Hop group Run-DMC—was her major source of inspiration and model.

Salt-N-Pepa's mainstream success offered a spotlight for women deejays. And yet even with that spotlight, commercialization (and often appropriation) has frequently targeted rappers most closely, enabling the deejay to preserve the culture in ways that have often eluded other pillars of Hip Hop. We see women Hip Hop deejays as especially crucial to the longevity of a specific expertise because of the sociopolitical context in which they have to represent their dexterity. DJ Reborn—a twenty-year deejay veteran who has rocked a variety of clubs, served as the Russell Simmons's *Def Poetry Jam* tour DJ from 2004 to 2005 and was also a DJ instructor at New York City's DJ school Dubspot—especially offers a critical context in which to understand skills and the marginalization of women deejays.

As a woman deejay, Reborn argues that as soon as you arrive to the turntables or any given DJ set, you are seen as a novelty, as someone "just standing up there to be cute." Thus, women have to prove themselves each time they show up, almost as if starting from the beginning all over again. "Being skilled" is a crucial way for a woman deejay to assert dignity and value. Being skilled is about something much more than a minimalistic equality equation where a woman strives to be as good as a man. "Skilled" in this context means controlling what Reborn calls the language of Hip Hop deejaying and therefore how an audience will consume a woman deejay's presence and body. Reborn stresses that when she arrives at any set, she needs to know and command a range of techniques that include how to let a mix ride out, address an audience on the mic, set up and break down equipment, masterfully use a mixer and turntables, troubleshoot technical difficulties, carry crates, hook and unhook RCA cable cords, choose relevant music, navigate the new equipment of new spaces, and know when to spin or blend or mix. For example, as a woman, when her sound system has blown out, she has to immediately show herself as someone who can handle that setback instantaneously. Failure to do so would mean a loss in credibility not merely for her professional self but for women deejays in general. For Spinderella, as an earlier deejay who traveled with female MCs and female dancers and performed on multiple stages, she had to contend with jumping and skipping needles, a constant challenge of the deejay technology at that time. Again, lack of ability in these domains hurts the entirety of women Hip Hop deejays. "Skill" in these contexts means knowing how to recover right away from jumps and skips as part of the way you rock the party, forcing deejays to also acquire new strategies that sustain and add new creative twists to the music and to an audience's experience.

Since most audiences know Spinderella and her reputation before she arrives, she no longer faces the same kind of credibility challenges her more junior successors still face. However, Spinderella still argues longevity is not promised to her and she must still be careful in the ways she renews herself and in the kinds of jobs she chooses. As a sixteen-year-old high school student touring the world as a deejay over thirty years ago, she immersed herself in Hip Hop culture without knowing the influence she would someday have, especially since every woman deejay interviewed in this study cites her as inspiration. Spinderella is proud of the expanse of women deejays she sees today "rocking it," and she vows to make sure "the light stays always on for the new deejays out there."

"Nothing Like Vinyl": New Technologies, Same Ol Misogyny

"Create your own style, create your own sound." ~Pam the Funkstress

"The needle is the pen . . . the needle writes that music that you are putting in from your thoughts, your mind, your heart . . . by the time the needle gets to the end of the groove of that last track playing, that's the story right there. That's the ink." ~Kuttin Kandi

"You don't just use the culture and throw it away." ~Reborn

Looking at the work of the deejay allows us to focus on the ways the beat is an integral part of African-American political resistance and survival (Neal, *Songs in the Key*; Weheliye). Because we treat Hip Hop beats as a culture and thought system (Chang, *Can't Stop Won't Stop*; Kun, "Two Turntables"), we see Hip Hop deejays as cultural producers who work from and transform a distinct ethos of rhythm and sound. Like what is commonly called a "blues idiom" (Murray), we believe Hip Hop deejays represent a "Hip Hop idiom" that integrates multiple and oftentimes disjointed sounds and experiences using the most cutting-edge technologies available to them (Rabaka).

Deejays are inherently savvy technologists given the unique history of scratching, mixing, and blending that is central to the very sonic history and beingness of Hip Hop culture (Weheliye). The women deejays interviewed for this study all see the deejay as central to the culture and coin a variety of monikers to get this point across. Spinderella calls deejays the "backbone" of Hip Hop. Shorty Wop has been a DJ for over twenty years and most recently served as Tour DJ for Grammy Award–winning singer-songwriter Estelle. Shorty Wop argues that deejays are "embedded in the DNA strand" of Hip Hop; thus these women deejays experience themselves as central to the sonic philosophies of culture. Pam the Funkstress also calls deejays the people "who teach you how to hear the music"; Reborn sees her work as "sound-collaging," where she places "sound-materials" in conversations with one another to write a new text. Based on these deejays' very own terminologies for their purposes and processes, we must treat their platforms as new technologies that push rhetoric, writing, critical educational, and informational purposes (Alim, *Roc the Mic Right*; Alim, Ibrahim, and Pennycook; Petchauer, "Starting with Style"; Richardson, *Hiphop Literacies*). As Pam the Funkstress, a twenty-six-year veteran who was also the DJ for Hip Hop revolutionary group The Coup, so adamantly stresses, the music—its lineage, form, story, and importance—must be taught to you, and so deejay practices, as inherently technologically based, must be construed as informational and pedantic. While each of these deejays are certainly collectors and call themselves such, we see them as doing more than just creating music libraries by the nature of what *they do with these collection technologies* in order to educate public audiences (Lingel).

Ironically, the newest technology designed to help or increase deejays' productivity works as both an impediment and resource (Katz). In this case, we are referencing technologies like the software Serato, a topic that reverberated across all of the interviews. Fifteen years ago, Serato's founders/inventors (see http://serato.com/about) tell a rags-to-riches story of itself as a digital system that has transformed the experience of deejaying without supposedly losing any of its impact and craft. Hip Hop deejays, however, tell a different story. Deejays have traditionally played vinyl records, which are heavy and costly. CDs seemed to ease these burdens but could not be manipulated in the way that vinyl could be. Serato thus invented what it calls "vinyl emulation technology," which it has followed with the digital promotional music distribution service Whitelabel.net that, in most brutally simplistic terms, imagined itself as the alpha and omega of mp3 storage (until its discontinuation sometime around 2017); an all-in-one compact DJ controller system that allows deejays to engage the crowd more and not just a computer screen and keyboard; and programs that allow DJs to play digital video files such that audio and visual can work together (Montano; Swiss and Farrugia). With vinyl emulation, it maintains a deejay's ability to operate with vinyl and turntable; other than a digital catalogue of music, the foundational aspects of DJing can be maintained, if overtly chosen. The gift of this technological innovation lends convenience to deejays who travel (both in fees for carrying records as well as safeguarding invaluable records from being stolen while en route from Airport A to Airport B). Now, one can travel with a laptop, hard drive, and control vinyl in order to rock a party on turntables while having virtual access to a digital catalogue only limited by the size of the portable hard drive. The curse is that many can (and have) utilize(d) the technology without ever engaging in studying the craft or technique of DJing. One can even play music at a party without ever touching a turntable. This is where the technology gets quite dicey. The women deejays in this collection of interviews chronicle complex narratives of the role of new deejay technologies in their lives.

Each of the deejays interviewed offers a nuanced and complicated evaluation of what we are calling the newest additions to their information technologies. While each unanimously values the ease with which they can travel since they do not have to carry as many heavy crates of albums or 45s, they also acknowledge the limitations. Kuttin Kandi is a twenty-five-year veteran

DJ and turntablist who rocked with the DJ scratch crews the 5th Platoon and the Anomolies. Currently located in San Diego, Kandi identifies how regressive economies of travel (heightened airport security and costly baggage charges) make it impossible for her to travel back and forth to the East Coast with her records and equipment. Because San Diego does not host the range and number of music stores as other big cities, Kuttin Kandi has capitalized on the access to a digitized music catalogue that Serato gives her. Like Kuttin Kandi, each deejay notes these specific travel and mobility advantages of access but also works to make up for what they lose with the seeming disappearance of vinyl.

Since each deejay here uses both Serato and vinyl, most often using both for any given deejay set, these women Hip Hop deejays challenge commonly held notions that we are witnessing "the death of vinyl" (Attias). Natasha Diggs is known for her vinyl stylings; a twenty-year veteran, Diggs is a club and radio DJ and is resident DJ of "Soul in the Horn" and "Mobile Mondays"—an all-vinyl 45 party in New York City. Natasha Diggs is known for her reputation of playing 7-inch records (also known as 45s). Like Spinderella, Natasha Diggs explicitly calls the work that deejays do to find music and know artists her "research" (cited in Denise). While she values the ability to access mp3 files so readily, she argues a deejay's research and craft suffer, because many times the mp3 files do not include information about an artist's name, history, or band. Artists, therefore, become nameless, faceless entities for a kind of corporate consumption, limiting the stories that deejays want to tell with their music because they have no context in which to situate a track. For Pam the Funkstress, who has worked as a deejay since the 1980s, much of the older music she preferred could not be found on mp3, and so Serato could not help her achieve her full goals as deejay. Put simply, Pam argued, "There's nothing like vinyl."

We contend here that there is a specific politics in which these women Hip Hop deejays frame the new technologies available to them via software like Serato. The ethos of what we earlier called a Hip Hop idiom becomes visible to us. Technologies here are intimately tied not merely to the practices and techniques of being just a deejay but to the role of being a deejay in and for Hip Hop, to the very history and role of Hip Hop. In her July 2012 interview at *Offbeat. com*, Spinderella responds this way when asked what gets lost when deejays no longer use two turntables and a mixer:

> Technology makes it all easier and you cannot discount what it's become. We've taken advantage of it, but everything's so fast. "I don't need to learn the foundation, all I need is the controller and a computer and speakers and we're good."

The hard part is learning the history. Don't call it hip-hop if you don't know the foundation. It's a labor of love for our culture, for the legends that came before us. (Boyles 27)

Likewise, in the interviews with these women Hip Hop deejays, you get the sense that if the deejays do not control the technologies and make the technologies do what the culture needs it to do, then Hip Hop culture can no longer truly exist.

Kuttin Kandi further offers an important community context in which vinyl has been shared and understood by deejays. For her, deejays are the "heartbeat of Hip Hop culture" that put Hip Hop on the map in the first place. They work to connect "everyone together: bboys, graf writers, and the MC" (DJ Kuttin Kandi). Kandi argues that the center of gravity for deejay communities was the Hip Hop record store. While there has been a recent reemergence of vinyl in the past few years, vinyl stores struggled to remain open in the era of Serato's introduction and initial rise to popularity, so the community of deejays who shared stories and ideas in vinyl stores gradually disappeared. Kuttin Kandi remarks the work of searching for records, knowing the label colors, reading the visuals designs of covers has real value (DJ Kuttin Kandi). The removal of this process changes the literate practices and social responsibilities of the deejay if Serato is all a Hip Hop deejay knows.

As the youngest deejay of those interviewed, Shorty Wop offers a different lens of gender and this role of crate digging. Shorty Wop notes that the craft of deejaying is really exploited with Serato because deejays who are not talented, not connected to the history of Hip Hop, and not part of a record collecting tradition now insert and assert themselves as deejays. Of particular note for Shorty Wop is that women deejays often substitute their sexuality for such deejay research skills. Women who are scantily clad are devoured as new digital deejays, though they have not developed any real skills in the craft and do not really know (or spin) Hip Hop history (Benard).

Female Hip Hop deejays discuss the limits of Serato and other new deejay technologies in ways that echo the politics of male Hip Hop deejays (Craig, various interviews). These traveling women embrace constant motion, change, and technological transition, not as passive and distant recipients of these processes but as active interpreters who decide deliberately how they will embody and transform new digital forces for Hip Hop. They take on the disruption and discontinuity of new technologies and shape their own new expressions, refusing to embrace technological determinism or fatalism. New sounds, multiple places, and multiple experiences are welcomed. However, gender and sexuality become arenas for exploitation in markedly divergent ways. As women who see themselves as telling stories and teaching their audiences about music, they have sharp critiques of and practices against new deejay technologies that remove their skill, craft, and knowledge and, instead, (re)inscribe the misogynistic requirement that women hypersexualize themselves instead of learning how to tell and spin stories as skilled deejays. We believe the ways they praise the ease with which technology helps them work *alongside* a critique of the consumption of their sexuality offers an important reminder for how to situate the new roles of information technologies. In relation to twenty-first-century communication paradigms, women Hip Hop deejays complicate new technologies in specific relation to Hip Hop and offer new lenses into the ways new technologies can mobilize misogynistic hierarchies of gender and sexuality.

The "Living Document": The Mix Is the Story, the Language, and the Rhetoric

"I do my research." ~Natasha Diggs

"We write the story for your whole night." ~Shorty Wop

"I take the crowd with me on my ride." ~Spinderella

"You have a responsibility to have a conversation in that space. You are speaking with your turntables and your choices. You are mixing, responding to what is happening in the room and other people are speaking back to you." ~Reborn

Each deejay in this chapter explicitly calls herself a storyteller. Pam the Funkstress even makes the distinction between Hip Hop and rap, arguing that the difference must be critically noted by all who choose to be a part of Hip Hop. Rap tells the truth about life in the streets and the social realities that the urban, Black poor must navigate there. Hip Hop, on the other hand, represents lyrical expressiveness, the clever use of metaphors, tragedy, comedy, and fusing new words. In these descriptions of Hip Hop and rap, Pam critically assesses and understands the roles of stories and words in the atmosphere that she creates with each of her deejay sets; her heuristic organizes how she chooses and delivers the stories of the music she plays.

Further extending Pam's definition of the deejay as an obvious reader of Black culture and creativity, Natasha Diggs and Spinderella explicitly call themselves "researchers" who study music and composition in order to create the story they present to the crowd in a deejay set. Diggs and Spinderella's self-defined roles as researchers connect most explicitly to Adam Banks's argument that the Hip Hop deejay works as a digital griot who learns the history and stores it in her very being and body so as to chronicle it publicly, methodically, and creatively for an audience. Reborn further explains she has explicitly called and treated deejays as griots after witnessing the off-Broadway play, *The Seven*, the Hip Hop musical adaptation of Aeschylus's *Seven against Thebes* which follows the struggles of Eteocles and Polynices, the two sons of King Oedipus who fight for the throne of Thebes (McCarter). Will Power writes the play entirely in rhyming verse with a deejay-griot who weaves the story together with Calypso, Doo-wop, R&B, Funk, and Blues with choreography designed by Bill T. Jones. Thus, for DJ Reborn, the cultural currency of deejays as griots resonates with the ways she experiences her own storytelling processes and interactions with audiences, what she defines as a "call-and-response relationship," a foundational strategy of African-American rhetoric as well as an important repeating trope in key Black cultural artifacts from *Call and Response: Key Debates in African American Studies* to *Call and Response: The Riverside Anthology of the African American Literary Tradition*. While call-and-response has often been central to the ways scholars rhetorically situate the power and histories of Black sermons, speeches, literary texts, and general discursive styles (Jackson and Richardson; Richardson and Jackson; Smitherman), we are not as often inclined to center the sound philosophies and performances of Hip Hop deejays in that same tradition in the way that Reborn defines her role.

This nature of the deejay's storytelling and story-crafting are further illuminated by Shorty Wop, who explains that every record she plays is relevant and explicitly connects to the next record. Shorty Wop and Spinderella both call their deejay sets a "journey" their listeners "travel," a "journey" they deliberately craft for them. Meanwhile, Kuttin Kandi calls her story a kind of "movie." We highlight this craft and role of storytelling because storytelling is often described within the purview of the Hip Hop MC rather than in the very nature of what the culture calls for, a role that deejays originally inhabited and explicitly represent. As Pam the Funkstress argues, deejays tell their own story in the mix; *the mix itself is a story*. Like what Ball (2011) argues in *I Mix What I Like! A Mixtape Manifesto*, we treat the "mix" as these deejays describe and enact it as a source of Emancipatory Journalism: a form of media and communication disbursement that revolves around decolonizing practices.

There are times, however, when an audience's interests do not match a deejay's interests, as Kuttin Kandi and Spinderella both explain. Spinderella, who aligns herself with Old Skool sounds, admits she does not often like much of the new music that comes out. In such cases, the deejay must mix the song so she can still be herself but connect with the audience at the same time. Kandi argues her job is to "tell a story so others can relate to it" and gives the example of the times when she might play an artist such as Brittney Spears, a musician she doesn't particularly like but who her audience may enjoy and value. In those instances, Kuttin Kandi mixes the track in a new way with new beats and backgrounds that the audience might not even know. She shows her audience a new way to view the song because, as she puts it, you can "always rock your style" even when the audience does not know a piece. Reborn calls this ability to educate people about music they don't know how to access while also providing them with familiar sounds a matter of "personal integrity." Since deejaying is "a live art form," Reborn researches her audience beforehand but makes sure she connects to the energy and vibe of the space, even when a crowd is not necessarily deeply and consciously listening to just the music. For Reborn, this "art form" is a living "document" that leaves a "new canvas" behind.

No deejay in this chapter creates a definite, final set prior to meeting her audience. In each case, they read the crowd, both what the crowd likes and what the crowd needs. Each setting also has a different function: a themed gathering, a wedding, a sweet sixteen party, a birthday party, a formal gathering, or a club/dance scene. The deejays research their events and their audiences before the event, making some mental notes on the kinds of aesthetic tastes the audience may have (based on age, location, party promoter, and setting). All of these deejays have traveled across the globe, but they rely most heavily on what the crowd is communicating in the moment at each event.

The communication between audience and deejay is very nuanced. Natasha Diggs describes herself as reading her audience but also offering her audience inspiration and a model, thereby also inviting them to read her. Shorty Wop similarly describes an emotional connection she is making with the music she is offering to her audience, while Pam the Funkstress describes her connection with the audience as a sharing of music and, therefore, passion. Kuttin Kandi describes audiences and deejays as "working in tandem" by "reading" one another. She gives the audience a message about who she is and takes audience members on "an emotional ride."

Because Kuttin Kandi is also a turntablist, her understandings of the differences between being a turntablist and being a deejay are particularly critical, especially in light of the role of the audience and the ability to "rock the party." As a battle deejay, Kandi has crafted her turntablist skills in quite deliberate ways. Turntablism, as she notes, is about the self and a sharing of a skill set as a musician. However, being a deejay and honing in on the value of carrying record crates and working with a crowd has taught her how to really connect with people. Because she does both, she creates her own language and her own sound and communicates in many ways.

By focusing on the mix as a story and the deejay as a storyteller rather than the written or spoken word, we hope to push for a more fluid notion of text, textuality, and DJ Rhetoric and Literacy. We consider deejays storytelling as a process for setting texts in motion. Though he was not focused on Hip Hop or deejays, Henry Louis Gates Jr. proposed the notion of "texts in motion" in the now canonical *The Signifying Monkey: A Theory of African American Literary Criticism*. Thus, the concept of fluid texts is not new or original to us when tracing African-American cultural traditions. We are simply suggesting that a focus on the primacy of the MC or the written word has often overshadowed the texts that deejays are also constantly rewriting and putting in motion. In this case, we mean motion literally since deejays are constantly crossing territories and boundaries with their archives/records in tow, as well as manipulating a variety of sources that rotate on turntables at various speeds and pitches while reverberating sonically through speakers. This focus requires us to invoke DJ Rhetoric, DJ Literacy, and sonic lineage in order to share a deep and rich perspective on DJ sensibilities.

The women deejays construct DJ rhetorical strategies as a language that speaks new insights and connections into the worlds of their audiences. They are not offering their audiences a mere mimicry or cover of songs. Instead, these women integrate multiple sounds and sources as they craft a collective ethos that rocks the crowd. They are uniquely positioned in the ways they observe, interpret, and musically comment on Hip Hop as they shape audiences in real time and, as Shorty Wop argues, "Write the story for your whole night."

Loving Hip Hop: The Public Pedagogies of Women Hip Hop Deejays

"I educate and bring my turntables along." ~ Kuttin Kandi
"I've been able to find my voice through deejaying and I've used deejaying to be able to communicate—to write—in a certain kind of way." ~Reborn

It is obvious to us that deejays are twenty-first-century multimodal readers and writers (Wakefield), but it is also worth noting here that they perform these roles for the purpose of a public pedagogy. Though most of the deejays in this group never explicitly link themselves with state-sponsored "educators," we see them as teachers based on the fact that every deejay in this study describes herself as *teaching her audiences* about the music. Her deejay set has a special function for Pam the Funkstress: it teaches people how to *hear* the music. When Natasha Diggs plays a set, she consciously and deliberately takes people back to teach about a certain moment in the history of the music and, thereby, the history of their own lives. She writes a new moment with her set and takes her audience some place in particular with the collective memories of the participants of this moment. Shorty Wop makes the important distinction that having the music in your possession and playing the music are altogether different things. We are inspired by the ways these women deejays describe their love of the music, where DJ Reborn even argues deejaying requires a kind of "unselfishness" that comes with committing to the crowd. Like Pam the Funkstress, Reborn also contends that you always share your love of the music and the culture with your audience. Teaching in these models is thus an explicitly scaffolded experience. It is in the scaffolded playing of the music where these deejays compose their curriculum, a self-conscious act that each deejay critically calls teaching.

In addition to educating their audiences with their deejay sets, Kuttin Kandi and DJ Reborn work directly in classrooms and with young people. Kuttin Kandi's experiences have ranged from her time teaching spoken word and poetry to high school students at El Puente Leadership Center in Brooklyn to working at the Women's Center at the University of California, San Diego (Hisama). As a youth mentor, activist, and Hip Hop Feminist, Kandi sees her primary role as one of "educating our communities about Hip Hop," preserving Hip Hop culture, and building social justice platforms with the music and art. As she argues: "I educate and bring my turntables along."

Reborn teaches in two capacities: as a deejay instructor for Dubspot and as a workshop facilitator for UrbanWordNYC. At Dubspot, she uses both vinyl and Serato to teach "the language of deejaying," namely, song structure, sound, beats, range of motion, bars, dropping on the one, stamina, muscle memory, and reading a crowd. She began at UrbanWordNYC by deejaying youth open mic shows and gradually moved to teaching girls-only deejay and creative workshops where young women learn deejaying, lyrical analysis, and creative writing in the service of cultural critique of images of women in media. When Kandi and Reborn are working in state-official capacity as teachers, they make sure that Hip Hop, education, and social justice are always functioning simultaneously in their lives.

Given the specific, feminist classrooms of Kuttin Kandi and Reborn inside of a continuum where every woman deejay in this collective defines herself as a teacher, we see their public pedagogies as part of the wider teaching continuum in communication studies. We especially appreciate the ways these deejays center themselves and their bodies outside of the voyeuristic and cannibalistic gaze that comes when women of color perform. Reborn reminds us that deejaying is a very "exposing craft" that has taught her to communicate more directly and fluidly when at one point in her life she was more shy. In contrast, deejaying forces you to open up as you must learn to communicate your love of the music and who you are as a person. This communication ethic and ethos of women Hip Hop deejays point to the ways that women enter male-dominated closed systems of meaning and (re)define themselves and educate other young women to do the same.

Whether they are assessing new deejay software, describing themselves as storytellers, arguing for the role of invention, or explaining their relationships with immediate audiences, women Hip Hop deejays are always highly cognizant of the dynamic exchanges within DJ Rhetoric and Literacy that occur between word, sound, and audiences. These deejays act as both theorists and practitioners who challenge and reinvent lives. They continually construct themselves as dynamic authors of their sets and self-conscious teachers of their audiences.

Toward a Hip Hop Feminist Deejay Methodology

Using hiphopography as a methodological lens for these interviews with women Hip Hop deejays reaffirms that their perspectives are "meaningful, knowable, and able to be made explicit" and that as researcher-writers, our job is to "capture how those being interviewed view their world, to learn *their* terminology and judgments, and to capture the complexities of *their* individual perceptions and experiences" (Patton 341–348). This methodology thus encouraged the deejays themselves to tell their own stories and reflect on their day-to-day experiences based on an interviewer's deeply rooted and strong "interest in subjectivity and . . . people's life histories or everyday behavior" (Silverman 6–10). In listening to the interviews repeatedly, several overarching questions that emerged:

- What roles have women Hip Hop deejays assumed in, for, and against Hip Hop culture?
- How do women Hip Hop deejays complicate notions of race, gender, and sexuality as new media readers and writers?

- What are the implications of women Hip Hop deejays' rhetorical, digital, and pedagogical practices?

While growing more and more inspired by the deejays' narratives, challenging the notion that the often-cited pitfall of qualitative research is the bias from the researcher's close contact and commitment to the respondents involved in the study became paramount (Bowen; Creswell; Patton). In direct contrast to this sentiment, "Sista Girl Rock" purposefully strives to achieve a Hip Hop deejay methodology that refuses to privilege distance from Hip Hop culture as synonymous with being able to construct knowledge about it and honors multiple voices.

Kuttin Kandi offers perhaps the most provocative reading of the state of Hip Hop scholarship in academia. As a staff member of a college Women's Center, she visits many college classrooms and interacts with many college students who sit in classes about Hip Hop. Kandi is both alarmed and incensed at just how much of the information is misrepresented, distorted, or downright inaccurate. The very spaces that imagine they are passing on knowledge are not actually accomplishing this work in relation to Hip Hop. The legends of Hip Hop, when they are even included in a curriculum, are mere objects of study and never, as Kandi argues, "get to tell their own story." She reminds us her very skill and craft as a deejay came alongside these stories the legends gave to her, stories that seem omitted everywhere from Hip Hop curriculum as tenured bosses (i.e., university researchers) make their way up the scholarship chain.

Being inspired by the women Hip Hop deejays in this chapter evoked an attempt to ground the methods and polemics of this chapter in a specific movement: Hip Hop feminism (Cooper, Morris, and Boylorn; Durham, Cooper, and Morris; Lindsey; J. Morgan). We have no inclination to appease any of these oppressive camps that work against Hip Hop women who can stand on their own, generate their own theoretical dispositions, and spin the records of their own inclusion based on the unique locations they occupy in the world. In fact, the very process and purpose of "sound-collaging," as DJ Reborn coined it, works as the kind of intellectual and political process and style that writing about Hip Hop must embrace, a praxis that we situate in Hip Hop feminism.

The work of these women DJs offers new notions for the ways race and gender frame rhetorical strategies in communication. These women Hip Hop deejays have important stories to tell about education, technologies, race, and gender in the twenty-first century. The stories these women tell to their audience are also simultaneously a story they are telling us about life, work, and knowledge. The barred entry points that each woman in this chapter faces offer insights into how the very foundation of our culture works and strategies for breaking down that culture and remixing it. Everything that happens before, during, and after these women Hip Hop deejays spin a set offers us important techniques and perspectives that can rock multiple audiences.

What a DJ does is put music together to create a sound that creates a format just like a writer would create a story or something like that. Because when you write, you have to sit back and think about what you're going to write and how you're going to write whatever you're writing. As a DJ, when you're putting a set together, that's important. You don't just come and just go and just think you're going to play a song and everyone's gonna dance to it. You've got to create something that is going to get the crowd going. You have to make sure that at a certain point of the night, that these are the type of songs you're playing. You want to make sure the timing is right when you're mixing them.

You want people to groove!

So you have to really sit back as a DJ—or at least good DJs do—can sit back and go, okay. They don't have an exact set, but they know what they're going to play for the night, or what they have intentions on playing folks.

So when I am mixing and DJing, not only am I just mixing and DJing. I get a little scratch here, I do a little trick, I may double it up a little bit. And just kind of make the record or the song fun. So that people can really enjoy the song. Suppose it's a popular song, you don't want to just play it and go through. You want to make that song last a little bit—you can lower the volume, so people can sing a certain portion of the song, certain hook of the song, and you just kind of go back and forth and play with the crowd. So you got to kind of play with the crowd a little bit. That's what I do, I give them a show. So if anybody has ever seen me DJ, you'll just know I'm not just standing there, mixing songs. My body is moving, I'm grooving to everything. And I'm also just pretty much giving you a show, because I'm so into it. It just shows you the passion that I have, and how I'm into making the crowd dance.

Pam the Funkstress, personal interview, 6 Dec. 2011

6

THE GET DOWN PARTS
KEEPS GITTIN' DOWN
The DJ in the Center of the Comp "Contact Zone"

It look like I been cookin'!!!
   It look like I been cookin'!!!
      It look like I been cookin'!!!
         It look like I been cookin'!!!

Fat Joe and Remy Ma featuring RySoValid, "Cookin'," *Plata o Plomo*, Terror Squad / E1
Records, 2016.

. . . when you listen to Fat Joe and Remy Ma's song "Cookin'," you quickly realize its
message is simply about celebrating the success of the work they've been putting into their
craft in order to maintain top-tier status in Hip Hop culture.
In the music video, RySoValid attacks the one-line refrain in the hook, repeating,
"It look like I been cookin'! It look like I been cookin'!"
while Fat Joe, Remy Ma, and French Montana navigate the lush urban and desert
landscapes of Dubai, with a small brigade of dancers stirring the pot to a military-esque
cadence of drums and regal horns produced by iLLA . . .
what makes this happening noteworthy
is it shows Fat Joe and Remy Ma's ability to draw from
different moments in Hip Hop culture while also staying true to themselves.
Remaining relevant for various decades allows them to infect ear waves with anthem after
anthem that reverberates with multiple generations' worth of listeners . . .

https://doi.org/10.7330/9781646424849.c006

In the previous chapter, we examined the concept of #BlackGirlMagic through the lens of the female Hip Hop DJ. The ways in which these women DJs not only maneuver but also thrive in a male-dominated industry demonstrates how they engage in the Hip Hop DJ's rhetorical and discursive practices in order to serve as cultural practitioners, curators, and sonic producers. Continuing in a similar vein, this chapter will utilize DJ histories, modes, and techniques for construction of an in-depth commentary on the positionality of the Hip Hop DJ as new media reader, writer, and cultural critic. When furthering this conversation, it is critical to keep the discussion situated in the landscape of the DJ.

What I found most useful in envisioning this chapter was a moment on my way to LaGuardia Airport a number of years ago, traveling to a conference. I was listening to Hot 97's morning show, which back then was *The Cipha Sounds & Rosenberg Show with K. Foxx*. One of the promotional segments was called "the Cold as Ice MC," a contest that entailed an MC calling into the show and being given fifteen seconds to spit "some cold as ice" rhymes. On this Wednesday morning, the spitter of the day was this dude AimsLee. When DJ Cipha Sounds said, "Ready, set, go!" AimsLee immediately broke into rhyme. And he had it all: dope flow, ill cadence, witty punch lines, and great delivery. Cipha Sounds, Peter Rosenberg, and K. Foxx were all making the usual rhyme-cipher-observer noises like "oooooh . . . uuuuuuh . . . aaaaaaah" and a few moments of occasional laughter based on AimsLee's wit. The moment of interest for me, though, was when Cipha Sounds said, "Aight AimsLee, that's 15 . . . stop . . . STOP!!!" Rosenberg was like "Yo, dude's REALLY gonna keep rhyming" . . . and AimsLee did so until he finished his verse. While Ciph, Rosenberg, and K. Foxx kinda laughed and made jokes about it, AimsLee's response was most significant. When Cipha said, "Yo sun, you only got 15 seconds . . . you dope, but you gotta stop at 15 seconds," AimsLee's response was "Yo, I was supposed to stop? Yo, my fault—you the DJ sun, you need to stop me, knaimean?" In this moment, AimsLee demonstrated the significance of the DJ and what the DJ means to Hip Hop culture. And while it was great to see a younger MC acknowledge this paradigm, it's one that is seldom elaborated upon.

We see at any given time, people talking about Hip Hop from various perspectives—we also see the DJ's imprint and existence in various contemporary settings—be it popular culture, with DJ D-Nice appearing in the Ford F-150 commercial campaign; or even academic circles, for if you look very closely at the cover of Dr. E's book entitled *Hiphop Literacies*, the small pictorial band that separates the upper pink portion of the cover from the lower maroon quarter is a DJ's hand scratching a record on a 1200 right next to a mixer. After very close examination, I'ma say that these are not my fingers, although they do bear a coincidental resemblance. Similarly Hill and Petchauer's book cover for *Schooling Hip-Hop* also pictures a hand hovering over a record.

And as we see Hip Hop Nation Language now functioning as popular culture's language, we still see the DJ. For example, you can't tell me Charlie Sheen ain't start to say, "I'm WIIIIIIIIIIIIIIIN-ING!" without the subliminal message of DJ Khaled's radio spins of a song with a hook that goes "All I do is win-win-win, no matter what," with the infamous chorus "everybody's hands go UP . . . and they stay there!!!" (DJ Khaled, "All I Do Is Win"). Skip stage to over a decade later and add to this equation the Intuit QuickBooks and Mailchimp commercial, where the middle-aged woman and man do a spectacular job of appropriating Khaled's iconic hook (in the most orchestratedly horrible way), and yet again we see another example of how culture is premised on an action initiated by the DJ.

A universal truth is that most intellectuals, academics, historians, and anyone making some formative (or even nonformative) commentary on the history of Hip Hop will start with the source being located somewhere in the early to mid-'70s with Kool Herc. After Godfather Herc, some may talk about Afrika Bambaataa . . . and a few may mention Grandmaster Flash, or even go a step further with Grand Wizzard Theodore. But from there, people swiftly move to what seems to be the other "cooler" elements of Hip Hop. We all love the Hip Hop modern-day Master of Ceremonies, otherwise known as the MC/emcee. We are all intrigued with the historical connections and cultural relevance of the b-boys and b-girls. The aesthetic value of the artistic movement called graffiti even gains much light. And don't get me wrong, I love all the work my brothers and sisters in this cultural movement called Hip Hop have done to illuminate the importance of these elements. However, the phenomenon that I continue to notice that continues to take place is that we leave the DJ out of the conversation—once the historical flags are planted, it's like a Nubian or a Dominican with mad bobby pins . . . it's a wrap for the DJ. What becomes most critical about this conundrum is the DJ actually created the landscape for what we know today as Hip Hop. It was Kool Herc who won the projects Triple Crown: he was the dude, as DJ Mr. Len so eloquently described to me in conversation, "That jockeyed the beat. Dudes like Herc rode the shit outta that ten second break." Out of that break-riding springs forth the artistic and cultural field . . . let's keep it 100—ain't no chicken and egg confusion here. Clark Kent hit the nail on the head when he said, "The cornerstone of all Hip

Hop is the DJ. No break dancers if there's no DJ, no rappers if there's no DJ. The DJ, first—always! I just want to be clear" (Clark Kent). The history has it that the MC was the icing on the cake . . . the DJ was *always* the one who rocked the party, and the one people came to see. As Rich Medina stated, "With regard to talking about music, at times it feels like the DJ is like the 600-pound gorilla in the room that nobody wants to talk about."

"Brothas from a Hip Hop Mother": The DJ Community Linked through Craft

In order to make this chapter possible, I have included the voices of DJs in Hip Hop culture as well as the Hip Hop diaspora to advance the scholarly archive *on* the DJ *by* the DJ. Here, I will share research and excerpts of conversations with five DJs in particular. I have found these DJs epitomize specific aspects of the craft of DJing, and thereby aspects of the rhetorical milieu of the DJ. They embody the DJ's multifaceted work, as each has an artistic life that stems from, but also functions outside of, the parameters of strictly being DJs. They also serve as "your favorite DJs' favorite DJs." These individuals are well respected and highly revered as masters of their craft; frankly, their track records speak for themselves. They are DJs I've shared highly intellectual conversations with before all these interviews I conducted with the myriad of DJs began. These dudes serve as fact-checkers, cultural sponsors, and supporters of my work. Last but not least, some of these guys are family. I could give a laundry list of other reasons. Instead, I'll just give you their voices.

First is a dude by the name of Mr. Len. For those who don't know, in 1994, Mr. Len was one-third of a group named Company Flow. CoFlo was the *first* rap group signed to Rawkus Records and is considered one of the most influential underground Hip Hop groups of its time. The success of CoFlo ushered in the Hip Hop age for Rawkus Records, who released collaborative projects including *Lyricist Lounge* and *Black Star* (Yasiin Bey and Talib Kweli), and *Reflection Eternal* (Talib Kweli and Hi-Tek), as well as albums for artists including Mos Def (currently known as Yasiin Bey), Talib Kweli, Hi-Tek, Pharoahe Monch, DJ Spinna, Big L, and others. After CoFlo disbanded, Mr. Len worked with Chubb Rock, Jean Grae, Murs, Prince Paul, and many other artists. As well, Mr. Len is a member of the CM Famalam: this is the crew who would continue the legacy of the *Stretch Armstrong and Bobbito Show* on 89.9 (89 tech 9) WKCR (Columbia Radio) on Thursday nights from 1 a.m. to 5 a.m. This show was responsible for breaking artists including Biggie, Nas, Big L, a dude by the name of Big Dog Punisher (Big

Pun), Mobb Deep, and countless others. This is the same show that was voted by the *Source* magazine (when the *Source* was still truly "The Source" and pulse of Hip Hop culture) as "The Greatest Hip Hop Radio Show of ALL TIME." This same show has been immortalized in a documentary called *Stretch and Bobbito: Radio That Changed Lives*. Len also started an independent label called Smacks Records, which was the *first* label to do "30 in 30": thirty songs in thirty weeks; unfortunately, if you think Ye (aka Yezos aka Yeezy aka Kanye West) was the first one to do this with his "Good Music Good Friday" trend, you are sadly mistaken . . . Mr. Len was the first one who did it and got away with it. Mr. Len has traveled the world and back as both a DJ and producer, from DJing one of the first Hip Hop shows in Africa, to opening for the Beastie Boys and Portishead, to working as Jean Grae's DJ for a tour with her, Pharoahe Monch, and DJ Boogie Blind (for Pharoahe's album *W.A.R. [We Are Renegades]*). Len went on to become one-third of the DJ crew "Dirty Disco Squares" alongside DJs Rhettmatic and Prince Paul. Soon after, Len served as tour DJ with Everlast on the "Everlast Presents: Whitey Ford's House of Pain" tour. His production has landed in the score of the *Empire of Blood* podcast. A formally trained drummer and saxophonist—although he'll tell you, "I haven't played sax in a while"—Len is presently working on a series of multimedia projects. Engaging with the idea that people do listen but more people watch, Len has begun to collaborate with different artists, spearheading both the music production as well as curation of all the visuals that accompany the music. He is currently working with Murs, Fatboi Sharif, and Jimi Hazel (of the Funk Metal group 24-7 Spyz) and Corey Glover (from Rock band Living Colour). Reminiscent of "maxi-singles" in the 1990s, Len's goal is to create concept-driven three-song multimedia projects with each artist, as a way to further continue his sonic and visual artistic output.

The second DJ is Rich Medina, who has been a DJ for over three decades and has also done work as a poet/spoken word artist and producer. Some of Rich's accolades include long-standing DJ residencies in New York; one of the most popular was "Little Ricky's Rib Shack," which lasted over a decade at Club APT before the club closed. This party was rebirthed as a weekly event called "Propz" at Le Poisson Rouge with DJ Akalepse. As a poet, Rich has worked with the Roots and as he says, he's even crushed some of your favorite Def Poets when it was just popping off. He released an album entitled *Connecting the Dots* and compilation projects including *Rich Medina Presents Jump N Funk* and *Rich Medina and Bobbito: The Connection Volume One*. Medina has also contributed to the 89 tech 9 *CM Famalam Show* and also played alongside various DJs, including Q-Tip during their residency at Club Santos for five years (2005–2009). He was also a DJ on the premier season of Smirnoff's *Master of the Mix* (MOTM) DJ contest/reality series. Of the eight DJs, Rich made it to the top three with DJs Vikter Duplaix and DJ Scratch—to situate Rich, in one of the first episodes, DJ Scratch (winner of *MOTM* Season 1) said on the show, "Rich is my FAVORITE club DJ." As well, Medina is most known for his two-decade-strong party entitled "Jump N Funk"—this event has given Rich the title of the first American club DJ to introduce to and celebrate within American club culture the music, life work, and philosophies of Fela Kuti. So you understand how real it is, when the Fela show opened on Broadway, Rich DJed the opening night after party. As one of five DJs highlighted in the long-running New York City party called "The Originals," Rich spins records alongside powerhouse DJs Clark Kent, Tony Touch, D-Nice, and Stretch Armstrong. Rich holds a BS in Business Management from Cornell University's College of Agriculture and Life Sciences and is also the first Cornell alum to sit on the advisory board of Cornell's Hip Hop Collection Archive. Rich Medina was awarded a 2021 PEN Fellowship and is currently serving as music director of Dante's HiFi in Miami, Florida.

The third and fourth DJs, Mr. Sonny James and Phillip Lee (originally known as DJs Statik and Phillee Blunt, respectively), are two of the founding members of the six-man DJ crew called Illvibe Collective out of Philadelphia. Both James and Lee are two veteran DJs who fell in love with Hip Hop and DJ culture. As a child hanging with his older sister, who was cool with a well-known Philadelphia DJ, Sonny was exposed at a young age to Hip Hop music and DJ practice sessions. This would lead him to an early desire to delve into DJ culture and practices. Phil grew up in Nutley, New Jersey, and found himself as one of the few people who was tuned into Hip Hop music and culture at a young age. He pieced together his journey toward Hip Hop culture in four different events over the course of a year: a friend lending him a Run-DMC album; his cousin's graduation party in Staten Island, New York, which featured a Filipino DJ Soundsystem; a *Yo! MTV Raps* interview where Dr. Dre talked about the specifics of DJing; and attending a summer party where he watched a DJ spin and peppered him with questions for the entire event. By that Christmas, Phil had begged his parents for a mixer and by age twelve, he hooked up two mismatched belt-drive turntables into his new mixer in order to start his journey as a DJ. Both James and Lee started DJing in 1992; they met at Philadelphia College of Textiles and Science, where Phil studied audio engineering and Sonny studied graphic design. In college, they would connect with DJs Panek, Skipmode, and lil'dave to form the DJ crew Illvibe Collective. This crew would later include DJ Matthew Law into their fold in 2011.

Sonny James has traveled the globe as a tour, club, and radio DJ. He's DJed for artists including Grand Agent, Bahamadia, Hezekiah, Jay Live, Camp Lo, Smif-N-Wessun, and the legendary James Brown. James has DJed a series of events from Shawn Stockman (Boyz II Men) and Babyface's gala for autism awareness and Stevie Wonder's prewedding party, to the Obama Administration's White House events that include the US-Africa Leaders Summit (alongside Lionel Richie) and Susan Rice's fiftieth birthday celebration (with Aretha Franklin). Sonny is currently one of four people responsible for educating and servicing artists, producers, and DJs with the digital music software brand Serato. The global staple of DJ digital software, Sonny is based out of Los Angeles and handles Artist Relations and Support for the West Coast—but on any given day, you can catch Sonny supporting an A-list DJ who's about to start an event, presenting new products to DJs at Jazzy Jeff's PLAYLIST Retreat (Sonny is the only person to be invited as a DJ and then also work the event as a Serato representative), or even lending a hand to a regular college professor trying to buy his eleven-year-old daughter the proper DJ controller. Sonny has also contributed as a co-creator and DJ for radio shows including *The SureShot* on Illvibe Radio back in 1998 (this show functioned as an early podcast before the term "podcast" was created). He also DJs and cohosts *Across The Tracks* with Fat Nice, a show they started in 2006. He continues to thrive as a DJ and producer in Los Angeles.

Phillip Lee has been the most underrated DJ of Illvibe and was once described by Mr. Len as one of DJ culture's "best kept secrets." Arguably one of the most technically savvy DJs in his crew, Phil has formal training as an audio engineer, which has allowed him to thrive as a sound technician and equipment point person for Illvibe Collective. He has spent decades serving as a top-notch DJ for clubs, parties, radio, and mixtapes alike, as well as an engineer in a series of studio sessions, including the recording of Illvibe Collective's album *All Together Now* and various other Illvibe remix projects. Phil resides in New Jersey, where he continues to DJ and currently works with Apple.

Finally, DJ Boogie Blind (who has a gazillion akas, including "The X Factor") has been a stalwart in the New York City DJ scene. Blind was introduced to records as young as age five. Cutting his teeth with DJ Roc Raida (RIP) of the X-Ecutioners—as well as with DJ Precision, DJ Cutfucious, Lord Finesse, and others—Boogie Blind is one of the most ingenious DJs of the culture. His DJ savvy has allowed him to tour the globe many times over, playing various events and festivals worldwide. He has served as tour DJ for Pharoahe Monch, Busta Rhymes, and D.I.T.C. crew; worked with other Hip Hop artists, including Jean

Grae and Busta Rhymes; and also plays for radio platforms including SiriusXM. For the past ten years, Blind's weekly "Drunk Mix" and "Sober Mix" segments have appeared on Shade 45's *Lord Sear Special* show. He also remains in a small rotation of DJs who are called upon to appear on shows, including DJ Premier's *Live From Headqcourterz* and Statik Selektah's *ShowOff Radio*. Recently, Blind has consistently participated in New York City happenings, whether at community events for WNBA's Shannon Bobbitt or rocking Summer Stage courtesy of Eric Elliot. One of the newest members of DJ Enuff's NYC-based DJ crew The Heavy Hitters, Boogie Blind can be found at his monthly residency called "Easily" at Friends and Lovers in Brooklyn. When Large Professor found himself scoring the movie *All the Streets Are Silent*, he called in Boogie Blind to record all the live DJ scratches throughout the score. Whether Blind is playing in Japan alongside DJ Koco—or playing in Australia, Brazil, or the UK—his ability to tour globally lends itself to shaping a musical ear that has always remained on the cutting edge of music and DJ culture. This has allowed Blind to engage not only with Hip Hop but also with other genres of music, including Dubstep, Drum & Bass, Brazilian Samba, Bali Funk, UK Drill, and Grime. Boogie Blind has taken the past few years to step into production, crafting beats for artists the likes of Jean Grae, as well as working on remix production for Jarreau Vandal and David Rodigan. Most important, Blind is one of few DJs who consistently sounds the same on *all* DJ mediums: he manipulates 12-inch vinyl in the same way he rocks on Serato and Traktor, DJ controllers, and even 7-inch vinyl at a speed of 45. His residency at "Easily" allows him to showcase his uber-high-level skill set and talents.

Cuz This Push Kicks: The DJ and Contact Zone in Contemplation

The goal of this chapter is to analyze the thoughts, modes, and methods of these five DJs in order to highlight and propel the significance of the DJ's rhetorical, discursive, and communicative practices. Normally, I would work to make this point with two 1200s and a Mixars DUO. And while I could make the argument that this statement alone is an intricate form of rhetoric that only DJs would really understand, I'll just let that thought marinate on the page for a hot second, and keep it moving. There is a clear decision made here in how the DJ set is constructed in this conversation. At the heart of it is always the turntable (mental note); however, this chapter will substitute auditory vinyl with tangible textual syntax . . . the crate of records I've carried with me here to this chapter functions off the premise of original data I've collected in interviewing DJs in conjunction with scholarship from English Studies.

As with the last chapter, it is the presence and voices of these DJs—not to be confused with the "wax poetics" of what you may think the DJ *might* be saying or doing, but their actual voices—that will steer this journey back toward some interesting moments in scholarship from a few scholars and theorists.

On one turntable, the classic record from 1995 that spins is labeled by Joseph Harris, entitled "Negotiating the Contact Zone." In describing this negotiation, Harris argues that the goal of writing courses should focus toward "the creation of a space where the conflicts between our own discourses, those of the university, and those which our students bring with them to class are made visible" (Harris 31). He uses Mary Louise Pratt's definition of the "contact zone" in identifying a location where and how this critical work in learning and writing takes place. The questions I ask here are "Why move towards 'creating' a contact zone, when we already have a living and breathing example which is readily available?" And "Why are people so drawn to 'creating' this zone when DJs already BEEN mastered this craft?" What becomes noteworthy is the DJ is the quintessential "Contact Zone" creator and facilitator, in that every DJ set is a contact zone: it is an intertextual and intersectional location where all these varying thoughts, ideas, and paradigms collide. It becomes the job of the DJ to make sense of how this contact zone called "DJ set" works itself out.

The DJ thus becomes a great example of writer and researcher in terms of being able to navigate, negotiate, organize, critically process, and critique varying collections of data and information. It can be envisioned in the same way depicted by Kermit Campbell in his book *Gettin' Our Groove On*; in describing the "virtual gold mine of knowledge and experience involving various oral and literate media" that our students bring to the table with them in the college classroom, he notes, "They possess a wealth of cultural knowledge in desperate need of intellectual inquiry and critique. Just consider what many of these students consume from Hip Hop alone: besides the music and videos (oral and visual media) . . . the sound (a deejay's mixes and scratches, which in itself is a kind of art requiring specialized knowledge)" (Campbell 139). The DJ is both creator and source of cultural capital, weaved together to form a site of inquiry; is this not the same work we ask of our students as writers, researchers, and critical thinkers? While many may envision the rapper or the emcee as the creator of an oral-tradition-focused contact zone, it's important to acknowledge the DJ at the forefront of this movement—the mix-master or Grand Wizard of the culture who stuck the picket sign up in the air, while the rapper read a line that said, "Eff Standard English" in pushing forth the voice we know as Hip Hop. As well, this mix takes on a new dimension in 2023, as Hip Hop culture is the dictator of and tastemaker to global popular culture. Make no mistake about it: the DJ weaves both hands in and out of this blend.

Part of the difficulty we see with Hip Hop is that as it has evolved into the tastemaker for popular culture, people tend to forget that it was and continues to be a cultural phenomenon turned practice that originated *solely* as a voice for Black folx (African-American, Caribbean, and African, and even members of the Latinx communities) living in the urban underclass of New York City, specifically in order to give voice to the voiceless. While I do appreciate and acknowledge the work of authors and academics like Jeff Rice and Paul Miller (aka DJ Spooky), my work moves to both further and complicate their ideas. For example, I would argue that the proliferation of DJ equipment in the 1977 Bronx Blackout led to the ascension of the DJ (Chang, *Can't Stop Won't Stop* 84). This event might lead us away from Rice's assertion in regard to the "whatever moment," which depicts that the DJ comes out of nowhere, "unattached" to anything. In Jeff Chang's book *Can't Stop Won't Stop*, he shows us that the dearth of resources in the area known as the "burnin'-down Bronx" leads to a special set of circumstances that find poor and disenfranchised BIPOC communities looking for a way and means by which to tap into a creativity that was longed for, when arts and education as well as extracurricular programs were removed from the schools (Chang, *Can't Stop Won't Stop*). This is a historical piece of Hip Hop culture rooted in a very particular geographic landscape. The best way for me to articulate this is by moving directly to the source and playing a Hip Hop record from artist Busta Rhymes. On his album *The Big Bang*, Busta featured megaproducer, occasional hook-spitter, and Verzuz cofounder Swizz Beatz on a song that dominated the Mid-Atlantic airwaves: a Hip Hop anthem called "New York Shit" (interestingly enough, this record was produced by DJ Scratch . . . not to be confused with MC, b-boy, or graf artist Scratch). In this song, Busta and Swizz run through a number of things that have been affected, dictated, or influenced by Hip Hop culture, and what they see as "New York Shit"—mainly, "Yeah, yeah, I'm on my New York shit / Kid Capri on my New York shit / DJ Red Alert on my New York shit / Funkmaster Flex on my New York shit" (Busta Rhymes featuring Swizz Beatz). My equivalent sits in two spots. On the one side, the saying "real recognize real" is important; both Rice and Miller are two scholars and thinkers who make early contributions to research on the DJ. At the same time, in the mix on the other side is the premise of the song, which for this writing, would sound like "I'm on my Hip Hop DJ shit!" as spoken directly from the DJ's mouth. This is something both writers neglect in their work. My objective here is to not only examine the importance of the DJ but also to envision the DJ as an example of twenty-first-century new media reader, writer, and literary critic. This work simply cannot be accomplished without DJ voices at the epicenter of this inquiry.

HSTRY Is More Than Just Clothes: How These DJs Git Down with the Git Down (RIP Tame One)

Mr. Len started DJing when he was twelve years old and when asked what initially prompted him to be a DJ, he tells a story of how his dad, who was an engineer, made an 8-track six days before Len was born, an 8-track dedicated to his birth. When Len was old enough to listen and understand it, he was determined to find all the records on the 8-track, which included "songs like The Ohio Players, Jackson 5, Harold Melvin and the Blue Notes, Booker T and the MGs, Kool and the Gang—an amalgamation of Soul and Funk records" (Mr. Len). It was this amalgamation that prompted Len to become a DJ. This moment sits in conjunction with another moment in Rich Medina's interview. When asked about what goes into his thinking when it comes to choosing the records he buys and/or plays, his focus is on filling holes in his record library—an archive that holds upward of fifty thousand records (50,000):

> I'm trying to fill out catalogues now. I'm trying to have all the Michael Jackson albums, all the Michael Jackson 12 inches, all the Michael Jackson 45s. I'm digging on that level. I want ALL the James Browns: the imports, the exports, the 7 inches, the white labels, the obscure label joints that people don't know he wrote. On and on and on: Marvin Gaye, Stevie Wonder, all the Staples stuff . . . at this point for me in my digging, I'm filling holes. I'm trying to round off my library to make it more fundamentally complete. (Medina, interview)

Phil Lee also lent critical dialogue in terms of the temporality of finding records to add to one's collection (aka catalogue, aka arsenal, aka lineage), as everything was not readily available as it might be today with the advent of digital music. He shares, "It was much more exclusive back then. Cuz you knew that [a record] wasn't coming back into the store after it sells out. So either you pick one up, or you're never going to get it . . . you would go on a quest, and it was like that *every* weekend" (Phillip Lee).

In looking at these moments together, we see emerging out of the DJ's voice an echoing of Alfred Tatum's concept of textual lineage. Tatum argues that one way to keep African-American adolescent males engaged in the education process—specifically reading—is to introduce them to books that relate to them so they can begin to build a textual lineage of books and stories (both textual and nontextual) that engage them deeper in the reading process. Here we see how these DJs—in the stages of both inception of and longevity within the craft—highlight the integral nature of understanding the textual (or even musical/sonic) lineage they spring from as Hip Hop DJs. Whether it is Mr. Len doing the research on his "Birthday 8-Track" recorded by his father, or the archive completion work to which Medina is tending, interestingly enough, all of these DJs mention one another as influences and part of their understanding of DJ tradition. For example, Sonny James and Phil Lee mention Rich Medina as an influence. Boogie Blind states, "There's DJs that inspire me now actively, like Statik from Philly" (DJ Boogie Blind). Mr. Len has praised Phil on many occasions, in the same way that Rich Medina has applauded Mr. Len. Thus, these DJs are actively engaged in a circle of sonic lineage when reflecting on their craft.

As we connect the idea of sonic lineage, both Sonny and Phil add critical perspectives. In thinking about aspects of research that go into building one's sonic lineage as a DJ—especially around identifying, researching, and acquiring records—Sonny states:

> You had to go to a club in order to hear a certain record and you had to wait for it to come on. There are certain records that Rich Medina plays now, that you're not going to hear anybody else play. It's always been like that—that's why he is where he's at. And you go out and it would be like 11:30 p.m., and you'd be like "I hope Rich is going to play that record because I need to hear that record." And then once he plays it, you're like "oh my God I gotta try to get up there to ask him what it is!" And then you hope that you remember it so you can get to the store the next day and be like "oh yo, there's this record by" and you mess up the name. And you know, your guy there that you trust will be like "Oh no, it's not called that! It's called this, and I got one copy and it's yours!" And you felt like you triumphed. (Sonny James)

The excitement around this victory is the enthusiasm that great DJs bring to the table when it comes to expanding their auditory knowledge of music. This expansion lends itself to an elevated and enhanced sonic lineage and DJ Literacy.

Another moment that comes out of Len's interview really puts the idea of this lineage and literacy into practice: "Most DJs are—and I say this humbly—a wealth of knowledge. There are things that we're privy to in records, from reading, that most people don't pay attention to." Len goes on to explain the following scenario: he's addicted to the show *NCIS*. He notes an actor on NCIS—David McCallum, who was the coroner on the show (Ducky) . . . David McCallum was also on a show called *The Man from Uncle*. Len went onto explain that

[McCallum's] a well-known actor from the 60s, but he also made records. One of the records that he made is with David Axelrod called "The Edge," that was sampled by Dr. Dre for "The Next Episode." So a lot of times when people reference the song "The Edge," they always reference David Axelrod, but it's on David McCallum's album. The song is written by David Axelrod, but it's composed and performed by Dave McCallum and his orchestra . . . so as a reader, you're now delving deeper into the record. We nerd out and dig deeper into the song. (Mr.Len)

Again, this idea of moving through the connection between a collection of sources not only speaks to Tatum's idea of textual lineage or Lynnée Denise's concept of DJ research but also begins to segue into thinking about Pratt's notion of "the contact zone": this location where all these different ideas and discourses come into play with one another.

In speaking to this idea of Pratt's contact zone, Medina explains,

A large dynamic in the culture is the gathering, the dancehall, the block party where all these different elements of the culture are brought together—and the fans and the components of it as well. But the one person who's conducting the space that all of those people are existing in is the DJ. And originally the MC was just to interact with the crowd and to get them involved in the moment to make the crowd feel ownership in what was going on. (Medina, interview)

This remark comes from a DJ who is known for what we call a "three shot deal" mentality; Rich will play three records of one genre, then switch, then switch again every three records. In his work and grounded in his reputation as a DJ, Rich brings forth this sort of auditory textual hybridity, bringing various genres together intertextually, with each genre lending to and sharing with another in order to create the story of Rich Medina's sets.

When it comes to set creation, Boogie Blind shares,

I just really try to create a feeling . . . I wouldn't say I pre-program, you know. I definitely practice, but it's more so knowing how I'm going to make my transitions, you know what I'm saying? Like, if I gotta go on before somebody, or I gotta go after somebody, or whatever. Because, sometimes there's a situation where you have someone spinning a different type of music, or you got to blend into what he's playing or what have you. So I just try to be prepared for everything, because you never know what's going to happen. Because people say, "Oh, this is a Hip Hop party" but it'll be like, eight to one girls. I don't think they would want to hear underground Hip Hop all night long. So it's like that sometimes. (DJ Boogie Blind)

What Blind's analysis gets at is both the idea of practice in set creation (hence, drafting a sonic text) and also understanding the importance of audience when writing these live sonic critiques.

As well, when Sonny and Phil are thinking about set creation for events, they envision the idea of the contact zone in terms of "creating a vibe." Long before the latest iteration of slang for creating a mood, these two DJs were engaging in contact zone vibe creation (after all, they are founding members of the IllVibe Collective). When depicting the sentiments involved in playing and selecting music for events, Phil shares that

> one thing that any DJ or musician or artist that really cares about what they're doing—they're creating a vibe. And that's something that you'll hear all the time if you're talking to people like us or other DJs that we always look up to. People like Rich [Medina] or King Britt or anyone, any DJ or artist who's in that league of being a tastemaker, so to speak, they're the ones who think about it in terms of creating the right energy for that audience. And when you're putting sets together, you're creating that vibe and building off of it. If there's a DJ who played before you, you have to pay attention, because you can't just slam people with a different story. You have to kind of tell off of that other story. So I always think about it in that way of creating a mood and certain types of energy so that you can carry it out through the rest of the night, or at least the rest of your set. (Phillip Lee)

Here, Lee not only identifies the importance of facilitating the mood and vibe of an event, but he also leans into the idea of the DJ as griot and storyteller. The sonic choices that any good DJ will make (especially during an event where multiple DJs are playing) bear in mind the auditory storytelling of the DJ who played before, and sometimes they will set the stage for the DJ who might be playing after. What we clearly see here is the DJ as reader, writer, and storyteller: orchestrating and overseeing the mood that gets established in the event or gathering as contact zone. Boogie Blind also addressed this idea, when he states,

> I feel it's like that because if you know you're doing your own solo set, you don't have to worry about this DJ playing this [record] or, you know, this DJ trying to play the hits before you get on or whatever the situation may be, you know? You still gonna have a way to start your set, you're still going to try to make a transition to keep at an even flow. I usually don't just bounce around from one tempo to another tempo, because it confuses people. You know? (DJ Boogie Blind)

Contact-Zone-Collab'ing: The Record Store and the Recordings Stored

While Medina identifies the party, or "the gathering" as the contact zone, both Sonny and Phil also illuminate the record store experience as a contact zone.

When thinking about the importance of the process of purchasing records (which in itself is a research/archivist moment), Phil shares:

> I feel so bad for DJs that are coming up now that are never going to experience this: there was something that you can't really put into words about *being* in the record store, because it was a physical social thing. And one way that you could tell the record was good was because everyone in the record store showed that energy physically—whether it was verbally or just head nod or body language, whatever it was. There was someone who worked in the record store, that all their job to do all day was just push records, and they would play what they have. And you could see, you could just hang out in there for an hour or two and just look and whenever something hot came on, everyone was feeling it, you'd say "lemme get one of those." You know what I mean? And that was a big part of it . . . you know you're either at school or you were at work on Thursday, Friday, or even Saturday morning, you were like "I gotta go to the record store." And then you walked in and just the smell of it. You know, the brand new plastic and the cardboard and everything—you just walk in and you're like "thank God! I'm finally gonna get some new records." (Phillip Lee)

This idea from Phillip Lee connects back to Kuttin Kandi's comments on the importance of record stores. It also resonates with Lynnée Denise's conception of the DJ as researcher and archivist, specifically when she chronicles her own experiences in records stores: "Working those stores, one of which was the legendary Tower Records, provided me with two skills that support my now professional love of music today. First, it gave me the ability to catalogue and categorize music with the attentiveness of a librarian; second, it taught me how to search for music in record stores all over the world" (Denise 62).

Similar to the DJ's collaborative efforts with call-and-response in the gatherings that Medina identified, the DJ has always held a collaborative (and almost symbiotic) relationship with the MC. Mr. Len describes this moment in terms of a trusting relationship between the MC and the DJ:

> The one thing that most DJs especially back then felt was you had to be original. We DON'T ever want you to sound like anyone else. Because if you sound like this record, I'll just play THAT record and I'll NEVER play your record because it sounds just like that one. But if you want to MIX with this record, I'm gonna tell you "this record is 96 BPMs": so you're either gonna stay between 94 and 97 so that the record is mixable but DON'T sound like it . . . this was a great time where DJs were an integral part of the culture. (Mr. Len).

Both of these ideas echo the negotiation described by Harris earlier. It's worth repeating here that the DJ thus becomes a great example of reader, writer, and researcher in terms of being able to navigate, negotiate, organize, critically process, and critique varying collections of sonic data and information.

The collaborative conversation between the DJ and MC that Len pinpoints (and also appears back in chapter 4) is a similar contact zone to the one described by Phil Lee in the record store. Sonny James pushes the idea further by likening the contact zone collaboration with the record store employees and buyers, who also served as sonic sponsors for DJs. James identifies the relationship that any good DJ fostered within the record stores they'd frequent:

> There's a lot to be said about the relationship that you built with people who were like buyers at record stores. Because you trusted that person like you would trust a Reverend or something, you know? They knew what they were talking about. And they knew what their word meant in the club, and to DJs who were playing in the club. So they knew not to push stuff just because it was the popular jam right now. It was like, "We're gonna push joints that are dope music that you should know." So I think that person who played that role was always sort of underappreciated if you ask me. Because people like Stef Tatas, like Randy Flash (RIP), like Joey Blanco, and I'm just speaking for Philadelphia. I know up in New York, you had your [DJ] Eclipse of Fat Beats, you had your dudes at Rock and Soul. And, you know, there's a ton of people who, who are really just like, supplying deejays with their ammo. And without that person, you were kind of like, guessing your way through it sometimes. So, I think that played a tremendous role, then. (Sonny James)

This moment is very reminiscent of how sponsors and fact-checkers continued to help DJs with creating the rhetorical savvy they built when constructing their contact-zone club-narratives. This idea also reminds me of my own record store excursions and those sponsors in the stores who helped me navigate my own record curation. It started with the guy who would sell me my tapes at QP's flea market on those Sundays after I'd leave from church. That relationship continued with people like Rich at Rock and Soul, who sent me more than a few boxes of records up to my Williams College SU Box. I also think of my man Marcus Todd in Providence, Rhode Island, in this moment as well—whether it was Skippy White's Records, Scott's or Glenn's stores in Providence, or even when he got up to Boston Beat. Those cultural practitioners were also critical to DJs' ability to understand sonic sources that would help them write the auditory narratives of the night in any given contact zone setting.

Another fruitful location of inquiry brought about by these DJs comes in the question "What genres of music do you play as a DJ?" While each of the DJs speaks to this moment at different times, they approach the concept in very similar ways. Mr. Len discusses his DJ practice in tandem with the changing climate that came with the emergence of the Hip Hop DJ as

I play everything. I hate to sound like it's masturbatory, but I only care about pleasing me. If I feel like hearing Reggae, I play Reggae. Meringue, Hip Hop, House, Rock, Soul . . . and you know there's a change coming. You're in these clubs that were mostly Rock venues. None of these places are designed for Hip Hop shows, and we're going into these places and packing these rooms. So we DEMANDED respect. I don't get the same respect that Run-DMC gets yet, but the operative word there is YET. So it was one of those things where you knew that this was the new New York sound, it was the new Tri-State area. Everyone's got something to prove, but no one's trying to kill each other. And there's competition, but it's so intellectual at the time. Even the hard-core gangsta dudes when you listen to them, you're like "yo, did you catch his wordplay? The way his usage of the similes" . . . Everyone was breaking out their Oxford Dictionaries to write about Hip Hop . . . in those years, the DJ was still part of the group . . . there is no Run-DMC without Jam Master Jay. EPMD is EPMD, but if DJ Scratch ain't there, you're gonna be let down. 3rd Bass had Richie Rich, De La Soul got Maseo, Stetsasonic had Prince Paul, Boogie Down Productions after Scott La Rock passed, they ran with D-Nice who was already part of the group, and then Kenny Parker. (Mr. Len)

Sonny James approaches the idea by stating:

In terms of the genres that we play. I always say that I play everything but obviously that excludes Country music, and Polka, you know. I'm not taking gigs where I'm playing like Accordion music. But you know, it ranges from House to Samba to Bossa Nova to Salsa and Merengue. It could be, you know, Hip Hop, Jazz, Broken Beat. New Jazz, Funk, Classic Soul, New Soul, Hip Hop classics, Dubstep, Drum and Bass. It ranges depending on what the scenario is. (Sonny James)

The sonic hybridity in conjunction with the vast musical knowledge of Hip Hop DJs is displayed throughout these conversations. It's also important to note how each DJ describes what they play in connection to studying various genres of music. Phil Lee captures this idea when he states:

I had originally really just known about Hip Hop music when I first started. So for the beginning I guess four or five years of when I was a DJ, it pretty much all was that, and playing Reggae, Dancehall Reggae, because you could always fit the two together . . . playing those two things together was always a given, especially at house parties, around here like North Jersey, or in New York. Like, we always played those styles together. Once I went to school in Philadelphia, and I met Sonny and Cliff, and then after meeting Dave and Skip and everybody, they definitely put me on to a whole different range of music. So now everything that [Sonny] mentioned, I'm still a student of learning how to play that. But my foundation was in Hip Hop. (Phillip Lee)

Finally, Boogie Blind shares the same sentiments in terms of his multi-genred approach to DJing: "Recently, I've been, you know, just trying to be creative with different genres of music, but I play Hip Hop, Funk, Jazz, R&B, Disco, Drum and Bass, Dubstep, House, Progressive House, Smooth House, Funky House, whatever! '90s Hip Hop, you know, whatever! Samba, Salsa, Merengue, Cumbia, you know, everything. Afrobeat, whatever. I just never really touched Trance or Country like that though, to be honest with you" (DJ Boogie Blind). What becomes clear is that these DJs, who play with a Hip Hop sensibility, recognize the necessity to study, understand, and play from a wide swath of genres. As students of Hip Hop culture, they realize Hip Hop's sonic lineage is connected to many of these musical categories they name.

When describing the process of creating DJ sets, both James and Lee give poignant commentary. For example, Sonny James shares,

> I think there's a lot to be said for how a group of things are put together, you know? If we're talking about 100 songs, you can give even our crew, you can give five of us the same 100 songs, and you're going to be told a different story. Five different ways, you know? And I think there's a lot to be said for that, because I'm going to play things according to my style. And, you know, my style is based on my experience. Phil may hear songs go together differently. He may hear the orders completely differently. So, you know, I think there's a lot to be said, for that: each person's original interpretation of how they put the songs together to tell the story. (Sonny James)

Phil immediately responds with "And that's really what people are doing when they go to hear a DJ that they like. They don't realize it, but they like that DJ's interpretation. And that's why they follow them: not because they play the hot joints. They like how they put it together" (Phillip Lee). Lee's ideas here, with the identification of partygoers preferring a particular sonic interpretation, lends itself to the notion of the DJ as writing within set creation and functioning as a sonic literary critic. The DJ is, in essence, interpreting a series of texts through an individualized lens that is steeped in a Hip Hop cultural history and sonic awareness. The embodiment of the DJ set at the event is an articulation of *why* that set should be heard a certain way—just like James details how his sonic analysis will differ from Lee's or Medina's, or other DJs. In the same way an avid reader might look to a critic who reviews books for the *New Yorker* or the *New York Times*, listeners will flock to the sonic stylings of one DJ or another. That DJ's sonic interpretation becomes a critique of the various sonic sources they have at their disposal. But it's equally important to recognize what's at their "disposal" is also a carefully crafted curatorial choice. By privileging what *to* include, DJs are also inherently making a critique based on what gets left out or *doesn't* get heard.

"I'm out here ridin' for my freedom like Stokely": Sonic Liberation in the Mix

When you listen to Fat Joe and Remy Ma's song "Cookin'," you quickly realize its message is simply about celebrating the success of the work they've been putting into their craft in order to maintain top-tier status in Hip Hop culture. In the music video, RySoValid attacks the one-line refrain in the hook, repeating, "It look like I been cookin'! It look like I been cookin'!" while Fat Joe, Remy Ma, and French Montana navigate the lush urban and desert landscapes of Dubai, with a small brigade of dancers stirring the pot to a military-esque cadence of drums and regal horns produced by iLLA. This phrase and iconic hand gesture stems from James Harden during his moments of uncanny scoring streaks in NBA games, with one hand making a pot and the other hand stirring a spoon to symbolize a cooking motion. This specific hand gesture can be traced back to 2015, with Chedda Da Connect's viral song "Flicka Da Wrist." What makes this happening noteworthy is it shows Fat Joe and Remy Ma's ability to draw from different moments in Hip Hop culture while also staying true to themselves. Remaining relevant for various decades allows them to infect ear waves with anthem after anthem that reverberate with multiple generations' worth of listeners. This mentality resonates with the work that DJs do, as the DJs featured in this chapter all have to figure out ways to remain relevant, and (re)invent themselves for changing listeners, but also maintain a sonic integrity that allows them to sound timeless as cultural sonic curators. The outcome of mixing all the aforementioned ingredients shows exactly how DJs write their own sonic realities with a recipe for an outstanding musical meal each and every time we may encounter them in a contact zone when engaging in their craft.

The philosophy of boundless sonic inclusion, alongside the intellectual demeanor involved with assessing and critiquing sonic sources, are attributes exhibited by the DJ and demonstrated by the example of Rich Medina's career. When asked what type of music, or what genres of music he plays, Medina's answer was quite simple:

> I think I've been blessed that I haven't been pigeonholed into a categorization box as an artist. I play records with the Hip Hop guys, I play records with the House

music guys, with the 45s guys, with the obscure strange-Jazz-record guys . . . I'm able to function on a higher level in ALL those worlds . . . I dictate the way I play based on those parameters, not necessarily genre. (Medina, interview).

When Blind, James, and Lee talk about the vast expanse of music they both study and play, or when Mr.Len talks about the early years of Hip Hop and the DJ demanding the respect of club owners as Hip Hop emerged and solidified itself in popular culture, and when Medina talks about how he dictates what and how he plays, you can hear the rhetoric of Scott Lyons and his idea of rhetorical sovereignty. In highlighting and accessing what Indigenous students want and deserve in their education, Lyons argues that "rhetorical sovereignty is the inherent right and ability of *peoples* to determine their own communicative needs and desires in this pursuit, to decide for themselves the goals, modes, styles, and languages of public discourse . . . it also requires a radical rethinking of how and what we teach as the written word at all levels of schooling, from preschool to graduate curricula and beyond" (Lyons 449–450). This record must be mixed in conjunction with Karla Holloway's "Cultural Politics in the Academic Community: Masking the Color Line," in which Holloway discusses a graduate class she teaches called

"Diaspora Literacy: Black Women's Writing of the Third World." (I borrow the term "Diaspora literacy" from VèVè Clark, who defines it as a reader's "ability to comprehend the literatures of Africa, Afro-America, and the Caribbean from an informed, indigenous perspective.") . . . in that class, "reading" means educating ourselves, sometimes outside of our own cultures, so that we may appreciate the cultural expressivity and ways of representation of others. I believe that reading within the United States means the same thing. (615)

With both Lyons's and Holloway's work in the mix, it becomes critical to see how these DJs not only reach throughout various genres of music but also bring the Hip Hop DJ back to its rightful seat at the head of the African diasporic roundtable, carving the same positionality that has been long documented for the other elements of Hip Hop (MCing, breaking/b-boyin'/girlin', and graffiti). All of these DJs consider the DJ as reader and writer. When we delve deeper into their thoughts, the ideas they express uncover the aspect of the DJ as literary and cultural critic. Boogie Blind captures this sentiment well, when he shares:

Definitely there are DJs that should be considered writers. All DJs should, because all DJs have a certain way of how they do their thing. But when you talking about turntablism, for example, there are scratch notations. There are people that write out the scratches and actually, you know, scratch off the chart.

Like, you can read it like it's sheet music . . . depending on who you have—it's gotta be people that are qualified, that have *really* done it. But yes, I actually do. I think definitely—because you have to outline. There's always an outline, you know? There's an introduction, there's a beginning, there's a middle, and then it's like "peace out y'all, somebody's coming on next" (DJ Boogie Blind).

Hopefully this chapter helps to illustrate and solidify the Hip Hop DJ's specific cultural literacy with its own unique rhetorical and discursive practices. In closing, I will use three anecdotes:

Rich says he started playing records for people at age eight . . . but he started DJing at nineteen. By age three, Rich's son, Kamaal, had traveled with him to various parties and festivals in the front-facing baby carrier. Soon after, Rich was showing me video of Kamaal scratching records at age three—and scratching 45s, not to be confused with 12-inch records. Young Kamaal then developed to scratching and moving the crossfader. It was only a matter of time before—at age three—he was able to put both together in order to exhibit an elementary understanding of the modes and methods of DJ Rhetoric.

Boogie Blind was another DJ who tapped into the culture at a very young age (and he has the receipts to prove it). When I asked him how long he's been a DJ, his response was:

All my life. Starting around like five, six years old. I was able to blend directly. Like if you want to, call my uncle and have him verify that! When I grew up, that's all I knew—music. There was records everywhere. You know? My uncle DJed, my moms would supply the records. My grandmother had records, my grandfather had records. That's what it was. I can remember breaking needles, getting on punishment and all that shit. You know?

Finally, the outcome of Mr. Len's "Birthday 8-Track" research culminated in his actions early on in his career. Mr. Len's reputation in the inception of his DJ years was to come through to your party with some records, and he'd rock until he was tired. Then, his last song was ALWAYS a Company Flow record, from beginning to end, and then it would be dead silence. And Len would collect his records and leave the party completely, walking right out the door to silence after a CoFlo record . . . the name of the Company Flow album was *FunCrusher Plus*, so the folklore became "Yo—Len came through to funcrush my party."

I've just funcrushed "The Get Down Parts Keeps Gittin' Down: The DJ in the Center of the Comp 'Contact Zone'."

(Note: press play on "Funcrush Scratch" and listen to the entire 2:50 track)

Mr. Len of Company Flow, "Funcrush Scratch," *Funcrusher Plus*, Rawkus, 1997.

7

"LEARN LEVELS TO THIS WHOLE THANG . . . TRYING TO MAKE A SLOW CHANGE"
Spinnin' the Words for Comp3.0

> . . . just imagine where the state of Hip Hop is
> gonna be when the DJ jumps out the window.
> *I'm jumpin' out the window wit' this one!* Jump out the window man.
> Y'knowhutimsayin'? Jump out the window! . . . the DJ is and always will be
> responsible for Hip Hop. And that's it, Y'knowhutimsayin'?

P. Diddy (Combs), "Diddy Blog #37—A Message to the DJ," February 9, 2009, Web.

https://doi.org/10.7330/9781646424849.c007

Figure 7.1a and 7.1b. February 25, 2005, party flyer for an event: "The Legendary DJ Premier of Gang Starr with The Record Player and T. O. Double D" at Fluid Nightclub, Philadelphia.

Yo . . . this is flavor for the non-believes / Sit back, take a seat, and don't forget to pass the weed / And by the way, this is all the way live / and the way that I survive . . .

Havoc of Mobb Deep, "Flavor for the Non-Believes," *Juvenile Hell*, 4th & B'way / Island / Polygram Records, 1993, Vinyl/LP.

In concluding this journey, we find there are a few things to cover on the way to the last page. First, I want to make sure I leave some parting words on the Hip Hop DJ, and DJ Rhetoric and Literacy. Second, I want to expand on the implications of DJ Rhetoric and Literacy as they relate more broadly to Hip Hop scholarship and its positioning in Comp/Rhet. In true Hip Hop album fashion, no good outro is complete if it's not replete with chock full o' shout-outs. Finally, it's imperative to depart this project (although, as Nip would say, "the Marathon continues . . .") with a vision of what future possibilities and unrealized spaces could be beyond what I hope here is a solid contribution to how we see Hip Hop scholarship functioning in the academy in the twenty-first century. So in order to do this work, I aim to embody this entire textual sentiment based on a series of specific instances in this outro.

I'm really not sure how else to say this other than by spitting out the statement that Hip Hop saved me. It was the music and the culture that have always brought me through the toughest moments and the darkest days.

Being able to DJ has been the action that has always
sustained me. From that first time I saw those two turntables
in WSGS and fell into an indescribable love, to those first blends I
was making in my dorm room on the first floor of Auchincloss on my DJ
starter kit, through to the first outdoor party I DJed in the park in Newport,
Rhode Island, to the first solo party at Williams in Dodd and the first pair of
1200s compliments of the Williams College Black Student Union via Mecha
Brooks in 1993. From my first club gig at David's, through every party at
Williams, Harvard, and beyond, the craft of DJing has sustained me. It supported me through college, graduate school, and other times.

And to be honest, I don't know who or where I'd be without it.

So it just didn't feel right to complete a book on the DJ without including the flyer in figure 7.1. Clearly, it's important to a lot of different people
for a lot of different reasons. While it may seem minimal to some, my career
as a DJ culminated in a party when Matt Braun (aka The Record Player)
and I (T. O. Double D.—the name Havoc first called me) opened up for DJ
Premier. At this point, most people know who DJ Premier is, but in case you
don't, he is a legendary Hip Hop DJ and producer. Preem is arguably one
of the most influential DJ/Producers of all time when it comes to Hip Hop
culture. From his involvement as one half of the legendary Hip Hop group

Gang Starr (RIP to Guru), to his production credits that include a vast array
of musicians across over thirty years: Nas, The Notorious B.I.G. (RIP), Mobb
Deep, Anderson.Paak, AZ, Big Daddy Kane, Big L, Bumpy Knuckles, Bun B,
Christina Aguilera, Common, D'Angelo, Dilated Peoples, D.I.T.C., Dr. Dre,
Fat Joe, Game, Janet Jackson, Jay-Z, Joey Bada$$, Kanye West, KRS-One,
The Lady of Rage, Limp Bizkit, Lord Finesse, The LOX, Ludacris, Mac Miller
(RIP), M.O.P., Mos Def, O.C., Papoose, Rakim, Royce Da 5'9", Snoop Dogg,
Westside Gunn, Xzibit, and many, many more. And some might argue a
simple look at the flyer, the chain, and the star should do it. The second rea-
son including this flyer is integral to the text is it speaks to the ways in which
K for the Way ebbs and flows. It's evidence that demonstrates this project isn't
coming from a place that's ill-mannered or uninformed.

What makes me most proud of this image
is that you don't get your name on one of these flyers
during that time period if you're a wack DJ, simple and plain.
It also brings me to a place that allows me to reminisce on Preem's peoples,
who approached me in the booth and said, "We know who you are cousin. We
hearing you! Plus we know you Hav's cousin—real recognize real sun, word."
After opening up for Premier, the ways in which I played out as a DJ began to
wind down. After over a ten-year run, I opened up for one of my favorite all-
time DJs, one of my favorite DJs' favorite DJ. This is part of both the homage
but also the lineage that exists within our community. But for me, this was
when I moved further into teaching, writing, and interweaving the 1s and 2s
into both of those categories. It was at this time when I also began to figure
out I would need a doctorate to teach college English full time. But make no
mistake about it, there is a HUGE difference between "wind down" and "cease
and desist." I still buy records to this day. I still rock on 12s to this day (there
are four in our home, as well as two Vestax portables, a Hello Kitty Columbia
gp3 portable, a Fisher Price Classic Record Player, and an old "Record Player
in a Box" joint that's probably from a public school or somewhere no one can
remember). I still make mixtapes to this day. I still dig in the crates to this
day. I still have a radio show to this day (which is currently being relocated,
but *soon come, Starr . . .*). It is part of my constant rhetorical situation and
literacy that will always remain, that I will always carry with me. After all,
this DJ Literacy got me through high school, undergrad, grad school, up
and down the Eastern Seaboard and into Fluid nightclub in Philadelphia
(traveling that same corridor that Marley traveled), in the elevated DJ booth,

looking down on a crowd that I was rockin' with while sayin' to myself,
"Damn, in not too long, I'ma step down and Primo's gonna be up in here.
How real is *THAT?*"

DJ Premier is one of those great DJs who came before me; and no DJ is
worth his or her weight in vinyl if he or she didn't try to duplicate the "Code
of the Streets" test-tone scratch that Preem laid as the hook to the song back
in 1994. His legacy is a springboard to many DJs after him, and his existence
becomes a landmark in Hip Hop DJ textual/sonic lineage and in DJ/Producer
textual/sonic lineage as well. He is also a great testament to the fact that the
ways in which a DJ decides to express him- or herself and communicate that
expression among members within and outside of DJ culture via turntables
and the sounds they create with their arsenal/archive/collection of music has
everything to do with the sonic quality of the choices they make. So it moves
beyond just what gets said in songs by an MC or singer, and into the actual
sonics of the song: the frequency of what gets said in the song in conjunction
with the landscape of the musical background. How that DJ works and interacts "in the mix" with other pre-fixed songs and their sonic quality is what
comprises how a DJ communicates. Thus, DJ Rhetoric becomes the quality of
oral, written, and sonic language that displays and expresses sociocultural,
historical, and musical meanings, attitudes, and sentiments. From what gets
said in the songs to what gets looped in the break in the mix, from the part of
the song that gets cut up and scratched on the 1s and 2s to what gets chopped
and flipped in the sample . . . from what gets sprayed and laid on the walls
to what gets captured physically in the ambidextrous movements. Thus, DJ
Rhetoric communicates the values of Hip Hop culture, (re)shaping it as we
have known, now know, and will continue to know it. As Grandmaster Caz
said, if Hip Hop has (re)invented everything, the language used to describe
that scene and paint that picture comes directly from the culture's shaman-
istic cornerstone: the DJ. With this in mind, identifying DJ Literacy becomes
clear: the sonic and auditory practices of reading, writing, critically thinking, and speaking through and with the rhetoric of DJ culture. I have argued
in past years, still argue today as I type on this page, and will continue to
argue from tomorrow and beyond that we must begin to overstand this
chamber of Hip Hop, this most sacred element of the four (or five) if we are
to truly historicize and document our beloved music and culture. You can't
do it without acknowledging this science as actual fact . . . and that's word to
Matthew Africa, Timbuck2, Pam the Funkstress, and mad other mixologists

and turntable technicians, beat-blending specialists, scratch scientists, and musical grandmasters.

I've been blessed and fortunate enough to have a series of DJ landmarks, including a guest set on *Squeeze Radio* in front of DJs who acknowledged my turntable competencies; these are folks who would have told me I sounded like trash in a heartbeat if that was the case, for real. This good fortune extended into the roots of this book: a research project that spanned over about two years and involved me being in conversation with over *ninety* DJs across Hip Hop, across race and gender, across ethnicities, nationalities, and orientations. Those ninety people who opened their doors and homes, their offices and studios, and finally their phone lines and iChat audio and video connections to build with me on DJ culture were a set of people who really understood what I was trying to do and where I was trying to take this work. What also became humbling was that almost every one of these DJs at the end of the interview thanked me for including them in this project . . . to all of y'all: to have the time to rock with each of you, please know that the honor was really and truly all mine. But most important to me about opening up for DJ Premier is simply the idea that it allowed me, in my own small way, to inscribe myself into a small piece of Hip Hop music and culture (as well as DJ culture). Because the fact of the matter is not everyone gets to open up for Premier.

On the next record, the story that spins comes from my Hip Hop Worldview class. In an effort to help students think about sampling and the importance of the DJ/Producer, I assigned a YouTube video of a TEDx Talk with DJ/Producer Mark Ronson. After watching the video with the class, I opened up the discussion with my usual open-ended, "So what do y'all think?" The first response was from someone I'll call Joss. Her response was also the most powerful:

"Well, he's white, so at least people will listen to him."

I moved onto a few more students, not dismissing this comment but giving it a few seconds to breathe. Joss jumped back into the dialogue after a few students made comments about what they thought about sampling, getting a sense of how a piece of something could be reconfigured in the same way that Mark Ronson took the TEDx Talk theme song and reconfigured it sonically, live during his talk.

She came right back with "Yes, I agree with all that, with what everyone said. But let's be honest. Dude is white, so he is able to have the conversation in a way that other people can't. And when he talks, people will listen because he's white. But I guess that can be a good thing for Hip Hop."

The class went on, and we had formative discussion about race in Hip Hop culture. And class may have ended, but for the next forty-six hours, I could *not* stop thinking about Joss's statement. At the same time this was happening, I was simultaneously in the midst of a Hip Hop focused exchange in my group chat. We have a thread that consists of a group of Black men from my high school; because there were so few of us, we've continued to share a bond that spans from brothers who graduated from 1989 to 1995. I shared with the crew what happened in class. When I mentioned the part of the conversation where we discussed Mark Ronson, Miley Cyrus, Snoop Dogg, Nas, and Kanye, the Hip Hop heads amongst us were intrigued. One dude in our crew—who swears the UMCs were the best and only thing that happened in Hip Hop—was beefin' with me about inviting him to the class; we all know his appearance in my class would be like having that uncle everyone has and tries to keep contained to family functions. To keep it honest, you can't be havin' Uncle Pookie show up at your place of employment; you *will* get fired that day! One person said, "Point deduction for giving Cyrus legitimacy. Come on, man!"

My response was "Ronson mentioned her. I brought it back to Slick Rick. From Slick Rick over to GFK [Ghostface Killah]. Students went to Nas and Kanye." The next response was the handclapping emojis in triplicate, which was a sign I could carry on. Another question emerged: "If Miley Cyrus is being mentioned, is there some element of the conversation that touches on the term/concept 'culture vulture'???"

I explained that Ronson presented Cyrus, as he discussed her sampling of the song "La Di Da Di." I ended on a pensive note, sharing with the group that "one student went RIGHT in on the fact that Ronson's perspective was super white." With a very surface-level glance, one might try to read this as a race-based indictment on both Cyrus and Ronson. But this is not that at all. The fact that I included Ronson on my syllabus for a Hip Hop class speaks to the work he's done as both a DJ and producer. He's had his fingerprints on many a sonic soundtrack with some of my favorite artists. But there's no way I could deny Joss's words here, especially in a climate where there is an erasure of Black and

Brown voices speaking on Hip Hop scholarship in Comp/Rhet. Combine these actions with Rapsody and Talib's conversation about "Culture Over Everything" with regard to the foundation of Hip Hop culture, and Joss's words resonate even truer.

Joss's statement had already burrowed into my mental framework. As I continued to replay the quote over and over in my head, it finally dawned on me that it was resonating so much because of Nelson Flores and Jonathan Rosa. In their article "Undoing Appropriateness: Raciolinguistic Ideologies and Language Diversity in Education," they highlight the idea of raciolinguistic ideologies, which "conflate certain racialized bodies with linguistic deficiency unrelated to any objective linguistic practices" (Flores and Rosa 150). What's particularly interesting about Flores and Rosa is when they describe the effect of raciolinguistic ideologies on Heritage-language learners, long-term English Learners, and standard English learners, and when they mention Tamara—a long-term English learner who fluidly adjusts her language based on her listening public—they state the following:

> We find that these so-called long-term English learners are adept at using their bilingualism in strategic and innovative ways—indeed, in ways that might be considered quite appropriate and desirable were they animated by a privileged white student . . . were Tamara a privileged white student engaging in English linguistic practices in the ways that she did in this interview, her linguistic practices would likely be perceived differently. In fact, were she a privileged white student who was able to engage in the bilingual language practice that she described, she might even be perceived as linguistically gifted. (Flores and Rosa 158)

When I made this connection, the comment in the class began to loom even heavier on my psyche. I began to wonder if in a moment in front of a multicultural class of primarily Black and Brown students, I had created a situation that devalued each and every student of color, when all they are doing sitting in my "Hip Hop Worldview" class is trying to figure out a way to (re)inscribe themselves into a small portion of the academic fabric and landscape . . . knowing that they feel most comfortable making that move through the lens of Hip Hop culture?

This (re)inscription is steeped in the rhetoric of social justice and equity and is evident in Carmen Kynard's book *Vernacular Insurrections: Race, Black Protest, and the New Century in Composition-Literacies Studies*. I am drawn to how Kynard sees the rhetorical site of her classroom as acutely and uncompromisingly Black: a much-needed space for Black and Brown students in urban educational systems, one that is empowering for and nurturing within the Black community, with Hip Hop (and specifically in this case, the Wu-Tang Clan) as the spectrum by which this critical and culturally relevant education unfolds. When Kynard talks about her high school teaching experiences and reflects on her Hip Hop conversations with students (which mostly entail her trying to make fun of kids' love for the Wu-Tang Clan), she highlights her student Raynard, who is able to write a fifteen-page essay that included narrative of how Hip Hop helped to save the day when brought into conversation with a funny-looking teacher that resembled her. After hearing Raynard read his essay aloud to the class, Kynard recalls:

> I never snapped on the Wu again, though I have thought about it from time to time. Raynard, place, time, language, and culture now had a different place in this class and so did the role of African American Language (AAL) and rhetoric in writing: you could convey fiction, fantasy, sociological perspectives, and personal narrative all in one fell swoop and get all of your audience—your homies and your foes—to move their thinking and style your way. If we take Raynard and transpose him onto the histories of black protest literacies in higher education, we will see that there is nothing new about the ways that Raynard is shifting the landscape of the classroom with his knowledge system, his literacies, and his language. Black students have always done this, whether we want, welcome, understand, require, study, or like it. (Kynard, *Vernacular Insurrections* 23–24)

It is this common thread, one that starts in a space long before Raynard, and continues on past him and into spaces with Joss, and continues on even past my classroom spaces, that made me think about the importance of Hip Hop's rhetorical power and savvy and the work that people of color in the academy continue to do by any means and at all costs. It is not only Black students but Black people (and Black culture) who have always done this work; I argue Hip Hop—as part of a Black cultural, musical, and radical tradition—has also done this work. And since the Hip Hop DJ sits in the forefront of the movement, this is work that the DJ does in exemplifying both rhetoric and literacy through a specific lens.

This brings us back to Talib and Rapsody's conversation about the phrase "Culture Over Everything" and how the pro-Black sentiment baked within it functions sans "anti-white" philosophies and is predicated on their mutual agreement in describing the essence of the culture as starting "with Black and Brown people, and anyone in the culture has to recognize that . . . Black and Brown, disenfranchised and poor" (Talib Kweli and Rapsody, qtd. in Kweli). It is, after all, the work that allows us to (re)define and (re)inscribe ourselves in the academic fabric and landscape. So as Joss and Raynard and Flores and Rosa continue to flood my mental, I got to thinking about what Comp3.0 (Craig, "The Intergenerational Blunder") might look like.

I envision Comp3.0 based on the conversation that started this text: the erasure of critical voices of color in the field when thinking about who gets to tell our story . . . and why. This is a question Adam Banks grappled with as well, dating back to his own scholarship. Banks gave us the blueprint to Comp 2.0 in *Digital Griots: African American Rhetoric in a Multimedia Age*; in Comp3.0, I contend that we have to push the scope of writing and rhetoric—with or without the field's permission or acknowledgment. Moments like Drs. Khirsten Scott and Louis Maraj creating DBLAC (Digital Black Lit and Composition) ask no permission while moving homies and foes toward that power and style, self-care, and collective agency required of writing and rhetoric. An organization created *by* Black and Brown graduate students of color *for* Black and Brown graduate students of color as well as other BIPOC scholars, writers, and thinkers, DBLAC never once in its formation or progression *asked* the field what it could do. Instead, as a collective, members created and forwarded an agenda based on the needs of graduate students of color in the twenty-first century, using both physical landscapes and digital spaces to (re)inscribe themselves into the fabric of the field . . . with or without permission. Dr. Bilal Polson, an elementary school principal who is broadening the canon on culturally sustaining and relevant pedagogies, has been going strong with the #literacylineage movement; a daily IG post with the picture of a record label is bringing people from academics to music moguls into a conversation about the music that has changed our lives. Polson and I have been cookin' up expanding the idea of textual lineage (Tatum) into sonic lineage (Craig, "Stacks"; Polson): using sonic compositions and expressions of Hip Hop and its roots to (re)inscribe the writing and rhetoric of African-American culture in the field and beyond. All of our abilities to congregate in cyberspaces that, oftentimes,

Black folks aren't credited with being able to initiate and nimbly navigate
with the BOOM-BAP as our Wakanda Forever signal, has been happening
since before #HipHopEd was a few heads talking about beats and rhymes in
academia . . . with and without permission . . .

This work becomes critically important for scholars like DJ Kuttin
Kandi—aka "the People's Hip Hop DJ Scholar" (who was also recently dubbed
"Dr. Kuttin Kandi" by her West Coast peers)—who, as a graduate student
at UC San Diego, was having difficulty finding her way into teaching a Hip
Hop course, even though Hip Hop culture knows her as cultural practitio-
ner, organic intellectual, and bad-ass turntable-rockin' Kuttin Kandi. She's
already solidified, deeply inscribed into the cultural landscape of DJ Rhetoric
and Literacy—a certified veteran in the culture. Somehow, there is a push
to (re)write herstory, instead of honoring her legacy in a way captured by
Rapsody, when in "Oprah," she states, "I'ma Master / y'all should gimme hon-
orary masters / rapper work the green like the Masters" (Rapsody).
Seeing this take place and allowing it to unfold is dangerous for the culture
in the worst way. That's why we need to advocate for folks like Popmaster
Fabel, 9th Wonder, and Wes Jackson, as they're opening doors for Ca$h
Money and Rich Medina, April Walker, and Bobbito Garcia to come through
and talk about Hip Hop culture within college classrooms, especially when
we know other Hip Hop cultural practitioners and organic intellectuals like
Kandi have been gatekept. For me, bringing BreakBeat Lou and
Mr. Len onto my college campus to discuss DJing as an
act of writing was paramount to what
a Comp3.0 could look like.

So sonic lineage moves my work
to extend outward toward Sound Studies and
Sonic Rhetorics. Comp3.0 has the potential to allow us to move
through myriad field(s) in ways that situate and validate the importance
of our work and contributions, while widening the ideas of what scholarly
research and dialogue can look like through the lens of Hip Hop—with or
without permission. I see hope for this movement in moments like A. D.
Carson dropping an album on University of Michigan Press: uncompromisingly scholarly . . . uncompromisingly authentic . . . uncompromisingly
Hip Hop . . .

Artist/scholars like A. D., Kandi, and Jason Rawls (aka DJ/Producer J. Rawls) are embodiments of the rhetorical practices of Hip Hop. In their work, they will always engage with a critical lens that is grounded in Hip Hop culture. The scholars of Comp3.0 won't be scholars who have an affinity for Hip Hop listening, or even thinkers who occasionally partake in Hip Hop stylings from time to time. Scholars coming up in Comp3.0 *have only ever* known Hip Hop as global popular culture. This means that music, images (both still and moving), social media, clothing, style aesthetics, and linguistic functionalities are both entrenched in and predicated on a music and culture that was once deemed "a passing phase" and sometimes "a fad that'll soon die out." But Hip Hop has always provided and infused the much-needed ingredient to popular culture's recipe. This idea sits at the core of the Mobb Deep song "Flavor for the Non-Believes." We knew what it was since a seventeen-year-old Havoc scrawled the words on the page in 1991, spitting: "Yo . . . this is flavor for the non-believes / Sit back, take a seat, and don't forget to pass the weed / And by the way, this is all the way live / and the way that I survive . . ." (Havoc in Mobb Deep, "Flavor"). The song speaks to the premise of giving the doubters and nonbelievers yet another instance that proves them wrong. This has been the life trajectory of Hip Hop: proving all who had no faith in its power and relevance . . . wrong . . . never asking, and *always* without permission. To quickly put it in perspective, think about how President Obama continues to have a year-end playlist that heavily incorporates Hip Hop, while our forty-fifth president claimed to intervene on A$AP Rocky's behalf with his international arrest, and his subsequent release. For me, that trajectory is quite similar to the way Detroit wordsmith eLZhi sums it up in the song "Pros and Cons." My positionality emerges from "the pro-Black self-proclaimed freedom fighters / that licked the shot after prohibition toward aggressors / that created programs for the kids whose now professors / who otherwise wouldn't be prone to make it out on they own" (eLZhi and Muldrow). Indeed, Hip Hop was that program for me. And it gave me permission when no one else in the academy would . . .

Even in this space, as we reflect on the Hip Hop DJ in *K for the Way*, writing this text cannot be complete without the voices of the DJs who are present on the page and exist in the spirit of the project. In conjunction with this marriage, there is no way that this text could honor the Hip Hop DJ without each and every song quote and reference, that, when sequenced together, do the work of Hip Hop DJ mixtape rhetoric. As I type this chapter, I aim to embody the rhetorical savvy of the Hip Hop DJ, even as the words shift left to right, like records cycling through on the turntables in a DJ set . . . like Rich Medina talking about the "left hand–right hand motion" that every DJ aims to perfect.

When I originally embarked on this journey and interviewed the first DJ in my research study, I never thought I'd be engaged in this process for over ten years. In the decade that this book was created, revised, and finalized, so much has happened: I completed a doctoral degree, earned tenure, and helped to raise my daughters Kaylee and Julia, ushering them into this world. We've also had to live through a global pandemic and public health crisis not seen in almost a century. Who would've thought the landscape of DJ culture would change so dramatically in ten years? It was an idea I discussed recently with the homie DJ A.Vee: a stalwart in the New York City DJ community, who is well known and respected globally. When talking about just how deep the changes are to DJ culture, A.Vee was clear: "Things will NEVER go back to how they were pre-pandemic." The exponentially decreased attention span of the average clubgoer has made the DJ experience less about a DJ leading you through a moment and more about documenting (with video footage) being in a moment that just so happens to include a DJ. Then, there's the immediate captioning of said video, followed by instant uploading of the video. A.Vee shared with me that while one could argue that captioning and uploading could happen the next day, the modern sentiment is to stop and do it "right now"—to show that you were outside *right then*—and a part of the vibe right then. Ironically, by the time you complete the video, the captioning, and the uploading, you've probably disconnected from the vibe you're trying to show you're a part of. How does a DJ even maneuver when *this* behavior is the wave? When addressing this new climate, A.Vee put it real simple. He said, "I'm fortunate enough to have really good friends and some great long-lasting relationships. And as a DJ, you learn
to adjust and adapt as needed. And when the time comes
when I no longer want to make those adjustments,
I'm sure I'll be the first to know . . ."

We could look at these words
as an ominous foreshadowing of an impending
end of an era. But hasn't this *always* been a narrative that serves as an
undercurrent for DJ culture? Fifteen years ago, we wondered how Serato
would "change the DJ game." Yet here we are, with 99 percent of the DJs with a
computer in front of them using Serato (which will probably be on its twenty-
second anniversary when you're reading this). Thus, the shrinking attention
span seems to be just another fork in the road for how DJ culture will adapt

and evolve. But inherent in this moment is still the premise that the DJ must captivate, tell a story, educate the partygoers, and figure out how to do that work in a unique and creative way . . . while adapting and adjusting, yet remaining steadfast in *not* compromising one's sonic integrity.

This, too, is a critical element of
Comp3.0—doing the educational work and engaging in the
liberatory practices that people **need** in order to take their mind
off the oppressive nature of the pandemic and the mundane stop-and-go of
repeated quarantines. D-Nice led the way during the Lockdown of
2020 phase. DJs like A.Vee carry that torch now that we've
made our way back outside.

In the book *Hip-Hop within and without the Academy*, authors Karen Snell and Johan Soderman reference a series of interviews with some of the people considered the first wave of scholars doing work in the emerging field of Hip Hop studies. At one point, in discussing the concerns that early "hip-hop scholars" had with the label, Hip Hop scholar Ted says, "When I met Alexandra in the 90s, she said something that struck me for years. She said: I hope ten years from now that I'll not be talking about hip-hop" (Snell and Soderman 90). Interestingly enough for me, I actually hope I'm able to still do this work ten years from now—so that the next graduate student persevering racism in a doctoral program might see these words and feel a better sense of belonging to a lineage that allows them to push a little further, and strive just a little bit harder. I hope this work can continue to resonate for the undergrads who need it, too. And for emerging scholars in the field on that tenure track, too. By 2023, Hip Hop will be living and breathing as a culture that has thrived for fifty years. Be clear that Comp3.0 includes a new wave of scholars who *only* know a world with Hip Hop in it. How we, then, make sense of this in the academy is important. We all need to work together to nurture and cultivate one another, to continue to advance the bounds of where our work can go with Hip Hop as the lens. When I envision Writing Studies and Rhetoric, I hope to be relevant, writing both timely and meaningfully about Hip Hop because through that global culture will come the scholars who will give us the full-blown version of Comp3.0 and beyond. I hope to be a part of helping that movement along, by situating the Hip Hop DJ and the rhetorical savvy that comes along with that role, and by helping emerging scholars to navigate both the joys and pitfalls

of the field . . . and learning how to move through it all,
with Hip Hop in their hearts and souls,
through their pens and onto pages . . .
with or without permission . . .

As I skate, I leave you with the words of Hip Hop artist/producer Oh No:

Feel it! It's been a long time comin', but we are here now! Uh-huh, yeah, we are here now! Uh-huh! Yeah, listen . . . (Oh No)

English Studies . . . the DJ has just exited the building . . . infinite thanks for listening, word . . .

. . . cli-click . . . cli-click . . . cli-click . . .

(the sound the needle makes at the very end of the record when it's hitting the label)

"Most evenings, I be staring at a beat and seeing murder /
       I was gifted as a child / Granny listened and said it /
             told me to never bury my talents / give it and spread it . . ."*

Carson, A. D., "Ampersand," *I Used to Love to Dream* (University of Michigan Press, 2020).

BIBLIOGRAPHY

Achebe, Chinua. *Morning Yet on Creation Day: Essays*. Garden City, NY: Anchor Press. 1975. Print.

Ahmad Jamal. "Jamal Plays Jamal." *Swahililand*. 20th Century, 1974. Vinyl/LP.

Alexander-Floyd, Nikol G. "Disappearing Acts: Reclaiming Intersectionality in the Social Sciences in a Post–Black Feminist Era." *Feminist Formations* 24.1 (2012): 1–25. Print.

Alim, H. Samy. "'The Natti Ain't No Punk City': Emic Views of Hip Hop Cultures." *Callaloo* 29.3 (2006): 969–990. Print.

Alim, H. Samy. *Roc the Mic Right: The Language of Hip Hop Culture*. New York: Routledge, 2006. Print.

Alim, H. Samy, and John Baugh, eds. *Talkin Black Talk: Language, Education, and Social Change*. New York: Teachers College Press, 2006. Print.

Alim, H. Samy, Awad Ibrahim, and Alastair Pennycook. *Global Linguistic Flows: Hip Hop Cultures, Youth Identities, and the Politics of Language*. New York: Routledge, 2008. Print.

All the Streets Are Silent: The Convergence of Hip Hop and Skateboarding (1987–1997). Dir. Jeremy Elkin. Perf. Eli Morgan Gesner, Jeff Pang, Fab 5 Freddy, Rosario Dawson, and DJ Clark Kent. Music by Large Professor. Elkin Editions, 2021. DVD.

Anzaldúa, Gloria, and Cherríe Moraga. *This Bridge Called My Back: Writings by Radical Women of Color*. New York: Kitchen Table, Women of Color Press, 1983. Print.

Armani White. "Billie Eilish." Legendbound / Def Jam Records, 2022. Mp3.

Artifacts featuring Busta Rhymes. "C'Mon Wit Da Git Down." *Between a Rock and a Hard Place*. Big Beat Records, 1994. Vinyl.

A Tribe Called Quest. "Bonita Applebum." *Peoples Instinctive Travels and the Paths of Rhythm*. Jive Records, 1990. Vinyl/LP.

A Tribe Called Quest. "Bonita Applebum (Hootie Mix)." Jive Records, 1990. Vinyl.

A Tribe Called Quest. "Check the Rhime." *The Low End Theory*. Jive Records, 1991. Vinyl/LP.

A Tribe Called Quest. "If the Papes Come." *Peoples Instinctive Travels and the Paths of Rhythm*. Jive Records, 1990. Vinyl/LP.

A Tribe Called Quest. "Jazz (We've Got)." *The Low End Theory*. Jive Records, 1991. Vinyl/LP.

A Tribe Called Quest. "Scenario (Remix)." Jive Records, 1992. Vinyl/LP.

Attias, Bernardo A. "Meditations on the Death of Vinyl." *Dancecult: Journal of Electronic Dance Music Culture* 3.1 (2011). https://dj.dancecult.net/index.php/dancecult/article/view/321/315.

https://doi.org/10.7330/9781646424849.c008

Baker, Houston A. *Black Studies, Rap, and the Academy*. Chicago: University of Chicago Press, 1993. Print.

Ball, Jared. *I Mix What I Like! A Mixtape Manifesto*. Oakland, CA: AK Press, 2011. Print.

Banks, Adam. *Digital Griots: African American Rhetoric in a Multimedia Age*. Carbondale: Southern Illinois University Press, 2011. Print.

Barriball, Louise K., and Alison While. "Collecting Data Using a Semi-structured Interview: A Discussion Paper." *Journal of Advanced Nursing* 19.1 (1994): 328–335. Print.

Bartlett, Andrew. "Airshafts, Loudspeakers, and the Hip Hop sample: Contexts and African American Musical Aesthetics." *African American Review* 28.4 (1994): 639–652. Print.

Beacham, Kevin. Personal interview. 18 Jan. 2012.

Becker, Carol, Romi Crawford, and Paul Miller. "An Interview with Paul D. Miller a.k.a. Dj Spooky—That Subliminal Kid." *Art Journal* 61.1 (2002): 82–91. Print.

Bell Biv Devoe. "Poison." *Poison*. MCA Records, 1990. Vinyl/LP.

Benard, Akeia A. F. "Colonizing Black Female Bodies within Patriarchal Capitalism: Feminist and Human Rights Perspectives." *Sexualization, Media, and Society* 2.4.2016. https://doi.org/10.1177/2374623816680622.

Benja Styles. Personal interview. 22 Dec. 2011.

Berube, Michael. *The Employment of English: Theory, Jobs, and the Future of Literary Studies*. New York: New York University Press, 1998. Print.

Big Daddy Kane. "Young, Gifted and Black." *It's a Big Daddy Thing*. Cold Chillin' / Reprise / Warner Bros. Records, 1989. Vinyl/LP.

Bilge, Sirma. "Intersectionality Undone: Saving Intersectionality from Feminist Intersectionality Studies." *Du Bois Review: Social Science Research on Race* 10.2 (2013): 405–424. Print.

Bishop, Wendy. "Steal This Assignment: The Radical Revision." *Practice in Context: Situating the Work of Writing Teachers*, ed. Cindy Moore and Peggy O'Neill, 205–221. Urbana, IL: National Council of Teachers of English, 2002. Print.

Black Star. *Mos Def and Talib Kweli are Black Star*. Rawkus Records, 1998. Vinyl/LP.

Blue Sky Black Death and Jean Grae featuring Chen Lo. "Threats." *The Evil Jeanius*. Babygrande Records, 2008. Mp3.

Bobbito Garcia. Personal interview. 11 Jan. 2012.

Bobby Brown. "Don't Be Cruel." *Don't Be Cruel*. MCA Records, 1988. Vinyl/LP.

Bob James. "Nautilus." *One*. CTI Records, 1974. Vinyl/LP.

Boogie Down Productions. "I'm Still Number One." *By All Means Necessary*. Jive Records, 1998. Vinyl/LP.

Bowen, Glenn A. "Preparing a Qualitative Research-Based Dissertation: Lessons Learned." *Qualitative Report* 10.2 (2005): 208–222. Print.

Boyles, Brian. "Push It: DJ Spinderella Returns to Essence as an Ambassador of Hip-Hop's Golden Era." *Offbeat.com*, 26–27. 2012. Web.

Bradley, Adam. *Book of Rhymes: The Poetics of Hip Hop*. New York: Perseus Books, 2009. Print.

BreakBeat Lou. *Da Diggin' Ek-Suh-Bish-uhn: A Brief Revelation of The Genuine Article's Crates*. UBB Entertainment, 2012. CD.

BreakBeat Lou. Personal interview. 6 June 2011.

BreakBeat Lou, and Ben Ortiz. Personal Interview. 21 Aug. 2012.

Brewster, Bill, and Frank Broughton. *last night a dj saved my life: the history of the disc jockey*. New York: Grove Press, 2000. Print.

Brewster, Bill, and Frank Broughton. *The Record Players: DJ Revolutionaries*. New York: Black Cat, 2010. Print.

Brown, Lee Ann. *Polyverse*. Sun & Moon Press, 1999. Print.

Brownstone. "If You Love Me." *From the Bottom Up*. Epic/MJJ Records, 1995. Vinyl/LP.

Bumpy Knuckles aka Freddie Foxxx. "Change." *Leaks Vol. 1*. Gracie Catalog, 2011. Mp3.

Busta Rhymes. "Put Your Hands Where My Eyes Can See." *When Disaster Strikes . . .* Flipmode/Elektra Records, 1997. Vinyl/LP.

Busta Rhymes featuring Bell Biv Devoe. "Outta My Mind." *Extinction Level Event 2: The Wrath of God*. Conglomerate/Empire Records, 2020. Mp3.

Busta Rhymes featuring Swizz Beatz. "New York Shit." *The Big Bang*. Flipmode/ Aftermath/Interscope Records, 2006. CD.

Campbell, Kermit. *Gettin' Our Groove On: Rhetoric, Language, and Literacy for the Hip Hop Generation*. Detroit: Wayne State University Press, 2005. Print.

Capone-N-Noreaga. "Bloody Money." *The War Report*. Penalty Records, 1997. Vinyl.

Capone-N-Noreaga featuring Tragedy Khadafi. "T.ON.Y. (Top of New York)." *The War Report*. Penalty Records, 1997. Vinyl.

Carson, A. D. "Ampersand." In *I Used to Love to Dream*. Ann Arbor: University of Michigan Press, 2020. Print.

Ca\$h Money and Marvelous. "Ugly People Be Quiet." *Where's the Party At?* Sleeping Bag Records, 1988. Vinyl/LP.

Catalyst. "Uzuri." *Perception*. Cobblestone, 1972. Vinyl/LP.

CB4. Dir. Tamra Davis. Perf. Chris Rock. Universal Pictures, 1993. Film.

CCCC. "Students' Right to Their Own Language." Special issue of *College Composition and Communication* (National Council of Teachers of English). 1974. https://prod -ncte-cdn.azureedge.net/nctefiles/groups/cccc/newsrtol.pdf.

Chairman Mao. Personal interview. 12 Oct. 2012.

Chandrasoma, Ranamukalage, Celia Thompson, and Alastair Pennycook. "Beyond Plagiarism: Transgressive and Nontransgressive Intertextuality." *Journal of Language, Identity, and Education* 3.3 (2004): 171–193. Print.

Chang, Jeff. *Can't Stop Won't Stop: A History of the Hip-Hop Generation*. New York: St. Martin's Press, 2007. Print.

Chang, Jeff, ed. *Total Chaos: The Art and Aesthetics of Hip-Hop*. New York: Civitas Books. 2006. Print.

Charnas, Dan. *Dilla Time: The Life and Afterlife of J Dilla, the Hip-Hop Producer Who Reinvented Rhythm*. 2002. Print.

Chedda Da Connect. "Flicka Da Wrist." eOne Entertainment, 2015. Web.

Chinx Drugz featuring French Montana. "I'm a Coke Boy." *Cocaine Riot 2*. Coke Boys Records, 2012. CD.

Christie Z-Pabon. Personal interview. 26 Oct. 2011.

Clear, Duval. "Me & The Biz." *YouTube*, 10 Nov. 2007. https://www.youtube.com/watch?v=-mlLGsTNwmg.

Clinton, George. Interview by Mo'Nique. *The Mo'Nique Show*. BET, 26 Feb. 2010. Television.

Cobb, William Jelani. *To the Break of Dawn: A Freestyle on the Hip-Hop Aesthetic*. New York: NYU Press, 2007. Print.

Cohen, D., and B. Crabtree. "Qualitative Research Guidelines Project." July 2006. http://www.qualres.org/HomeSemi-3629.html.

Coleman, Brian. *Check the Technique: Liner Notes for Hip-Hop Junkies*. New York: Villard, 2007. Print.

Combs, Sean. "Diddy Blog #37—A Message to the DJ." *YouTube*, 6 Feb. 2009. https://www.youtube.com/watch?v=fssPp8xmV5U.

Common. "Testify." *Be*. G.O.O.D. Music/Geffen Records, 2005. Vinyl/LP.

Common featuring The Last Poets. "The Corner." *Be*. G.O.O.D. Music / Geffen Records, 2005. Vinyl/LP.

Company Flow. "Funcrush Scratch." *Funcrusher Plus*. Rawkus, 1997. Vinyl.

Cooper, Brittney. "Intersectionality." In *The Oxford Handbook of Feminist Theory*, ed. Lisa Disch and Mary Hawkesworth, 355–406. New York: Oxford University Press, 2015. Print.

Cooper, Brittney C., Susana M. Morris, and Robin M. Boylorn. *The Crunk Feminist Collection*. New York: Feminist Press, 2015. Print.

Cosmo Baker. Personal interview. 12 Oct. 2011.

Cosmo Baker. Personal interview. 14 Oct. 2011.

Craig, Todd. "The Intergenerational Blunder of Elitism as Fun(k)tionality, aka An Open Letter on Choices When 'Keepin' It Real Goes Wrong . . .'" *Composition Studies* 49.1 (2021): 125–205. Print.

Craig, Todd. "'Jackin' for Beats': DJing for Citation Critique." *Radical Teacher* 97 (28 Oct. 2013): 20–29. Print.

Craig, Todd. "'Makin' Somethin' Outta Little-to-Nufin'': Racism, Revision and Rotating Records—The Hip-Hop DJ in Composition Praxis." *Changing English* 22.4 (2015): 349–364. Print.

Craig, Todd. "'Stacks, Sounds and a Record a Day': An Introduction to DJ Rhetoric and Sonic Lineage in Praxis." *Rhetoric, Politics and Culture*. Forthcoming.

Craig, Todd. "'Tell Virgil Write BRICK on My Brick': Doctoral Bashments, (Re)Visiting Hiphopography and the Digital Discursivity of the DJ. A Mixed Down Methods Movement." In *Methods and Methodologies for Research in Digital Writing and Rhetoric Centering Positionality in Computers and Writing Scholarship*. Vol. 1, ed. Crystal VanKooten and Victor Del Hierro, 87–107. Fort Collins, CO: WAC Clearinghouse, 2022. Print.

Crenshaw, Kimberlé. "Demarginalizing the Intersection of Race and Sex: A Black Feminist Critique of Antidiscrimination Doctrine, Feminist Theory, and Antiracist Politics." *University of Chicago Legal Forum*, no. 1 (1989): 139–167. Print.

Crenshaw, Kimberlé. "Mapping the Margins: Intersectionality, Identity Politics, and Violence against Women of Color." *Stanford Law Review* 43.6 (1991): 1241–1299. Print.

Crenshaw, Kimberlé Williams. "From Private Violence to Mass Incarceration: Thinking Intersectionally about Women, Race, and Social Control." *UCLA Law Review* 59 (2012): 1419–1472. Print.

Creswell, John W. *Qualitative Inquiry and Research Design: Choosing among Five Traditions.* Thousand Oaks, CA: Sage Publications, 1998. Print.

Cymande. "The Message." *Cymande.* Janus, 1972. Vinyl/LP.

Cypress Hill. 1991. "How I Could Just Kill a Man." *Cypress Hill.* Ruffhouse/Columbia/SME Records, 1972. Vinyl/LP.

Da Youngsta's. "Pass Da Mic." *Somethin 4 Da Youngsta's.* East West / Atlantic Records, 1992. Vinyl/LP.

Dej Loaf. "Try Me." IBGM/Columbia Records, 2014. Mp3.

De La Soul. "The Magic Number." *3 Feet High and Rising*, Tommy Boy / Warner Bros. Records, 1989. Vinyl/LP.

De La Soul. "Plug Tunin'." *3 Feet High and Rising.* Tommy Boy / Warner Bros. Records, 1989. Vinyl/LP.

De La Soul. "Stakes Is High." *Stakes Is High.* Tommy Boy / Warner Bros., 1996. Vinyl/LP.

De La Soul. *3 Feet High and Rising.* Tommy Boy / Warner Bros. Records, 1989. Vinyl/LP.

Denise, DJ Lynnée. "The Afterlife of Aretha Franklin's 'Rock Steady': A Case Study in DJ Scholarship." *Black Scholar* 49.3 (2019): 62–72. Print.

Digable Planets. "Rebirth of Slick (Cool Like Dat)." *Reachin' (A New Refutation of Time and Space).* Pendulum/Elektra Records, 1993. Vinyl/LP.

Dimitriadis, Greg. *Performing Identity / Performing Culture: Hip Hop as Text, Pedagogy, and Lived Practice.* New York: Peter Lang, 2009. Print.

Diones, Jeff. Personal interview. 18 Mar. 2011.

DJ A.Vee. Personal interview. 5 Jan. 2012.

DJ Bear-One. Personal interview. 7 Jan. 2021.

DJ Boogie Blind. Personal interview. 7 Oct. 2011.

DJ Ca$h Money. Personal interview. 1 Nov. 2011.

DJ Clark Kent. Personal interview. 1 Aug. 2011.

DJ Eclipse. Personal interview. 12 Sept. 2011.

DJ Evil Dee. Personal interview. 14 July 2011.

DJ Jazzy Jeff. Personal interview. 21 Sept. 2011.

DJ JS-1. Personal interview. 5 Feb. 2012.

DJ Khaled. "All I Do Is Win." *Victory.* We The Best / Terror Squad / E1 Records, 2010. CD.

DJ Khaled featuring Drake. "For Free." *Major Key.* We The Best / Epic Records, 2016. CD.

DJ Krush. *Meiso.* Full Frequency / PGD Records, 1995. Vinyl/LP.

DJ Kuttin Kandi. Personal interview. 2 Dec. 2011.

DJ Matthew Africa. Personal interview. 14 Nov. 2011.

DJ Mick Boogie. Personal interview. 24 Jan. 2012.

DJ Reborn. Personal interview. 12 Sept. 2011.

DJ Revolution. Personal interview. 5 Aug. 2011.

DJ Rhettmatic. Personal interview. 27 June 2011.

DJ Scratch. *The Master of the Mix.* BET, 4 Dec. 2011. Television.

DJ Shortkut. Personal interview. 13 Oct. 2011.

DJ Shorty Wop. Personal interview. 7 Dec. 2011.

DJ Spinderella. Personal interview. 28 Dec. 2011.

DJ Spinna. Personal interview. 20 May 2011.

DJ Timbuck2. Personal interview. 10 Nov. 2011.

DJ Tony Touch. Personal interview. 10 Nov. 2011.

DJ Ultraviolet. Personal interview. 9 Nov. 2011.

Doug E. Fresh and the Get Fresh Crew. "La Di Da Di." Reality/Fantasy Records, 1985. Vinyl/LP.

DuBois, W. E. B. *The Negro Problem: A Series of Articles by Representative American Negroes of to-Day.* New York: James Pott and Company, 1903. Print.

Durham, Aisha, Brittney C. Cooper, and Susana M. Morris. "The Stage Hip-Hop Feminism Built: A New Directions Essay." *Signs* 38.3 (2013): 721–737. Print.

Dyson, Michael Eric. *Between God and Gangsta Rap.* New York: Oxford University Press, 1995. Print.

Ellison, Ralph. *Invisible Man.* New York: Vintage, 1995. Print.

eLZhi, and Georgia Anne Muldrow. "Pros and Cons." *Zhigeist.* Nature Sounds, 2022. TIDAL streaming service.

Emdin, Christopher. *For White Folks Who Teach in the Hood . . . and the Rest of Y'all Too: Reality Pedagogy and Urban Education.* Boston: Beacon Press, 2016. Print.

Eminem. "Untitled." *Recovery.* Aftermath/Interscope/Shady Records, 2010. CD.

The Fab 5 (Heltah Skeltah and O.G.C.). "Leflaur Leflah Eshkoshka." Duck Down / Priority / EMI Records, 1995. Vinyl.

Fabolous. "For the Love." *S.O.U.L. Tape II.* My Fabulous Life, 2012. CD.

Fashawn + Alchemist. "Po for President." *FASH-ionably Late.* Mass Appeal Records, 2014. CD.

Fat Joe and Remy Ma featuring French Montana and Infared. "All the Way Up." *Plata O Plomo.* Terror Squad / E1 Records, 2016. TIDAL streaming service.

Fat Joe and Remy Ma featuring RySoValid. "Cookin." *Plata o Plomo.* Terror Squad / E1 Records, 2016. TIDAL streaming service.

Flores, Nelson, and Jonathan Rosa. "Undoing Appropriateness: Raciolinguistic Ideologies and Language Diversity in Education." *Harvard Educational Review* 85.2 (2015): 149–171. Print.

Force MD's. "Itchin' for a Scratch." Tommy Boy Records, 1985. Vinyl/LP.

Forman, Murray, and Mark Anthony Neal. *That's the Joint!: the Hip-Hop Studies Reader.* New York: Routledge, 2004.

Freddie Foxxx. Personal interview. 30 Sept. 2011.

Freire, Paolo. *Pedagogy of the Oppressed: New Revised Twentieth-Anniversary Edition.* New York: Continuum, 1998. Print.

French Montana. "Shot Caller." *Mr. 16: Casino Life.* Bad Boy / Interscope Records, 2012. CD.

French Montana featuring Chinx Drugs and N.O.R.E. "Off the Rip." *Casino Life 2: Brown Bag Legend.* Coke Boys / Bad Boy / Maybach Music Group / Interscope Records, 2015. CD.

French Montana featuring Nicki Minaj. "Freaks." *Excuse My French*. Bad Boy / Maybach Music Group / Interscope Records, 2013. CD.

Fugees. "Killing Me Softly." *The Score*. Ruffhouse/Columbia Records, 1996. Vinyl/LP.

Fugees. "Ready or Not." *The Score*. Ruffhouse/Columbia Records, 1996. Vinyl/LP.

Gang Starr. "Code of the Streets." *Hard to Earn*. Chrysalis/EMI Records, 1994. Vinyl/LP.

Gang Starr. "Mostly Tha Voice." *Hard to Earn*. Chrysalis/EMI Records, 1994. Vinyl/LP.

Gang Starr. "The ? Remainz." *Full Clip: Decade of Gang Starr*. Virgin Records, 1999. CD.

Gates, Henry Louis Jr. *The Signifying Monkey: A Theory of African-American Literary Criticism*. New York: University Press, 1998. Print.

Gates, Henry Louis, Jr., and Jennifer Burton. *Call and Response: Key Debates in African American Studies*. W. W. Norton and Company, Inc., 2008. Print.

G-Dep featuring P. Diddy. "Special Delivery." *Child of the Ghetto*. Bad Boy/Arista Records, 2001. Vinyl/LP.

George, Nelson. *Hip Hop America*. New York: Penguin, 2005. Print.

Gramsci, Antonio. *Selections from the Prison Notebooks*. New York: International Publishers, 1997. Print.

Griselda. *WWCD*. Griselda/Shady Records, 2019. TIDAL streaming service.

Griselda featuring Novel. "The Old Groove." *WWCD*. Griselda/Shady Records, 2019. TIDAL streaming service.

Guru featuring Donald Byrd. "Loungin'." *Jazzmatazz*. Vol. 1. Chrysalis Records, 1993. Vinyl/LP.

GZA. "Liquid Swords." *Liquid Swords*. Geffen Records, 1995. Vinyl/LP.

Hardaway, Anfernee. "Nike Lil Penny Classic Commercial." *YouTube*, 16 Mar. 2007. Accessed Mar. 2010. https://www.youtube.com/watch?v=4MGXoh7eNhU.

Harris, Joseph. "Negotiating the Contact Zone." *Journal of Basic Writing* 14.1 (1995): 27–42. Print.

Harris, Travis T. "Can It Be Bigger than Hip Hop?: From Global Hip Hop Studies to Hip Hop." *Journal of Hip Hop Studies* 6.2 (2019): 17–70. Print.

Hartlaub, Peter. "Pam the Funkstress, DJ for the Coup and Prince, Dies of Organ Failure." 22 Dec. 2017. https://www.sfgate.com/music/article/Pam-Warren-DJ-for-the-Coup-and-Prince-dies-of-12451852.php#taboola-3.

Havoc and Alchemist. "Maintain (Fuck How You Feel)." *The Silent Partner*. Baby Grande Records, 2016. CD.

Hierro, Victor Del. "DJs, Playlists, and Community: Imagining Communication Design through Hip Hop." *Communication Design Quarterly Review* 7.2 (2019): 28–39. Print.

Hill, Marc. Lamont *Beats, Rhymes, and Classroom Life: Hip-Hop Pedagogy and the Politics of Identity*. New York: Teacher's College Press, 2009. Print.

Hill, Marc Lamont, and Emery Petchauer, eds. *Schooling Hip-Hop: Expanding Hip-Hop Based Education across the Curriculum*. New York: Teachers College Press, 2013. Print.

Hill, Patricia Liggins, and Bernard W. Bell. *Call and Response: The Riverside Anthology of the African American Literary Tradition*. Boston: Houghton Mifflin College Div., 1998. Print.

Hisama, Ellie. "DJ Kuttin Kandi: Performing Feminism." *American Music Review* 63.2 (spring 2014). https://www.brooklyn.cuny.edu/web/academics/centers/hitchcock/publications/amr/v43-2/hisama.php.

Hit-Boy. "Hit-Boy x The Alchemist—Slipping Into Darkness (Official Video)." *YouTube*, 10 Mar. 2023. https://www.youtube.com/watch?v=IqeK6BIS_pQ.

Holloway, Karla F. C. "Cultural Politics in the Academic Community: Masking the Color Line." *College English* 55.6 (1993): 610–617. Print.

hooks, bell. *Black Looks: Race and Representation*. South End Press, Boston, 1992. Print.

Howard, Rebecca Moore. "Plagiarisms, Authorships, and the Academic Death Penalty." *College English* 57.7 (1995): 788–806. Print.

Howard, Rebecca Moore. "Sexuality, Textuality: The Cultural Work of Plagiarism." *College English* 62.4 (2000): 473–491. Print.

Howard, Rebecca Moore, and Amy E. Robillard, eds. *Pluralizing Plagiarism: Identities, Contexts, Pedagogies*. Portsmouth, NH: Boynton/Cook Publishers, 2008. Print.

Ice Cube. "Jackin' for Beats." *Kill at Will*. Priority Records, 1990. CD.

Ice Cube. "Steady Mobbin." *Death Certificate*. Priority/EMI Records, 1991. CD.

The Isley Brothers. "Between the Sheets." *Between the Sheets*. T-Neck Records 1983. Vinyl/LP.

Jackson, Linda Susan. *What Yellow Sounds Like*. Sylmar, CA: Tia Chucha Press, 2007.

Jackson, Richard L., and Elaine Richardson. *Understanding African American Rhetoric: Classical Origins to Contemporary Innovations*. New York: Routledge, 2003.

Jadakiss, DJ Green Lantern, and DJ Drama. "Who Shot Ya." *The Champ Is Here Part 3 (A Gangsta Grillz Invasion)*. 2010. CD.

James, Lebron, and Kobe Bryant. "MVPuppets Kobe and Lebron—Handshake." *YouTube*, 8 Feb. 2010. Accessed Mar. 2010. https://www.youtube.com/watch?v=XQhn-nwjwNA.

Jay Electronica. "Somethin To Hold On To." *Victory*, 2008. Web.

J. Cole. "No Role Modelz." *2014 Forest Hills Drive*. Dreamville / RocNation / Columbia Records, 2014. CD.

J. Cole. "St. Tropez." *2014 Forest Hills Drive*. Dreamville / RocNation / Columbia Records, 2014. CD.

J. Period. Personal interview. 29 July 2011.

J. Personal interview. 13 June 2011.

Jay-Z. "D.O.A. (Death of Auto-Tune)." *The Blueprint 3*. RocNation / Atlantic Records, 2009. CD.

Jay-Z. "Roc Boys (And the Winner Is) . . ." *American Gangster*. Roc-A-Fella Records, 2007. CD.

Jay-Z. "Show You How." *The Blueprint 2: The Gift and The Curse*. Roc-A-Fella Records, 2002. CD.

Jay-Z. "Threat." *The Black Album*. Roc-A-Fella/Def Jam Records, 2003. Vinyl/LP.

Jay-Z and Kanye West featuring Frank Ocean. "Made in America." *Watch the Throne*. Roc-A-Fella Records, 2011. CD.

Jay-Z and Kanye West featuring Otis Redding. "Otis." *Watch the Throne*. Roc-A-Fella Records, 2011. CD.

Jay-Z featuring Jay Electronica. "We Made It." RocNation, 2014. Mp3.

Jeru the Damaja. "Come Clean." *The Sun Rises in the East*. Payday/FFRR/Polygram Records, 1994. Vinyl/LP.

Jeru the Damaja. "My Mind Spray." *The Sun Rises in the East*. Payday/FFRR/Polygram Records, 1994. Vinyl/LP.

Jidenna featuring Kendrick Lamar. "Classic Man (Remix)." Wondaland/Epic Records, 2015. Mp3.

Jidenna featuring Roman GianArthur. "Classic Man." *Wondaland Presents: The Eephus EP*. Wondaland/Epic Records, 2015. Mp3.

Jocson, Korina M. "Bob Dylan and Hip Hop: Intersecting Literary Practices in Youth Poetry Communities." *Written Communication* 23.3 (2006): 231–259. Print.

Kanye West. "Ultralight Beam." *The Life of Pablo*. Roc-A-Fella / GOOD Music / Def Jam Records, 2016. TIDAL streaming service.

Kanye West featuring Big Sean, Pusha T and 2 Chainz. "Mercy." *Cruel Summer*. G.O.O.D. Music/Def Jam Records, 2012. Mp3.

Kanye West featuring Jay-Z and Big Sean. "Clique." *Cruel Summer*. G.O.O.D. Music/Def Jam Records, 2012. Mp3.

Katz, Mark. *Capturing Sound: How Technology Has Changed Music*. Berkeley: University of California Press, 2010. Print.

Kendrick Lamar. "i." *To Pimp a Butterfly*. Top Dawg / Aftermath / Interscope Records, 2015. CD.

Kendrick Lamar. "Sing About Me, I'm Dying of Thirst." *good kid: m.A.A.d. city*. Aftermath/Interscope Records, 2012. CD.

Kendrick Lamar. *To Pimp a Butterfly*. Top Dawg / Aftermath / Interscope Records, 2015. CD.

Keyes, Cheryl L. *Rap Music and Street Consciousness*. Urbana: University of Illinois Press, 2004. Print.

Kid Potential. Personal interview. 13 June 2011.

Kitwana, Bakari. *The Hip-Hop Generation: Young Blacks and the Crisis in African-American Culture*. New York: Civitas Books, 2003. Print.

KOOL DJ Red Alert. Personal interview. 4 Feb. 2012.

KRS-One. "Hip-Hop vs. Rap." Jive Records, 1993. CD.

Kun, Josh. *Audiotopia: Music, Race, and America*. Berkeley: University of California Press, 2005. Print.

Kun, Josh. "Two Turntables and a Social Movement: Writing Hip-Hop at Century's End." *American Literary History* 14.3 (2002): 580–592. Print.

Kuttin Kandi. "Why Fat Beats Matter to Hip Hop." *Hip Hop and Politics*, 2010. http://hiphopandpolitics.com/2010/08/19/dj-kuttin-kandi-why-fat-beats-matter-to-hip-hop/.

Kweli, Talib. "Rapsody Talks MC Lyte and Lauryn Hill Inspiration, Being Pro Black, Mac Miller" ("Talib Kweli & Rapsody Talk Rap Influences, Being Pro Black, Kendrick, Jay Z, Eve | People's Party"). *The People's Party with Talib Kweli*. Uproxx. 2 Mar. 2020. https://www.youtube.com/watch?v=HDL9fx9fBX0&t=176s.

Kynard, Carmen. "'I Want to Be African': In Search of a Black Radical Tradition / African-American-Vernacularized Paradigm for 'Students' Right to Their Own Language,' Critical Literacy, and 'Class Politics.'" *College English* 69.4 (2007):360–390. Print.

Kynard, Carmen. "'The Blues Playingest Dog You Ever Heard Of': (Re)positioning Literacy through African American Blues Rhetoric." *Reading Research Quarterly* 43.4 (2008): 356–373. Print.

Kynard, Carmen. "'Looking for the Perfect Beat': The Power of Black Student Protest Rhetorics for Academic Literacy and Higher Education." *Changing English* 12.3 (2005): 387–402. Print.

Kynard, Carmen. "Teaching While Black: Witnessing and Countering Disciplinary Whiteness, Racial Violence, and Race-Management." *Literacy in Composition Studies* 3.1 (2015): 1–20. Print.

Kynard, Carmen. *Vernacular Insurrections: Race, Black Protest, and the New Century in Composition-Literacies Studies.* Albany: State University of New York Press, 2013. Print.

Large Professor. Personal interview. 10 Nov. 2011.

Lauryn Hill. "Lost Ones." *The Miseducation of Lauryn Hill.* Ruffhouse/Columbia Records, 1998. Vinyl/LP.

Lauryn Hill. *The Miseducation of Lauryn Hill.* Ruffhouse/Columbia Records, 1998. Vinyl/LP.

Lawrence, Tim. *love saves the day: a history of american dance music culture, 1970–1979.* Durham, NC: Duke University Press, 2003. Print.

Lil Wayne featuring Swizz Beatz. "Uproar." *Tha Carter V.* Young Money / Republic Records, 2018. TIDAL streaming service.

Lindsey, Treva B. "Let Me Blow Your Mind: Hip Hop Feminist Futures in Theory and Praxis." *Urban Education* 50.1 (2015): 52–77. Print.

Lingel, Jessica. "'We Realized We Had to Become Librarians': DJs, Information Practices and Music Libraries." In *Proceedings of the 2012 iConference* (iConference '12), 569–571. New York: ACM, 2012. https://doi.org./10.1145/2132176.2132292. http://doi.acm.org/10.1145/2132176.2132292.

Liu, Nelson, and Errol Anderson. "J Dilla: The Best That Ever Did It." *BOILER ROOM.* 23 Feb. 2016. Accessed 22 Mar. 2021. https://boilerroom.tv/j-dilla/.

L.L. Cool J. "Doin' It." *Mr. Smith.* Def Jam / RAL, 1995. Vinyl/LP.

Lonnie Liston Smith. "Expansions." *Expansions.* RCA/Flying Dutchman Records, 1975. Mp3.

Lord Finesse. Personal interview. 6 Oct. 2011.

Lord Finesse & DJ Mike Smooth. *Funky Technician.* Wild Pitch / EMI Records, 1990. Vinyl.

Lordi, Emily J. *Black Resonance: Iconic Women Singers and African American Literature.* New Brunswick, NJ: Rutgers University Press, 2013. Print.

Lords of the Underground. "Funky Child." *Here Come the Lords.* Pendulum/Elektra Records, 1993. Vinyl.

Lou Donaldson. "Pot Belly." *Pretty Things.* Blue Note Records, 1970. Vinyl/LP.

Love, Bettina L. *Hip Hop's Li'l Sistas Speak: Negotiating Hip Hop Identities and Politics in the New South.* New York: Peter Lang, 2012. Print.

Low, Bronwen. "The Tale of the Talent Night Rap: Hip-Hop Culture in Schools and the Challenge of Interpretation." *Urban Education* 45.2 (2010): 194–220. Print.

Lowney, John. *History, Memory, and the Literary Left*. Iowa City: University of Iowa Press, 2006. Print.

Lupe Fiasco. "KickPush." *Lupe Fiasco's Food and Liquor*. 1st and 15th / Atlantic Records, 2006. Vinyl/LP.

Lyons, Scott Richard. "Rhetorical Sovereignty: What do American Indians Want from Writing?" *College Composition and Communication* 51.3 (2000): 447–468. Print.

Mahiri, Jabari. "Digital DJ-ing: Rhythms of Learning in an Urban School." *Language Arts* 84.1 (2006): 55–62. Print.

Mark Farina. Personal interview. 7 Nov. 2011.

Marley Marl feat. Master Ace, Craig G, Kool G. Rap, and Big Daddy Kane. "The Symphony." *In Control: Volume 1*. Co-Chillin' / Warner Bros., 1988. Vinyl/LP.

Marshall, Wayne. "Giving up Hip-Hop's Firstborn: A Quest for the Real after the Death of Sampling." *Callaloo* 29.3(2006): 868–892. Print.

Martinez, Aja. *Counterstory: The Rhetoric and Writing of Critical Race Theory*. Champaign, IL: National Council of Teachers of English, 2020. Print.

Maru. "Masta Ace 'Me & The Biz'." *YouTube*, 21 Aug. 2008. Accessed 10 Nov. 2013. https://www.youtube.com/watch?v=gEjbuQVU9UY.

Mary J. Blige. "Amazing (feat. DJ Khaled)" [Official Video]. *YouTube*, premiered 21 Dec. 2021. Accessed 9 Jan. 2022. https://www.youtube.com/watch?v=CRZig-WX_U8.

Mary J. Blige featuring DJ Khaled. "Amazing." *Good Morning Gorgeous*. 300 / Mary Jane, 2022. Web.

Mas Yamagata. Personal interview. 14 June 2011.

Master Ace. "Me & The Biz." *Take a Look Around*. Co-Chillin' / Reprise / Warner Bros. 1990. Vinyl/LP.

McCallum, David. "The Edge." *Music: A Bit More of Me*. Capitol Records, 1967. Vinyl/LP.

McCarter, Jeremy. "Hip Hop and Musicals: Made for Each Other?" NewYorkTimes .com, 2003. http://www.nytimes.com/2003/06/08/theater/theater-hip-hop-and -musicals-made-for-each-other.html.

MC Hammer. "U Can't Touch This." *Please Hammer, Don't Hurt 'Em*. Capitol/EMI Records, 1990. CD.

MC Shan. "The Bridge." *Down by Law*. Co-Chillin' / Warner Bros., 1987. Vinyl/LP.

Meacham, Shuaib J. "Literacy at the Crossroads: Movement, Connection, and Communication within the Research Literature on Literacy and Cultural Diversity." *Review of Research in Education* 25 (January 2000): 181–208. Print.

Medina, Rich. "The State of Things—On the Road with Rich Medina." *Complex.com*. 20 Feb. 2012.

Medina, Rich. "TEDxPhilly—Rich Medina—Philadelphia: A City That Nurtures Our Creative Muscle." *YouTube*, Nov. 2011. Accessed 22. Jan. 2012. https://www.youtube .com/watch?v=kr4JvqCOEcw.

Meek Mill. "I'm a Boss." *Maybach Music Group Presents: Self Made Vol. 1*. Maybach Music Group / Warner Bros, 2011. Vinyl/LP.

Michael Jackson. *Off the Wall*. Epic Records, 1979. 8-Track.

Miller, Paul. *rhythm science*. Cambridge: MIT Press, 2000. Print.

Miller, Paul D., and Steve Reich. *Sound Unbound: Sampling Digital Music and Culture.* Cambridge: MIT Press, 2008. Print.

Miyakawa, Felicia M. "Turntablature: Notation, Legitimization, and the Art of the Hip-hop DJ." *American Music* 25.1 (2007): 81–105. Print.

Mobb Deep. "Flavor for the Non-Believes." *Juvenile Hell.* 4th & B'way / Island / Polygram, 1993. Vinyl/LP.

Mobb Deep. "Quiet Storm." *Murda Muzik.* Loud/RCA, 1999. Vinyl/LP.

Mobb Deep. "Shook Ones Pt II." *The Infamous.* Loud/RCA, 1995. Vinyl/LP.

Mobb Deep. "Survival of the Fittest." *The Infamous.* Loud/RCA, 1995. Vinyl/LP.

Mobb Deep featuring Big Noyd. "Give Up the Goods (Just Step)." *The Infamous.* Loud/RCA, 1995. Vinyl/LP.

Mobb Deep featuring Chinky. "Streets Raised Me." *Murda Muzik.* Loud/RCA, 1999. Vinyl/LP.

Monko, Kevin. 2011. "TEDxPhilly: The City, Philadelphia." Flickr. TEDxPhilly2011_291. Accessed 23 Dec. 2012. https://www.flickr.com/photos/tedxphilly/6352000667/in/photostream/.

Montano, Ed. " 'How Do You Know He's Not Playing Pac-Man While He's Supposed to Be DJing?': Technology, Formats, and the Digital Future of Digital Culture." *Popular Music* 29.3 (2010): 397–416. Print.

M.O.P. "Ante Up (Robbin Hoodz Theory)." *Warriorz.* Loud/Relativity Records, 2000. Vinyl/LP.

M.O.P. featuring Busta Rhymes, Remy Ma, and Teflon. "Ante Up (Robbin Hoodz Theory) Remix." Loud/Relativity Records, 2000. Vinyl/LP.

Morgan, Joan. *When Chickenheads Come Home to Roost: A Hip Hop Feminist Breaks It Down.* New York: Simon and Schuster, 1999. Print.

Morgan, Marcyliena. *Language, Discourse and Power in African American Culture.* Cambridge: Cambridge University Press, 2002. Print.

Morgan, Marcyliena. *The Real Hiphop: Battling for Knowledge, Power, and Respect in the LA Underground.* Durham, NC: Duke University Press, 2009. Print.

Morrell, Ernest, and Jeffrey MR Duncan-Andrade. "Promoting Academic Literacy with Urban Youth through Engaging Hip-Hop Culture." *English Journal* 91.6 (2002): 88–92. Print.

Mr. Len. Personal interview. 10 Mar. 2011.

Mr. Walt. Personal interview. 10 Nov. 2011.

Murray, Albert. *The Omni Americans: Some Alternatives to the Folklore of White Supremacy.* New York: Da Capo Press, 1970. Print.

N.O.R.E. "Nothin'." *God's Favorite.* Def Jam Records, 2002. Vinyl/LP.

Nas. "Back When." *Life Is Good.* Def Jam, 2012. CD.

Nas. "Halftime." *Illmatic.* Columbia, 1994. Vinyl/LP.

Nas. "The Message." *It Was Written.* Columbia, 1996. Vinyl/LP.

Nas. "Trapped in the 90s." *Life Is Good.* Def Jam, 2012. CD.

Nas. "The World Is Yours." *Illmatic.* Columbia, 1994. Vinyl/LP.

Nas. "The World Is Yours (Tip Mix)." Columbia, 1994. Vinyl/LP.

Nas featuring Olu Dara. "Bridging the Gap." *Street's Disciple*. Ill Will / Columbia Records, 2004. Vinyl/LP.

Nas featuring Victoria Monét. "You Wouldn't Understand." *Life Is Good*. Def Jam, 2012. CD.

National Centre for Sustainability. *Community Sustainability Engagement Evaluation Toolbox*. NCS, 2010. Accessed 8 Sept. 2012. https://www.amazon.com/Soul-Babies -Popular-Post-Soul-Aesthetic/dp/0415926580.

Neal, Mark Anthony. *Songs in the Key of Black Life: A Rhythm and Blues Nation*. New York: Routledge, 2003. Print.

Neal, Mark Anthony. *Soul Babies: Black Popular Culture and the Post-Soul Aesthetic*. New York: Routledge, 2002. Print.

Nielsen, Aldon Lynn. *Black Chant: Languages of African-American Postmodernism*. Cambridge: Cambridge University Press, 1997. Print.

Nipsey Hussle featuring Belly & Dom Kennedy. "Double Up." *Victory Lap*. All Money In No Money Out / Atlantic Records, 2018. TIDAL streaming service.

The Notorious B.I.G. "B.I.G. Interlude." *Life After Death*. Bad Boy / Arista, 1997. Vinyl/LP.

The Notorious B.I.G. "Juicy." *Ready to Die*. Bad Boy / Arista, 1994. Vinyl/LP.

The Notorious B.I.G. "Kick In The Door." *Life After Death*. Bad Boy / Arista, 1997. Vinyl/LP.

Oh No. "I'm Here (Intro) / Beat Interlude." *The Disrupt*. Stones Throw Records, 2004. Vinyl/LP.

Okawa, Gail Y. "Diving for Pearls: Mentoring as Cultural and Activist Practice among Academics of Color." *College Composition and Communication* 53.3 (2002): 507–532. Print.

Pam the Funkstress. Personal interview. 6 Dec. 2011.

Patton, Michael Quinn. *Qualitative Research and Evaluation Methods*. 3rd ed. Thousand Oaks, CA, 2002. Sage Publications. Print.

Pennycook, Alastair. "Borrowing Others' Words: Text, Ownership, Memory, and Plagiarism." *TESOL Quarterly* 30.2 (1996): 201–230. Print.

Perry, Imani. *Prophets of the Hood: Politics and Poetics in Hip Hop*. Durham, NC: Duke University Press, 2004. Print.

Petchauer, Emery. "Framing and Reviewing Hip-Hop Educational Research." *Review of Educational Research* 79.2 (2009): 946–978. Print.

Petchauer, Emery. *Hip-Hop Culture in College Students' Lives: Elements, Embodiment, and Higher Education*. New York: Routledge, 2012. Print.

Petchauer, Emery. "Sampling Memories: Using Hip-Hop Aesthetics to Learn from Urban Schooling Experiences." *Educational Studies* 48.2 (2012): 137–155. Print.

Petchauer, Emery. "Starting with Style: Toward a Second Wave of Hip-Hop Education Research and Practice." *Urban Education* 50.1 (2015): 78–105. Print.

Peterson, James Braxton. *Hip Hop Headphones: A Scholar's Critical Playlist*. New York: Bloomsbury, 2016. Print.

Pharaohe Monch. "Let My People Go." *W.A.R. (We Are Renegades)*. W.A.R. Media / Duck Down Music, 2011. CD.

Pharaohe Monch. *W.A.R. (We Are Renegades)*. W.A.R. Media / Duck Down Music, 2011. CD.

Pharaohe Monch featuring Styles P and Phonte. "Black Hand Side." *W.A.R. (We Are Renegades)*. W.A.R. Media / Duck Down Music, 2011. CD.

The Pharcyde. "The E.N.D." *Labcabincalifornia*. Delicious Vinyl, 1995. Vinyl/LP.

Phillip Lee (of Illvibe Collective). Personal interview. 20 Mar. 2011.

Planet Asia. "The Medicine." *The Medicine*. ABB Records, 2006. Vinyl.

Pleasant, Eric. "Literacy Sponsors and Learning: An Ethnography of Punk Literacy in mid-1980s Waco." *Young Scholars in First-Year Writing* 5.1 (2007): 137–145. Print.

Polson, Bilal. "Literacy-lineage: #literacy #literacylives #textual-lineage #JamesBrown #AlfredTatum." *Instagram*, August 12, 2019. Accessed 21 July, 2020. https://www.instagram.com/p/B1D_wLxgvf1/.

Pough, Gwendolyn. *Check It While I Wreck It: Black Womanhood, Hip-Hop Culture, and the Public Sphere*. Boston: Northeastern University Press, 2004. Print.

Power, Will. *The Seven*. Dir. Jo Bonney, 12 Feb. New York Theater Workshop, New York, 2006. Musical.

Pratt, Mary Louise. "Arts of the Contact Zone." *Profession* (1991): 33–40. Print.

Prince and the New Power Generation. "7 (acoustic version)." *Love Symbol Album*. Paisley Park / Warner Brothers Records, 1992. Vinyl.

Prince Paul. Personal interview. 19 Feb. 2012.

Prince Paul. *A Prince Among Thieves*. Tommy Boy / Warner Bros., 1999. Vinyl/LP.

Prince Paul. "Steady Slobbin.'" *A Prince Among Thieves*. Tommy Boy / Warner Bros., 1999. Vinyl/LP.

Prince Paul. "What U Got (The Demo)." *A Prince Among Thieves*. Tommy Boy / Warner Bros., 1999. Vinyl/LP.

Puff Daddy featuring The LOX, The Notorious B.I.G. and Lil Kim. "It's All About the Benjamins." *No Way Out*. Arista / Bad Boy Records, 1977. Vinyl/LP.

The Pursuit of Happyness. Dir. Gabriele Muccino. Perf. Will Smith, Thandie Newton and Jaden Smith. Sony, 2006. DVD.

Pusha T featuring Jay-Z. "Drug Dealers Anonymous." *King Push*. G.O.O.D. Music, 2016. TIDAL streaming service.

Queen with David Bowie. "Under Pressure." *Hot Space*. Elektra/Hollywood Records, 1982. Vinyl/LP.

Rabaka, Reiland. *Hip Hop's Inheritance: From the Harlem Renaissance to the Hip Hop Feminist Movement*. New York: Lexington Books, 2011. Print.

Raekwon the Chef featuring Ghostface Killer. "Shark Niggas (Biters)." *Only Built 4 Cuban Linx*. Loud/RCA, 1995. Vinyl/LP.

Rah Digga. "Tight." *Dirty Harriet*. Flipmode/Elektra Records, 1999. CD.

RAMP. "Daylight." *Come into Knowledge*. Blue Thumb Records, 1977. Vinyl/LP.

Rampage the Last Boy Scout featuring Busta Rhymes. "Wild for da Night." *Scout's Honor . . . By Way of Blood*. Flipmode/Elektra Records, 1997. CD.

Ramsay, Maureen, and Lionel Cliffe. "War on Iraq: An 'Honourable Deception'?" *Contemporary Politics* 9.4 (2003): 349–359. Print.

Rapsody. "Believe Me." *The Idea of Beautiful*. Jamla Records, 2012. CD.

Rapsody. *Eve*. Jamla/RocNation, 2019. TIDAL streaming service.

Rapsody. "Nina." *Eve*. Jamla/RocNation, 2019. TIDAL streaming service.

Rapsody. "Oprah." *Eve*. Jamla/RocNation, 2019. TIDAL streaming service.

Rapsody featuring Rocki Evans. "How Does It Feel." *The Idea of Beautiful*. Jamla Records, 2012. CD.

Rass Kass. "Soul on Ice" (Remix). *Soul on Ice*. Priority/EMI, 1996. Vinyl/LP.

Reighley, Kurt. *Looking for the Perfect Beat: The Art and Culture of the DJ*. New York: Pocket Books, 2000. Print.

Rice, Jeff. "The 1963 Hip-Hop Machine: Hip-Hop Pedagogy as Composition." *College Composition and Communication* 54.3 (2003): 453–471. Print.

Rice, Jeff. *The Rhetoric of Cool*. Carbondale: Southern Illinois University Press, 2007. Print.

Rich Medina. *Connecting the Dots*. Kindred Spirits, 2005. Mp3.

Rich Medina. Personal Interview. 18 Feb. 2011.

Rich Medina. *Rich Medina Presents Jump N Funk*. BBE, 2016. Mp3.

Rich Medina and Bobbito Garcia. *Rich Medina and Bobbito: The Connection Volume One*. R2 Records, 2009. CD.

Richardson, Elaine. *African American Literacies*. New York: Routledge, 2003. Print.

Richardson, Elaine. *Hiphop Literacies*. New York: Routledge, 2006. Print.

Richardson, Elaine, and Ronald Jackson. *African American Rhetoric(s): Interdisciplinary Perspectives*. Carbondale: Southern Illinois University Press, 2004. Print.

Rick James. "Superfreak." *Street Songs*. Gordy Records, 1981. Vinyl/LP.

Rick Ross featuring Dr. Dre and Jay-Z. "3 Kings." *God Forgives, I Don't*. Mercury Records, 2012. CD.

Rios, Victor M. "Stealing a Bag of Potato Chips and Other Crimes of Resistance." *Contexts* 11.1 (2012): 48–53. Print.

Rob Base and DJ E-Z Rock. "It Takes Two." *It Takes Two*. Profile Records, 1988. Vinyl/LP.

Rob Swift. 2011. Personal interview. 10 Nov. 2011.

Rodríguez, Louie F. "Dialoguing, Cultural Capital, and Student Engagement: Toward a Hip Hop Pedagogy in the High School and University Classroom." *Equity and Excellence in Education* 42.1 (2009): 20–35. Print.

Ronson, Mark. "TED—How Sampling Transformed Music." *YouTube*, 9 May 2014. Accessed 15 Nov. 2019. https://www.youtube.com/watch?v=H3TF-hI7zKc.

Rose, Tricia. *Black Noise: Rap Music and Black Culture in Contemporary America*. Middletown, CT: Wesleyan University Press, 1994. Print.

Rose, Tricia. *Microphone Fiends: Youth Music and Youth Culture*. New York: Routledge, 1994. Print.

Ross, Andrew, Frank Owen, Moby, Frankie Knuckles, and Carol Cooper. "The Cult of the DJ: A Symposium." *Social Text* 43 (Autumn 1995):67–88. Print.

Royce Da 5'9". *The Allegory*. eOne Music, 2020. TIDAL streaming service.

Royce Da 5'9" featuring Conway the Machine. "FUBU." *The Allegory*. eOne Music, 2020. TIDAL streaming service.

Royce Da 5'9" featuring Eminem. "Perspective (Skit)." *The Allegory*. eOne Music, 2020. TIDAL streaming service.

Ruff Ryders featuring the LOX, DMX and Eve. "Ryde or Die." *Ryde or Die Volume 1*. Ruff Ryders / Interscope Records, 1999. Vinyl/LP.

Sánchez, Deborah M. "Hip-Hop and a Hybrid Text in a Postsecondary English Class." *Journal of Adolescent and Adult Literacy* 53.6 (2010): 478–487. Print.

Schloss, Joseph. *Making Beats: The Art of Sample-Based Hip-Hop*. Middletown, CT: Wesleyan Press, 2004. Print.

Schoolly D. "P.S.K. (What Does It Mean?)." *Schoolly D*. Jive, 1986. Vinyl/LP.

Shusterman, Richard. "The Fine Art of Rap." *New Literary History* 22.3 (1991): 613–632. Print.

Silverman, David. *Doing Qualitative Research: A Practical Handbook*. 3rd ed. Los Angeles: Sage Publications, 2010. Print.

Sirc, Geoffrey. "Proust, Hip-Hop, and Death in First-Year Composition." *Teaching English in the Two Year College* 33.4 (2006): 392–400. Print.

Skeme Richards. Personal interview. 13 May 2011.

Smith, Sophy. *Hip-Hop Turntablism, Creativity and Collaboration*. London: Routledge, 2013. Print.

Smitherman, Geneva. *Talkin and Testifyin: The Language of Black America*. Boston: Houghton Mifflin, 1977. Print.

Snell, Karen, and Johan Soderman. *Hip-Hop within and without the Academy*. London: Lexington Books, 2014. Print.

Something from Nothing: The Art of Rap. Dir. Ice-T, perf. Grandmaster Caz, Ice T, Yasiin Bey. Indomina Media, 2012. DVD.

Sommers, Nancy. "Revision Strategies of Student Writers and Experienced Adult Writers." *College Composition and Communication* 31.4 (1980): 378–388. Print.

Sonny James (of Illvibe Collective). Personal interview. 20 Mar. 2011.

Spady, James G. "Mapping and Re-Membering Hip Hop History, Hiphopography and African Diasporic History." *Western Journal of Black Studies* 37.2 (2013): 126. Print.

Spady, James G., and Joseph D. Eure. *Nation Conscious Rap*. Vol. 3. New York: PC International Press, 1991. Print.

Statik Selektah. Personal interview. 18 Oct. 2011.

Stetsasonic. "Talkin' All That Jazz." *In Full Gear*. Tommy Boy / Warner Bros. Records, 1988. Cassette.

Stoever, Jennifer Lynn. "Crate Digging Begins at Home: Black and Latinx Women Collecting and Selecting Records in the 1960s and 1970s Bronx." In *The Oxford Handbook of Hip Hop Music*, ed. Justin D. Burton and Jason Lee Oakes. Oxford: Oxford University Press. 2018. https://academic.oup.com/edited-volume/34741/chapter-abstract/296543752?redirectedFrom=fulltext&login=false.

Street, Brian. "What's 'New' in New Literacy Studies? Critical Approaches to Literacy in Theory and Practice." *Current Issues in Comparative Education* 5.2 (2003): 77–91. Print.

Stretch and Bobbito: Radio That Changed Lives. Dir. Bobbito Garcia. Perf. B-Real, DJ Premier, Eminem, Jay-Z, Nas, Rosie Perez, and Raekwon. Saboteur Media, 2015. DVD.

Swave HMG. "Swave HMG - Blue Faces Remix (feat. Devvon Terrell) Prod. Dizzy Banko." *YouTube*, 13 June 2018. Accessed 20 June 2020. https://www.youtube.com/watch?v=395GvzfG-wk&t=48s.

Swiss, Thomas, and Rebekah Farrugia. "Tracking the DJ: Vinyl Records, Work, and the Debate over New Technologies." *Journal of Popular Music Studies* 17.1 (2005): 30–44. Print.

Tatum, Alfred. *Reading for Their Life: (Re)Building the Textual Lineages of African American Adolescent Males*. Portsmouth, NH: Heinemann, 2009. Print.

That Kid Named Cee. Personal interview. 30 Nov. 2011.

The Thomas Bell Orchestra. *The Fish That Saved Pittsburgh*. 1979. Mp3.

THE TWILITE TONE. 2011. Personal interview. 19 Nov. 2011.

3rd Bass. "Steppin' to the A.M." *The Cactus Album*. Def Jam / Columbia / CBS Records, 1989. Vinyl/LP.

Thompson, Celia, and Alastair Pennycook. "Intertextuality in the Transcultural Contact Zone." In *Pluralizing Plagiarism: Identities, Contexts, Pedagogies*, 124–139. Portsmouth, NH: Heinemann, 2008. Print.

Thompson, Celia, and Alastair Pennycook. "A Question of Dialogues: Authorship, Authority, Plagiarism." *Education Canada* 48.3 (2008): 20–23. Print.

Too $hort. "Blow the Whistle." *Blow the Whistle*. Up All Night / Jive Records, 2006. CD.

Tory Lanez featuring T-Pain. "Jerry Sprunger." *Chixtape 5*. Mad Love / Interscope Records, 2019. Mp3.

T-Pain. "I'm Sprung." *Rappa Ternt Sanga*. Konvict/Jive/Zomba Records, 2005. Mp3.

Tyra from Saigon. Personal interview. 20 Dec. 2011.

Ultimate Breaks and Beats: vols 1–26. Street Beat Records, 1986–1991. Mp3.

Vanilla Ice. "Ice Ice Baby." *To The Extreme*. SBK Records, 1990. TIDAL streaming service.

Verzuz. "Jadakiss freestyles to 'Who Shot Ya?' during #VERZUZ | The LOX vs Dipset." *YouTube*, 6 Aug. 2021. Accessed 28 Feb. 2023. https://www.youtube.com/watch?v= qo_wTGVmVdI.

Wakefield, Sarah. "Using Music Sampling to Teach Research Skills." *Teaching English in the Two Year College* 33.4 (2006): 357–360. Print.

Wallace, Riley. 2018. "'Special Delivery' Producer Ez Elpee Speaks on 'Uproar' Snub: 'They Stole My Shit'." *HipHopDX*, 24 Oct. Accessed 15 Feb. 2020. https://hiphopdx .com/interviews/id.3162/title.special-delivery-producer-ez-elpee-speaks-on -uproar-snub-they-stole-my-shit.

Wang, Oliver. *Legions of Boom*. Durham, NC: Duke University Press, 2015. Print.

Weheliye, Alexander. *Phonographies: Grooves in Sonic Afro-Modernity*. Durham, NC: Duke University Press, 2005. Print.

Welbeck, Timothy N. "People's Instinctive Travels and the Paths to Rhythms: Hip-Hop's Continuation of the Enduring Tradition of African and African American Rhetorical Forms and Tropes." *Changing English* 24.2 (2017): 123–136. Print.

Whodini. "Funky Beat." *Back in Black*. Jive/Arista Records, 1986. Vinyl/LP.

Williams, Justin A. *Rhymin' and Stealin': Musical Borrowing in Hip-Hop*. Ann Arbor: University of Michigan Press, 2013.

Young, Morris. *Minor Re/Visions: Asian American Literacy Narratives as a Rhetoric of Citizenship*. Carbondale: Southern Illinois University Press, 2004. Print.

Zulema. "American Fruit, African Roots." *Zulema*. Sussex Records, 1972. Mp3.

INDEX